Library of
Davidson College

Charles Tomlinson and
the Objective Tradition

Charles Tomlinson and the Objective Tradition

Richard Swigg

Lewisburg
Bucknell University Press
London and Toronto: Associated University Presses

© 1994 by Associated University Presses, Inc.

All rights reserved. Authorization to photocopy items for internal or personal use, or the internal or personal use of specific clients, is granted by the copyright owner, provided that a base fee of $10.00, plus eight cents per page, per copy is paid directly to the Copyright Clearance Center, 27 Congress Street, Salem, Massachusetts 01970. [0-8387-5249-7/94 $10.00 + 8¢ pp, pc.]

Associated University Presses
440 Forsgate Drive
Cranbury, NJ 08512

Associated University Presses
25 Sicilian Avenue
London WC1A 2QH, England

Associated University Presses
P.O. Box 338, Port Credit
Mississauga, Ontario
Canada L5G 4L8

The paper used in this publication meets the requirements
of the American National Standard for Permanence of Paper
for Printed Library Materials Z39.48-1984.

Library of Congress Cataloging-in-Publication Data

Swigg, Richard, 1938-
  Charles Tomlinson and the objective tradition / Richard Swigg.
    p.   cm.
  Includes bibliographical references and index.
  ISBN 0-8387-5249-7 (alk. paper)
  1. Tomlinson, Charles, 1927-   —Criticism and interpretation.
2. Objectivity in literature.   I. Title.
PR6093.O349Z86   1994
821'.914—dc20   92-56606
                                                                  CIP

PRINTED IN THE UNITED STATES OF AMERICA

To Virginia and Alex

Contents

Acknowledgments 9
Introduction 13

1. A Lucid Darkness 19
2. "Thus Men Make a Mountain" 38
3. In the Tutelary Spirit 78
4. Between Paradise and History 118
5. Contraries and Relations 146
6. Ends and Beginnings 185
7. To Marry with a Land 214

Notes 239
Bibliography 249
Bibliographical Appendix 255
Index 261

Acknowledgments

Grateful acknowledgment is made to the following for permission to reprint previously published material:

Carcanet Press Limited. Excerpts from Octavio Paz, *The Collected Poems: 1957–1987*, edited and translated by Eliot Weinberger, with additional translations by Elizabeth Bishop, Paul Blackburn, Lysander Kemp, Denise Levertov, John Frederick Nims, Mark Strand and Charles Tomlinson (© 1965 by Denise Levertov Goodman; © 1967 by Octavio Paz and Lysander Kemp; © 1968, 1981 by Octavio Paz and Charles Tomlinson; © 1970 by Octavio Paz and Paul Blackburn; © 1971 by New Directions Publishing Corporation; © 1972, 1973, 1978, 1979, 1986 by Octavio Paz and Eliot Weinberger; © 1979 by Editorial Seix Barral, S.A.; © 1979, 1985, 1987 by Octavio Paz; © 1983, 1984, 1985, 1986, 1987 by Eliot Weinberger). Excerpts from William Carlos Williams, *The Collected Poems of William Carlos Williams I: 1909–1939*, edited by A. Walton Litz and Christopher MacGowan: © 1986 by William Eric Williams and Paul H. Williams. Excerpts from William Carlos Williams, *The Collected Poems of William Carlos Williams II: 1939–1962*, edited by Christopher MacGowan: © 1944, 1948, 1949, 1950, 1951, 1952, 1953, 1954, 1955, 1956, 1957, 1959, 1960, 1961, 1962 by William Carlos Williams; © by William Eric Williams and Paul H. Williams.

David Higham Associates Limited: Excerpts from Dylan Thomas, *Collected Poems 1934–1952*. World English language rights administered by David Higham Associates Limited, London.

Faber and Faber Limited: Excerpts from W. H. Auden, *Collected Poems*, edited by Edward Mendelson: English language rights throughout the British Commonwealth including Canada (but excluding Canada for the extract from *In Praise of Limestone*). Excerpts from T. S. Eliot, *Collected Poems 1909–1962*: English language rights throughout the British Commonwealth including Canada. Excerpts from David Jones, *The Anathemata: Fragments of an Attempted Writing, In Parenthesis*, and *The Sleeping Lord and Other Fragments*: English language rights throughout the world. Excerpts from Philip Larkin, *The Whitsun Weddings*: English language rights throughout the world. Excerpts from *The Complete Poems of Marianne Moore*: English language rights throughout the British Commonwealth excluding Canada. Excerpts from Ezra Pound, *The Cantos of Ezra Pound* and *Literary Essays of Ezra Pound*, edited by T. S. Eliot: English language rights throughout the world excluding the United States of America. Excerpts from Wallace Stevens, *The Collected Poems of Wallace Stevens*: English language rights throughout the British Commonwealth excluding Canada.

Harcourt Brace Jovanovich, Inc.: Excerpts from "Burnt Norton" and "Little Gidding" in T. S. Eliot, *Four Quartets*. © 1943 by T. S. Eliot and renewed 1971 by Esme Valerie Eliot, reprinted by permission of Harcourt Brace Jovanovich, Inc. Excerpts from "Portrait of a Lady" and "The Love Song of J. Alfred Prufrock" in *Collected Poems 1909–1962*, reprinted by permission of the publisher.

Henry Holt and Company, Inc. Excerpts from *The Poetry of Robert Frost*, edited by Edward Connery Lathem. © 1969 by Holt, Rinehart and Winston. Reprinted by arrangement with Henry Holt and Company, Inc.

The Hogarth Press: The excerpt from Rainer Maria Rilke, *Sonnets to Orpheus*, translated by J. B. Leishman, reprinted by permission of the publisher.

Jonathan Cape Limited: Excerpts from *The Poetry of Robert Frost*, edited by Edward Connery Lathem. Copyright © 1969 by Holt, Rinehart and Winston. Reprinted by permission of Jonathan Cape Limited.

Macmillan Publishing Company. Excerpts from Marianne Moore, *Collected Poems of Marianne Moore*. Reprinted with permission of Macmillan Publishing Company from *Collected Poems of Marianne Moore*. © 1935, 1944, 1951 by Marianne Moore; copyrights renewed 1963 by Marianne Moore and T. S. Eliot; 1979 by Marianne Moore; and 1979 by Lawrence E. Brinn and Louise Crane.

New Directions Publishing Corporation, Inc. Excerpts from Ezra Pound, *The Cantos of Ezra Pound* (© 1934, 1937, 1940, 1948, 1956, 1959, 1962, 1963, 1966, 1968 by Ezra Pound). The excerpt from Ezra Pound, *Literary Essays of Ezra Pound*, edited by T. S. Eliot (© 1918,

1920, 1935 by Ezra Pound). Excerpts from Octavio Paz, *The Collected Poems: 1957–1987*, edited and translated by Eliot Weinberger, with additional translations by Elizabeth Bishop, Paul Blackburn, Lysander Kemp, Denise Levertov, John Frederick Nims, Mark Strand and Charles Tomlinson (© 1972, 1973, 1978, 1979, 1986, 1988, 1990 by Octavio Paz and Eliot Weinberger). The excerpt from William Carlos Williams, *The Autobiography of William Carlos Williams*, © 1948, 1951 by William Carlos Williams. The excerpt from William Carlos Williams, *In the American Grain*: © 1923 by James Laughlin; © 1933 by William Carlos Williams. Excerpts from William Carlos Williams, *The Collected Poems of William Carlos Williams I: 1909–1939*, edited by A. Walton Litz and Christopher MacGowan: © 1982, 1986 by William Eric Williams and Paul H. Williams. Excerpts from William Carlos Williams, *The Collected Poems of William Carlos Williams II: 1939–1962*, edited by Christopher MacGowan: © 1944, 1953, 1962 by William Carlos Williams; © 1988 by William Eric Williams and Paul H. Williams. The excerpt from William Carlos Williams, *Paterson*: © 1946, 1948, 1949, 1958 by William Carlos Williams.

Northwestern University Press. The excerpt from Maurice Merleau-Ponty, *The Primacy of Perception*, edited by James Edie. Translation © 1964 by Northwestern University Press. Excerpts from Maurice Merleau-Ponty, *Signs*, 1964 translated by Richard C. McCleary. Translation © 1964 by Northwestern University Press.

Oxford University Press. Excerpts from Basil Bunting, *Collected Poems*: © 1978 by Basil Bunting. Excerpts from Charles Tomlinson, *Collected Poems*: © 1985 by Charles Tomlinson. Excerpts from Charles Tomlinson, *Notes from New York*: © 1984 by Charles Tomlinson. Excerpts from Charles Tomlinson, *The Return*: © 1987 by Charles Tomlinson. The excerpt from Charles Tomlinson, *Translations*: (English translations) © 1983 by Charles Tomlinson. Excerpts from Charles Tomlinson, *Annunciations*: © 1989 by Charles Tomlinson.

Penguin USA, Inc.: Excerpts from D. H. Lawrence, *The Complete Poems of D. H. Lawrence*, edited by Vivian de Sola Pinto and Warren Roberts; © 1964, 1971 by Angelo Ravagli and C. M. Weekley, Executors of the Estate of Frieda Lawrence Ravagli. Excerpts from D. H. Lawrence, *The Captain's Doll*, *Etruscan Places*, *The Ladybird*, *Studies in Classic American Literature*, and *Twilight in Italy*. "Nottingham and the Mining Countryside," "Introduction to These Paintings," from D. H. Lawrence, *Phoenix: The Posthumous Papers of D. H. Lawrence* edited by Edward D. McDonald; © 1936 by Frieda Lawrence, renewed © 1964 by the Estate of the late Frieda Lawrence Ravagli. Used by permission of Viking Penguin, a division of Penguin Books USA, Inc. Acknowledgments to Laurence Pollinger Ltd., London, and the Estate of Frieda Lawrence Ravagli.

Princeton University Press. The excerpt from Dijkstra, Bram, *The Hieroglyphics of a New Speech: Cubism, Stieglitz, and the Early Poems of William Carlos Williams:* © 1969 by Princeton University Press. Reprinted by permission of Princeton University Press.

Random House, Inc.: Excerpts from W. H. Auden, *Collected Poems* by W. H. Auden, edited by Edward Mendelson. © 1934, 1941, 1951 and renewed 1962, 1969 by W. H. Auden. Reprinted by permission of Random House, Inc. Excerpts from Wallace Stevens, *Collected Poems* by Wallace Stevens. © 1954 by Wallace Stevens. Reprinted by permission of Alfred A. Knopf, Inc.

University of California Press. Excerpts from pp. 24, 76, 77, and 105, Charles Tomlinson, *Some Americans: A Personal Record.* © 1981, The Regents of the University of California.

Introduction

My subject is the poetry of Charles Tomlinson and the Anglo-American tradition that he illuminates. The lineage of concrete particularity to which he belongs is one that reaches back in verse to the English Augustans, and forward, through Blake, Whitman, and Hopkins, to William Carlos Williams. Above all, it is a tradition of objectivity that has special regard for the world in its solid, separate otherness—for a plurality of phenomena independent of our egotistic projection and unblurred by myth or symbol. Tomlinson, I believe, is unique among contemporary English poets in the way that he has provided the terms by which we see the distinctness of that world and the tradition that describes it.

Born 1927 in Stoke-on-Trent and teaching for most of his life at Bristol University, Tomlinson is not only a poet but also a painter. Indeed, when he began writing in the 1940s, his sense of concreteness and flux found no artistic kinship among contemporary poets such as Auden, Empson, Dylan Thomas, and Eliot, but in the work of Cézanne, the cubists, and the surrealists of painting and film. As a student at Cambridge and then as a schoolteacher in London, he gained temporary sustenance from the poetry of Blake and Whitman. But it was to be modern American verse, notably that of Wallace Stevens and Marianne Moore, which, by the mid-1950s in Tomlinson's first important collections, *The Necklace* and *Seeing is Believing*, had shown him a way toward the voicing of nature's textures, contours, and many-faceted surfaces.

Thus, while English "movement" poets like Philip Larkin and Kingsley Amis were settling for insularity or a "mild xenophobia," Tomlinson's internationalism was widening. This became especially important when, from 1957, he began to absorb the possibilities of William Carlos Williams's verse-line, both in the American's prewar poetry and the three-ply forms of *The Desert Music* and *Journey to Love*. All this gave Tomlinson a new, more flexible grip on chance-given fact and particularity. It was no accident, one feels, that Williams like Tomlinson was a poetic heir of Cézanne's art, as well as a whole artistic line of visually exact perception that goes back to Ruskin and Constable. But Williams's poetry moved Tomlinson's even more vigorously in the direction it was going: to language conceived as surface in its own right, where the reader, denied old linkages, is taught a fresh pace of relation, an earned way back to the phenomenal world.

My first three chapters, therefore, attempt to show how Tomlinson, as a developing poet, found his way to that world via the factual, objective tradition. By discussing what he gained, early and late, from Stevens, Moore, and Williams, I also seek to bring into view the scientific basis of particularity that precedes them in Ruskin and Hopkins. But, as a discussion of what an Englishman made of inheritances, native or American, these chapters lead to an examination of other poets who, like Tomlinson, sought New World precisions to speak their own Englishness. Hence, in chapter 4, I discuss the poetry of Ivor Gurney who, during the Great War and after, found a new breath and clarity in Whitman's verse that helped him escape his own decayed romanticism. Edward Thomas, Gurney's contemporary, gained also from America through the poetry and the encouragement of Robert Frost. It is of course a more celebrated Anglo-American literary relationship than that of Gurney and Whitman, but it is not one, I feel, that has necessarily been better understood, as regards the effect on Thomas's verse. Setting Thomas besides Gurney within the framework of Tomlinson's art, I attempt to suggest the way in which the earlier poets also found via America the limits and possibilities of their own distinctive speech.

In chapter 5 I return to Tomlinson's early development as a poet in order to consider, first of all, the place of Blake in his imagination, followed by that of Lawrence. However, my major concern is not so much the latter's influence on Tomlinson as their shared sense of contraries and relations, together with their artistic gain from America. In a previous book, *Lawrence, Hardy and American Literature* (Oxford University Press, 1972) I examined Lawrence's debt as a novelist to Hawthorne, Melville, Poe and others. But here the emphasis is on his poetry of the 1920s and a relationship with the poetry of Whitman that is more complex—indeed, more embattled—than Gurney's. Again, to see a poet like Lawrence within the Tomlinson framework is to become more precisely aware of what he won from the particularity of American art: in his case, as with Tomlinson, the uttering of a European Englishness.

That European quality is especially important in chapter 6 in which I discuss a group of political and historical poems by Tomlinson in the light of his literary relations with Octavio Paz and T. S. Eliot. It is Eliot the American expatriate—seeking a "mind of Europe" in a way that Williams did not—whose version of tradition is significant to, and given critical perspective, by Tomlinson's poetry. Here, as throughout the book, I am drawing on the standard of judgement that the Englishman's work provides. By this, I mean no rigidity, but rather a judicious play of mind that constantly reassesses the changing relations between self and world. Tomlinson's example as poet offers those flexible discriminations and judgements by which we can see Stevens, Williams, and Lawrence in earlier chapters. So now in chapter 6, as elsewhere in the book, we see the Eliot of *Four Quartets* with special clarity: a would-be transcender of time, history, and place, in a way that subverts a sense of temporal meaning and process. But if Tomlinson's portrayal of historical *deracinés* like Danton and Machiavelli has the effect of sharpening our view of the suprahistorical and exiled Eliot, it is also true that Tomlinson's example, with its Williams-like feeling for the localized, points to what Eliot did not abandon. Indeed, it is Eliot's commitment to history that becomes visible again when we consider the distinctive way that Tomlinson, in his politico-historical poems and elsewhere, embodies the individual talent at work in tradition. Less than ever is there reason to confuse the poet of *Four Quartets* with the Eliot of *The Waste Land* where he reaches not beyond time, but beyond myth, to Europe's temporal inheritance.

The terms of such discrimination are rooted in Tomlinson's own achievement. But they are also to be found in the art of two major British poets, Basil Bunting and David Jones, whom I discuss in my final chapter. As Tomlinson's contemporaries, although of an older generation—Bunting was born in 1900, Jones in 1895—they share with him the theme of native ground set within the vast dimensions of time and space. To this ground the traveler voyages back—marries it, so to speak, in sensibility and utterance, only by having journeyed beyond the insular in the first place. Thus Jones, in *The Anathemata* (1952), finds a way home to the British Isles, geologically and culturally, through an adventurous Catholic extension of Eliot's modernism. In *Briggflatts* (1965), Bunting is no longer the Poundian modernist that he was in the interwar years, but, journeying back to Northumbria, he is a poet who repossesses a ground and past in his own hard-won way. In this last chapter of homecoming, I attempt to show the appraising accuracy that Tomlinson's work brings to one's view of other poets and that it teaches implicitly about itself. To evaluate his poetry is also to grasp the abundance of a tradition; and yet, by our enlarged sense of the tradition, we see, as I now try to suggest, the "proper plenitude of fact" that he, individually and inimitably, sets before the reader.

Charles Tomlinson and
the Objective Tradition

1
A Lucid Darkness

I

Charles Tomlinson is a poet of many places, or simply of one:

> I have lived in a single landscape. Every tone
>   And turn have had for their ground
> These beginnings in grey-black: a land
>   Too handled to be primary—all the same,
> The first in feeling.

(At Stoke)

The Stoke-on-Trent where Tomlinson grew up in the 1930s and 1940s has remained very deeply "the first in feeling." Despite its blocked horizons, it was the starting point for a verse more open than that of any other English poet of his generation to the varied world—to Italy, France, the British Isles, Canada, America, and Mexico. Now that one can see the full range of the poetry produced by Tomlinson over nearly forty years, from 1951 to 1989, it becomes more evident that his internationalism has been not so much an escape from his native Midlands as a growing acknowledgement of its innate capacity to educate the mind, eye, and feelings. This is not a matter of nostalgia or class, but of primary realizations won, at first unconsciously, in a North Staffordshire town of "grey-black" fact that tempered even as it sharpened the sensibility.

Acceptance of objective fact—of the world's singularity beyond the ego's command—remains an essential principle in Tomlinson's art and goes back to the first lessons in recognition taught by a district that he describes as one of "smoke and blackened houses, of slag-heaps, cinder-paths, pitheads, steelworks," with its clay-kilns, canals, and "the great pools that formed in the pits where marl was dug for tile-making."[1] Growing up here, above Etruria Vale where Wedgwood had built his factory in the eighteenth century and where the Shelton Bar-Iron and Steelworks flared nightly, was for this poet the first step toward an art in which the self relates to the concrete world by an entry into—and illumination of—its dark solidity, its mass, weight, and tangible textures.

If the Potteries offered one kind of education to the sensibility, however, there was also another. At Longton High School during the war, where Tomlinson received especially good teaching in French and German, he had his first sight of a great literary perspective, "entering into conversation," as he says, "with all those mighty foreigners we'd been learning to read—Ovid, Racine, Hugo, Lamartine, Baudelaire, Heine, Rilke."[2] It was a widening that led him away from Stoke to Cambridge, travel, and university teaching. But expansion of view ultimately brought him back, closer to the center of the decay and the possibilities taught by Stoke, and which, much later, could now be seen to have a more fully British implication. For the Potteries, suffering the change wrought nationally by the decline of the old manufacturing industries, was to become in Tomlinson's poetry a way into a perception of the British city: a place of demolitions, dispossessions, and disorientation, in a country unsure of its future when directions had been brashly erased or routes hideously built over.

A poetry like Tomlinson's addresses that condition centrally. For his work, by its very nature, uncovers pathways, traditions, resources, and vitalities of mind supposedly buried. It also comes from a resilient sympathy showing particular breadth. For just as the poetry shares in the British experience, of a people enduring beyond an immense and potentially overwhelming past, so it also speaks to the state of other peoples as they surmount a crueler or more violent history: like the Mexicans in *The Well* (1966), the Hungarians in *Over Elizabeth Bridge* (1972), the Caribbean Londoners in *Portobello Carnival 1973* (1978), or the Oklahoma Indians in *Interpretations* (1987). Yet Tomlinson's feeling for possibility—and for those who assuage fate by finding freshnesses beneath the seemingly arid—has its distinct Stoke origin. People of the Potteries may have had to work all week in mines, potbanks, factories, or offices, but they also made the most of opportunities for recreation close at hand—as with the widespread cultivation of allotments (like those above Etruria Vale commemorated in Tomlinson's 1963 poem about his father, *John Maydew*) and with sports like fishing.

As a member of several angling clubs in his youth, Tomlinson has remarked on the ease of access to the pools and streams of Staffordshire, often reachable by walking out along the canals that cut through

Stoke. But such practical means touches on an image central to this poet: of a dark mass literally penetrated by water and where light, freshness or pastoral cannot be entered upon until the walker has also gone over the ground, step-by-step. In the poetry, similarly, an instinctive desire to flow through barriers toward an "Eden" of renewal, is accompanied by a discipline of the mind that knows it must negotiate contours and concreteness before it has earned a way forward. Patience goes hand in hand with desire, like the virtues involved in fishing that Tomlinson records, as he kept his shadow off the water and the self unobtrusive, "Silently . . . willing the fish to appear—or not willing, just letting the fish drift up, luring them in a peculiar will-lessness into one's mental orbit."[3] Fishing, indeed, like the process of certain Tomlinson poems, is the partnership of the unrushed mind and of all that is contained in the fluid unconscious. The poetry also shows a logic working with water, to acknowledge concreteness yet find a way through it (particularly where the concrete means deadlock or desolation) to a radiance that is not fantasy, but is built from the substance through which it has emerged. An early poem, with a Stoke setting, *The Slag Heap* (1951), attempts to suggest this way forward by breaking down an industrial waste mass—in the eye's imagination—through the colors of a setting sun. "Wash off the dross" is the aim as the heap is worked on: "Crushed-fruit-evening-red / Swealing the western slope." In the end, however, it is not a dying day that will cleanse: "Only the morning's lessive can / Wash out the gold from black so rich."

The "gold" in this poem, however, stays unidentified, no more attainable than the metal sought by the alchemists whose process of would-be purification has been borrowed as a metaphor. But twenty years later, in *The Marl Pits,* where the discovery of light in Stoke blackness, not "gold," is clearly the quest, Tomlinson needs no alchemy. For by now he has earned his own means of transformation—a process of language that is grounded in his knowledge of Stoke's working environment, where the excavators for clay have left behind "a landscape of disembowellings":

> Digging
> The marl, they dug a second nature
>   And water, seeping up to fill their pits,
> Sheeted them to lakes that wink and shine
>   Between tips and steeples, streets and waste
> In slow reclaimings, shimmers, balancings,
>   As if kindling Eden rescinded its own loss
> And words and water came of the same source.

Unlike his early attempt in *The Slag Heap,* Tomlinson now lets the sensibility work its way through density, with language itself taking on the quality of a tough but penetrable concreteness—plosively and sibilantly revealed in the hard-edged syllabic surfaces of *p*'s and *t*'s, with "pits," "tips and steeples, streets and waste." There is this same factlike opacity in "Sheeted," but one also hears watery stealth ("seeping") that has begun to accrete inside the substance hollowed open (like earth dug into) so that the fluidity of long-drawn *ee*'s is actually playing within solidity, "Between tips and steeples, streets and waste." The infiltration also lights up the space between things—a world of singularities, not a homogeneous mass. With space, there also comes the sense of time patiently revealed in the clean, luminous parts of its process "In slow reclaimings, shimmers, balancings." It is an equanimity of vision, a stability poised on transience, where the fluid participles ("—ings") twinkle within, and verify, the hard concreteness of *d*'s—not as a fancifulness indulged, but as the verbally proven steps that move in exactness with paradisal desire, "as if kindling Eden rescinded its own loss."

"Rescinded" has the precision of a law quickened rather than fantasy. Similarly, "Eden" speaks for accords grounded in live possibility, not an epiphanal glimpse of timeless moments or dream of the unfallen. For the wondrous, lit quality of relations, perfections, wholenesses, in "Eden" of *The Marl Pits,* and throughout Tomlinson's poetry, has the body of practical vigor, intent on recovering what Pound has called "the radiant world where one thought cuts through another with clear edge, a world of moving energies . . . magnetisms that take form, that are seen, or that border the invisible."[4] Such words (from the essay on Cavalcanti) have retained a special potency for Tomlinson—together with Pound's own recovery of light in the *Cantos,* as mythic, Dionysiac energies take body again in wave or grove. Yet, for all the importance of "Eden," Tomlinson is essentially a mythless poet, because he sees myth as potential evasion: a way of escaping direct encounter with singularities and the verifiable terms of relation. Neither the "tensile" light of the *Cantos*—nor the Poundian stress on a *paradiso,* nor the would-be magnetizing together of incoherent parts—have been as comparably important as Tomlinson's delight in the vitality of Pound's movement along the verse-line. It has been Pound's energy in dealing with materials—the transformation of the elements—that has mattered more than the actual myths of metamorphosis, as in *Canto II,* which Tomlinson read when, as a Stoke schoolboy in 1944, he bought Pound's *Selected Poems.*

1: A Lucid Darkness 23

> Lithe turning of water,
>   sinews of Poseidon,
> Black azure and hyaline,
>   glass wave over Tyro.

The writing's clean, lucid sinews, not those of Poseidon enveloping the nymph, were to point Tomlinson's art in its mythless direction. His was to be an art not of received frameworks but of new instancings: a poetry in which encounter and incident become central, in which relations with people, place, nature, and objects need different kinds of poetic form to suit the individual fact of each occasion. When the verse of William Carlos Williams showed Tomlinson in the late 1950s how a cleanly energetic verse-line could take the measure of American ground that was industrialized and semirural (New Jersey offering its own poetic way into the Potteries of Stoke), Pound's example became even more indirect in its effect on Tomlinson's development.

But the Poundian sense of Mediterranean light within solidity remained, to combine with Tomlinson's practical feeling for the way people work for a kinship with a ground—earth and concreteness illuminated, as it were, by a hard-won relation. This grounded quality is seen early on when, after a job in London as a schoolteacher, Tomlinson first went to Italy in 1950 and began to write the poems that were to compose *The Necklace* five years later. The concern of the verse to see the object clearly without blurring by the ego goes with the need to articulate the terms by which people, or "we," make right relation with the encircling terrain. The poems in *The Necklace,* far from being the lonely observations of an aesthetic purist, have behind them the substance of observed place, implicitly of Italy or the Ligurian coast near La Serra, that its people have farmed and terraced, often with great difficulty. To speak, then, as Tomlinson does in *The Necklace,* of a world "bodied over against one," is to mark its resistant identity yet also to enter it, with a language of contemplation that Tomlinson rightly sees as "dense in the usages of community." One also hears such "usages" in the more obviously peopled landscapes of *Up at La Serra* (1963), *The Return* (1987), and *The Compact: at Volterra* (1972), where Tuscan farmers rigorously till an earth of subsidence: "The crack in the stone, the black filament / Reaching into the rockface." In *this* Etruria, one is a long way geographically from the allotments in Stoke's Etruria Vale, but not so far from Tomlinson's native instinct for the way a people nurtures a relationship with their land, however formidable the task. The grape farmers of Volterra, as they "pit their patience against the dust's vacuity," make their "compact" with light, day, time, and fruitfulness that is part of their wary truce with a crumbling earth gripped and compacted—the perpetual reencounter with "black filament" and the nightly undoing of their efforts,

>   as if
> Unreasoned care were its own and our
> Sufficient reason, to repair the night's derisions,
>   Repay the day's delight, here where the pebbles
> Of half-ripe grapes abide their season,
>   Their fostering leaves outlined by unminding sky.

Tomlinson's trust in the possibility of light through blackness has another voicing in his memoir *Some Americans* (1981) where he recounts his experience of the place that inspired Pound to write "Gold fades in the gloom / Under the blue-black roof, Placidia's" (*Canto XXI*). Visiting the tomb of Galla Placidia in Ravenna, he found radiance inside stone: "The experience of a diaphaneity that, lost, can be recovered. Brick pierced by an alabaster not merely marmoreal. Alabaster as a touchstone—for light. A structure by no means weightless invaded by its opposite or its complement. Brick and mosaic suffering a sea-change."[5] The way forward, then, is to a poetry where contraries hold together, to a poetry of retrievable kinships where there can be space within density, a sky within the ground, a mind entering the textures of rock, leaf, or sea without losing its human self-responsibility or egotistically dominating what it finds. But the practical means for such tact and adventure were to be exemplified for Tomlinson at their fullest not by the model of another poet or another contemporary. Instead, at the back of all his endeavor to take his bearings on the English literary past and future directions lay the sustaining, educative force of John Ruskin.

II

Some of what Ruskin had to teach about the movement of water and clouds, Tomlinson already knew instinctively as a young fisherman who had learnt the importance of careful, self-effacing observation. More consciously, however, when he later came to read Ruskin's *Modern Painters*—especially the first book (1843) with its chapters on the "truth" of water, light, vegetation, and stone—he had before him, in Ruskin's attachment to the "singular veracity"[6] of pure fact, a whole attitude that might be developed further. Ruskin's emphasis on "truth," of course, was part of his strategy to champion the visionary exactness of Turner, as leader of a modern movement, above artists of the picturesque and sublime like Claude, Poussin, Salvator Rosa—painters whose reliance on careless detail or haunted wildness of scene showed Ruskin that they had failed to see the contingent world that exists outside the self and its fixed imaginings. Ruskin's adherence to fact over cliché expresses, therefore, that nonegotistic side of him freed from Victorian pathos and introspection, which had special interest for Tomlinson: a way of seeing that counters fatalism's excessive regard for the transitory by giving witness to constancies, solidities, textures, and multiplicities.

Science helped define for Ruskin his feelings with regard to the world's particularities and kept him, at his best, from emotional and religious confusion. As botanist, meteorologist, mineralogist, and geologist (characteristically taking a cyanometer to measure the blueness of sky on his visit to Switzerland in 1835), Ruskin was to show in *Modern Painters* how science could be a way of clarifying response while keeping a sensitive objectivity. This, as Tomlinson says with regard to Cézanne, was not the "outmoded objectivity of nineteenth century positivistic science—the objectivity which supposed a complete division between the observer and the observed," but "an outward gaze that would draw the sensuous world closer to the inner man and that would narrow the gap between abstraction and sensation, between intellect and things."[7] In this respect, Ruskin the scientist prefigures those such as Marianne Moore and D. H. Lawrence whose education in biology vitally partnered their intuitive, objective regard for the world's singularities—whether its birds, beasts, flowers, or mountains.

But Ruskin needed fact, and its clarifying of relation, as a sanity. One of his first publications is not a piece on art or architecture but, in significant sobriety, "Facts and Considerations on the Strata of Mont Blanc." This side of his sensibility is understood exactly by Patricia Ball in *The Science of Aspects* when she shows that Ruskin's science was implicitly at variance with—then later a conscious escape from—the self-tormenting intensities and egotistic overflow, which he had inherited as response from one strand of romanticism. "Not Manfred's agonies," she says, "but the stones and strata of the mountain on which he stands, now call to Ruskin for recognition."[8] Gaining that standpoint (despite his own Byronic inheritance and the belief in self-damnation derived from his Evangelical background), Ruskin could see with special clarity the age's "dreamy and sentimental sadness, tendency to reverie, and general patheticalness," which he attacks, in its literary manifestation, as part of the "Pathetic Fallacy" in book 3 of *Modern Painters*.[9] But if one looks more closely at Ruskin's characterization of the romantic poet projecting his misery into nature, it is evident that all such maudlin overhumanizing is perceived as compensation—sham linkages in place of the kinship that the sensibility has never tried to earn. Therefore, Ruskin's censure of artists who treat nature as the ego's repository—clamorously echoing human self-pity or turned into a savagery, the landscape as melodrama—is really an analysis of bogus affinities that have been created to hide failure, the inability to witness, either in a moral or visual sense. Unseen, never truly observed, the world becomes a blind, wild thing (like "The cruel, crawling foam" quoted by Ruskin from Kingsley's *Alton Locke*) or a harsh, impersonal process so separate from humanity that the Pathetic Fallacy must sentimentally cover the gap. Thus the garden roses in Tennyson's "monodrama" *Maud* are turned into a chorus to sing the pain of the Hamletian narrator.[10]

Ruskin suggests the failure of relation between poet and world more fully in his examples from Wordsworth, Byron, and Shelley. But his position is revealed at its keenest, and at its most vigorously antitragic, in his characterization of Keats as a violent drinker of nature who "has no more real sympathy for her than he has with a bottle of claret." This Keats is a poet of momentary sensation, never seeing nature except in terrible transience. He "'bursts joy's grape against it', gets nothing but misery, and a bitter taste of dregs, out of his desperate draught."[11] (One sees, with sudden force, the relevance of Tomlinson's comment that the romantics "virtually *swallow* the phenomenal world.")[12] There is a wasting of nature that Ruskin similarly sees in Oliver Wendell Holmes when the latter calls a flower a "spendthrift crocus . . . with his cup of gold."[13] Ruskin's correction—that, in fact, the crocus is "a hardy plant" and saffron in color, not gold—goes back to his energetic distrust of Keatsian practice, as in book 2 of *Endymion* where the fervid hero, his "dry palate" unslaked, takes refreshment from seeing the ocean unroll a wave

> Down whose green back the short-lived foam, all hoar,
> Bursts gradual with wayward indolence.

Citing this as evidence of an aesthetic malaise, Ruskin also writes with the authority of an observer who has learned through Turner's art—and his own science—how to look at the actual motion of the sea in its nonindolent hardiness, its unspent constancy. Already, in *Modern Painters,* he has spoken of water's impact on the shore, not as "a passive wave, rolling sleepily forward until it tumbles heavily, prostrated upon the beach, but a sweeping exertion of tremendous and living strength . . . which never perishes but recoils and recovers."[14]

Significantly Ruskin's quotation from *Endymion* comes in a chapter, "The Classical Landscape," where constancy is set against the momentary in a larger way, with Ruskin's evocation of Mediterranean agriculture and civilization: man actively collaborating with nature across the seasons. Indeed, here one comes closer to the values behind Ruskin's rejection not only of self-involved romanticism but also of those post-Renaissance painters who glory in savagely rugged landscape. For the Greek landscape that Homer shows him is one in which the highest virtues are "order, symmetry, and fruitfulness." This is a setting not for epic violence but for "utility," and the "practical common sense" seen in Homer's descriptions of husbandry and tillage, like the grove, vine, fountains, and violet meadow admired by Mercury in book 5 of *The Odyssey*.[15] Furthermore, in choosing to end his chapter on classical landscape with lines from Shenstone's *Rural Elegance* about the fruits due to cultivators, Ruskin shows even more clearly how far he is from romantic reclusiveness or rhapsodizing. The sympathy here is with that Georgic tradition in poetry that, through Dryden's (and Virgil's) example, took a markedly English character in, for example, *Windsor Forest, Epistle to Burlington* and *The Seasons*. Augustan energy and practicality also attracted Ruskin in his reading of Johnson. *The Idler* and *The Rambler*, he says in his autobiographical *Praeterita*, were his continual companions on his youthful trips to the continent, and it was Johnson, with his "adamantine common-sense," who saved Ruskin, it is said, from his own "sanguine and metaphysical temperament."[16]

By such an admission, one sees why, in *Modern Painters*, Ruskin had to put aside the picturesque, the subjective, the loosely wild, the epiphanal, or "the light that never was," and move toward a literature of encounter—a record of instances in nature met and seen by the human observer who owes the wonder of that world a clear-eyed, reasoned exactness. There can be a writing, as Ruskin shows, where the passionate mind is analytical yet instinctively reverent and where individual perceptions, holding off mere introspection, can be brought back into a renewed communal consciousness. By means of a prose devoted to instances of light, cloud, rocks, water, leaves—to a world of particularities not fleeting away but celebrated by a constancy of mind—Ruskin makes it ultimately possible for Tomlinson's poetry to take its bearings, for example, on those moments in Wordsworth when unexpected encounter (with the leech gatherer in *Resolution and Independence* or with the uprearing cliff in *The Prelude*, book 1) powerfully realigns the self to its place in existence. What is visionary can be seen as intrinsic to factuality, not in spite of it or above it. Where Ruskin sets against personal reverie an idea of Augustan "sense" or social consensus ("among men of average intellect the most useful members of society are the dissectors, not the dreamers"),[17] he opens the way not to gradgrindery, but to a nature that in poetry can be entered together by feelings *and* mind, without the necessity of pathos or mental arrogance.

Walter Scott, in Ruskin's eyes, had already shown healthy deference to things by not personalizing the thorn tree in his poem from *Marmion*. With the tree allowed to be itself—free from the observer's delight or misery—the poet, in his unselfish sympathy for the commonalty of old and young, has such thoughts, it is said, "as all sensible men ought to have in such places."[18] But Scott's "sensible" lack of poignancy is not the only cause of Ruskin's interest. For Scott, avoiding sentimental effusions, looks at nature objectively because to him it has no divine connotation. He is, sees Ruskin, a faithless figure in a faithless age, and that, in *Modern Painters,* is a mark of his value as a writer who never muddles together the natural object and creative Providence. Scott has almost the clarity of the Greeks, who, in Ruskin's account of the classical landscape, kept things apart, able to believe in a god of the sea, yet equally capable of treating the wave as a cold, salt water fact.[19] By such separateness, Ruskin himself largely avoids confusion. God is assumed to be there behind nature, but for all practical purposes, Ruskin treats what he sees with the zest of secular vision, his scientific practicality abetting that passion as he looks for an order, not divine rule, in apparent chaos.

This is not to forget (as Tomlinson does not, in *Frondes Agrestes*) the way that Ruskin can at times regard nature as a symbolic typifier of God's handiwork. His greatest energy, however, lies not in such shortcuts, but in the kind of groundlevel accuracy, working over the very contours and surface textures, that he so admires in Turner's careful portrayal of rocks, with his "perfect imaginative conception of every recess and projection." A man who can understand how Turner "*feels* the stone as he works over it; every touch . . . full of tender gradation," also has the sympathetic insight *and* geological rigor to take in as a whole a vastly larger mass of stone like the Alpine aguilles.[20] Here is an apparently overwhelming "inextricable complexity," but met and balanced by his tracing of "*some* authoritative principle . . . a system of structure." Indeed, all the corrugations, pinnacles, and intricacies set up against the mind by mountains can only be grasped by tracing in such labyrinths the "one mighty continuous caprice"[21] of Alpine form. Similarly, looking at the sea in ways taught by Turner, Ruskin notes the breakers' "irreconcilable mixture of fury and formalism."²² Speaking of Turner's *Long Ships Lighthouse,* he observes how, despite the waters' "dizzy whirl of . . . undirected rage," every one of the subdivided myriad waves "is not . . . a separate surge, but part and portion of a vast one."²³

Chaotic difficulty and the fragmentary need not overwhelm because, as Tomlinson has said, "The mind is a hunter of forms."²⁴ Indeed, it is by his awareness of Ruskin's investigation into the laws within phenomena, that one sees him appreciating one particular artist's "labour of observation / In face of meteorological fact," when presenting *A Meditation on John Constable* (1960). "Painting is a science, and should be pursued as an inquiry into the laws of nature,"²⁵ says Constable on landscape painting in an epigraph that Tomlinson reconsiders in his poem: "He admired accidents, because governed by laws." The laws are a constancy at work in ever-changing nature. But they also exist as the light of exactly judged relation, neither overradiant nor overdark, that the self makes with the opacity of fact, as when it sees the clouds "temper" the sun's blaze, "Massed darks / Blotting it back . . . until the source / Unmasks, floods its retreating bank / With raw fire." This, "As the mass thickens," and the sunlight narrows down from romantic overflow, is the pinpointed yet durable light, sensuously intelligent, that one gains from the darkness of fact. Reenacting what Constable had to teach, Tomlinson significantly commends him in terms that refer one back to the escape from the Pathetic Fallacy in Ruskin's celebration of Turner. For Constable's descriptive delight "wrings from the brush / The errors of a mind, so tempered, / It can forgo all pathos." Excess is squeezed to exactness: to that passionate steadiness by which this painter confronts abundance or (as seen by Ruskin) Turner keeps a staying power of consciousness in his depiction of water. For the latter artist "never loses himself and his subject in the splash of the fall, his presence of mind never fails as he goes down."²⁶ Instead of the visual style plunging into an "indiscriminate foam," there is a grasp of form's concavity and concentrity in the rush of water; so also in the catenary lines of Turner's *Upper Fall of the Tees,* where, according to Ruskin, analysis goes with perception as the fall begins to sweep out "in wilder stretching . . . to send down the rocket-like, lance-pointed, whizzing shafts at its sides, sounding for the bottom."²⁷

To take such soundings, without blind immersion, will become a major impulse of Tomlinson's poetry. Thus the human figure of *Swimming Chenango Lake* (1969) begins to spell out, as he cleaves the cold water, a lost instinctive language of mind and senses: "He reaches in-

and-through to that space / The body is heir to." It is the penetrative fluidity, the entry into nature's profusion and resistance, whose terms of access were first fully paced out in *Seeing is Believing* (1960) with Tomlinson's meditation on Constable and *Cézanne at Aix*. The latter poem, carefully paralleling in verse the way Cézanne's non-egotistic art takes the measure of Mont Ste. Victoire, implicitly carries forward, as with the Constable poem, Ruskin's example in celebrating Turner. The "stone bridgehead / To that which is tangible" is a point of entry into nature's mass and an artistic tradition, just as Turner's painting, *The Junction of the Greta and the Tees* gives Ruskin in its foreground detail, stepping-stones for the human sensibility and eye to move from the small standpoint into a colossal maze of solidities. "Every separate block" of stone remains a "study, chiselled and varied in its parts . . . without ever losing in a single instance its subordinate position," its place in the choked torrent bed where, in the larger view, resides a "mass of shattered rock, thrown down with the profusion and carelessness of nature herself."[28] There are, as Ruskin shows through Turner, important paths that the consciousness can travel from near to far, in its keeping relation to the whole. With Tomlinson, such means of transit will have to be clarified further as lucid, convincing passageways, in word and image, through labyrinthine nature. His poetry has to be more stylistically spare than Ruskin's prose of discovery needed to be. Ruskin, for instance, looking at a tree, finds that it is

> never opaque; it is always transparent with crumbling lights in it letting you through to the sky: then out of this, come, heavier and heavier, the masses of illumined foliage . . . then, under these, you get deep passages of broken irregular gloom, passing into transparent, green-lighted misty hollows . . . but all penetrable and transparent, and, in proportion, inextricable and incomprehensible, except where across the labyrinth and the mystery . . . falls, close to us, some solitary spray, some wreath of two or three motionless large leaves, the type and embodying of all that in the rest we feel and imagine, but can never see.[29]

Such entering into a recessed world, plane giving way to plane, made Ruskin a vital mainstay in the perceptions of the poet who was to write *The Necklace* and *Seeing is Believing*. But such a passage is also a reminder of the problems to be overcome by a poetry that, wanting to grapple with multiplicities and densities, must not confuse the eye or mind with overloaded syntax. Yet the "solitary spray" in the quotation is clue to the way that an image of particularity can be an Aeneas-like guide through a darkness: a lucidity of instance and style that might traverse complication without being a simplifying travesty. It is that penetrative possibility which Tomlinson was to develop in his own way, as Ruskin did in his, after he had seen, like a revelation, the small aspen tree that he records against the sky near Fontainebleau in 1842.[30] Here, indeed, was the exactness that took him away from a dissipating romanticism towards the great perceptions of *Modern Painters*—towards the passionate sobriety that was able to see, with all its implications, "a little flower apprehended in the very plain and leafy fact of it."[31]

III

Tomlinson's own way of apprehending fact was to take a particular direction with regard to English and American poetry that significantly did not include the one poet and student of *Modern Painters*—Hopkins—with whom he might be expected to have a special affinity. Yet Tomlinson's distance from Hopkins as a poet rather than as prose observer (from those very Hopkins qualities of sprung rhythm and syllabic wordplay that became increasingly prominent in his poetry of the 1960s onwards) helps to define the necessary divergence of both Ruskinians. What Tomlinson's early poetry could not directly borrow from Hopkins's art is as revealing as the two men's similarity of outlook.

After all, it was Tomlinson, echoing Hopkins, who decided to keep a journal of observations "from a Ruskinese point of view."[32] If Ruskin's viewpoint sharpened Tomlinson's insight into the forgoing of "pathos" by Constable, it also enabled Hopkins to distinguish between Pathetic Fallacy ("imposed outwards from the mind ... by melancholy or strong feeling"[33]) and his own attunement to the divine "instress" that he felt in nature. His was a remarkable trust in the apparent fortuitousness of the world's shapes and textures—seeing them clearly because of his belief in a law behind accidents, that, though more overtly Christian than the laws of Ruskin, Constable, or Tomlinson, did not interfere with his fidelity to fact. "Chance left free to act falls into an order as well as purpose," Hopkins noted in a journal entry of February 1873 as he described drifts fluted by the wind and "the random clods and broken heaps of snow made by the cast of a broom."[34] As open to the wayward givenness of things as William Carlos Williams, Hopkins can also show a Tomlinson-like patience in his watching of the sea: ready to follow the fall of the breakers (August 1872) so that he may "unpack the huddling and gnarls of the water and law out the shapes and the sequence of the running."[35]

But Hopkins's close, attentive verve in the journals—explaining and tracing the wondrous detail of flowers, leaves, clouds, water, glaciers, mountains, birds, sheep, fish—is overcome by more explicitly Christian considerations in the poetry. The man who noted in his journal (April 1871), "Just caught sight of a little whirlwind which ran very fast careering across our pond"[36] and then goes on to analyze and draw the two motions that compose it is markedly different from the poet who transformed a similar chance encounter ("I caught this morning morning's minion") into a celebration of Christ's immanence through the windhover. Moreover, Hopkins's poetic self, serving the holy symbol and humbled by awe, cannot come into full, equitable dealings with the nature he eagerly contemplates. The journal-like adherence to the shifts and surprises of birdflight ("how he rung upon the rein of a wimpling wing ... then off, off forth on swing") must turn into exaltation of the transcendental over the earthbound and all that seems plodding. There *is* a gleam shared between sky and ground; his heart has "Stirred for a bird." But Hopkins decisively moves away from an art of paired affinities and encounter—from the possibility of the mythless, nonsymbolic, secular yet religious poetry that Tomlinson sought.

For Tomlinson, the meeting between world and self would have to be truer to mutual interchange, where human consciousness can be reverently alert, letting things *be* in their singularity, yet earning a kinship and not simply subjugating the self to a Christian deference before things. Hopkins in the poem *To What Serves Mortal Beauty?* cannot but answer his own question, "how meet beauty?" by saying, "Merely meet it; own, / Home at heart, heaven's sweet gift; then leave, let that alone." It is the emphasis that shows Tomlinson's presentation of a land's variety in *Winter Encounters* ("House and hollow; village and valley-side: / The ceaseless pairings") more intimately engaged in relations, in time and place processes, than Hopkins with the variegations of *Pied Beauty*. Tomlinson's poem (from *Seeing is Believing,* 1960) takes the eye into the close network created by a country and its people together: "Lengthened shadows / Intersecting, the fields seem parcelled smaller / As if by hedgerow within hedgerow." Hopkins, by contrast, cherishes from afar, listing at a distance the dappled variety for which he praises God: "Landscape plotted and pieced—fold, fallow, and plough; / And áll trádes, their gear and tackle and trim."

In the journals, however, where he is less bound by the urge to celebrate, Hopkins is altogether more penetrative and tenacious in tracking the changes of phenomena. Also, Tomlinson-like, he can concern himself with the means by which, in image or comparison, one keeps pace with nature's speed, not losing one's self or simplifying what is seen. In an entry of July 1873 he notes "the bubble-jestled skirt of foam jumping back against the fall, which cuts its way clean and will not let it through, and there spitting up in long white ragged shots and bushes like a mess of thongs of bramble."[37] Two days later he describes lightning: "Flashes lacing two clouds above or the cloud and the earth started upon the eyes in live veins of rincing or riddling liquid white, inched and jagged as if it were the shivering of a bright riband string which had once been kept bound round a blade and danced back into its pleatings."[38] Catching this extraordinary dance, Hopkins feels no compulsion to heighten it into the drama of holy terror, with "lightning and lashed rod" in *The Wreck of the Deutschland,* or to sound any resurrective trumpet note, as with the end of *That Nature Is a Heraclitean Fire.* Instead, it is remarkable how well Hopkins approaches his best journal-like form at the beginning of the "Heraclitean" poem, when he allows the verse to show the metamorphic process of things. His Christian sense of the end to existence does not at this point overwhelm his delight in the way things happen—how the sky's movement is actually conveyed to the reader as shadows on a screen:

> Down roughcast, down dazzling whitewash,   wherever an elm arches,
> Shivelights and shadowtackle in long   lashes lace, lance, and pair.

It is here in particular that Hopkins and the Tomlinson of *Winter Encounters* share common ground. Theirs is not the praising of "pied beauty," but the entrance into the body of things, as also with the "pied / anatomies" in Tomlinson's poem of chance and incident, *The White Van* (1972). Encountered ahead of him on the road, a white van becomes a screen for the shadow play of trees upon it: the "black and white / abstraction of a coloured day," allowing the mind to grasp analytically, take purchase on, the profusion of the natural scene. Fullness is thus made realizable again, as the van turns off the road, unblocking the way ahead, so that "distance . . . re-opens its density / of gold, green, amethyst." One might imagine that Hopkins shares a similar concern when he continues the "Heraclitean" poem by tracing the changes in earth after rain:

>   in pool and rutpeel parches
> Squandering ooze to squeezed   dough, crust, dust; stanches, starches
> Squadroned masks and manmarks   treadmire toil there
> Footfretted in it.

But for Hopkins the poet, unlike Tomlinson, engagement in the flux is an ultimately tragic process. He has no Keatsian excess here ("Squandering ooze" being squeezed to dry, hard perceptions), but this overspeedy vision of nature, looking towards the world's end, subverts one's human standpoint. "Manmark" or consciousness can keep no footing, no hold: "Man, how fast his firedint, his mark on mind is gone . . . all is in an enormous dark / Drowned." The only saving light in all this rush to darkness is Christ's "eternal beam."

Hopkins's religious finality, however, was not the only factor that made Tomlinson remain at a distance (just as he would later oppose art devoted to grand endings, whether the suicidal, Promethean, or *Götterdämmerung* variety). Since Tomlinson's instinct was for continuity not rupture, for poetry as a vigorously awakened communal speech not a private intensity, his sympathies were less with Hopkins's eccentricity—the coinages, compressions, and verbal wrenchings— than with the attentive adventure of the journals, drawing upon "the naked thew and sinew of the language." Donald Davie, Tomlinson's tutor at Cambridge, characterized the physicality of Hopkins's poetry as a mark of his insufficient respect for the wider resources of English, describing Hopkins's language as being "crammed, stimulated and knotted together," subject to "Sandow-exercises until it is a muscle-bound monstrosity."[39] Such comments, in Davie's *The Purity of Diction in English Verse* (1952), with its emphasis on the shared ground of society's language and the individual writer in the Augustan age, would seem to reflect part of Tomlinson's position (and some, as has been seen, of Ruskin's pleasure in Augustan "common sense"). But Davie's antiromanticism and his unfairness to Hopkins had its own excess, and his book was not for Tomlinson the unofficial manifesto of the "moderate" style as it has since been viewed in regard to the "movement" poets of the 1950s like Philip Larkin, Kingsley Amis, and Robert Conquest. Tomlinson's own attack on their *New Lines* anthology, on a contented Little Englandism and underpowered tameness, serves to suggest how, despite his reservations, he remained intrinsically closer to Hopkins than they could be.

Even Tomlinson's motives in rejecting the poetry of Dylan Thomas, chief target for the movement's vilification of bardic extremism, went deeper than dislike of theatricality. For, with sympathetic spirit yet a strong sense of thwarted direction, he could hear in Thomas the crudified voice of Hopkins and a debased surrealism—a poetic speech of energy, wordplay, and image so bombastically corrupted that Tomlinson's own impulse towards such possibilities had to become emphatically separate from Thomas's art before he could develop them cleanly in his own style. *Seeing is Believing*, therefore, was a means towards a subtler tune than the sub-Hopkinsian clamor of Thomas and his apocalyptic ceremonializing of the self in verse such as this:

> Never until the mankind making
> Bird beast and flower
> Fathering and all humbling darkness
> Tells with silence the last light breaking
> And the still hour
> Is come of the sea tumbling in harness
>
> And I must enter again the round
> Zion of the water bead
> And the synagogue of the ear of corn

Effectively, Thomas was to distance Tomlinson even more from the verbally extreme qualities of Hopkins, setting inhibitions in the way of a metamorphic and acoustically alive poetry. As one hears in lines from Tomlinson's *Poem* (1951), this, very early, was the direction he was travelling toward—not to make an egotistic entrance into a "round / Zion," but to space out a terrain of neighborhood through the ear:

> Wakening with the window over fields
> To the coin-clear harness-jingle as a float
> Clips by, and each succeeding hoof fall, now remote,
> Breaks clean and frost-sharp on the unstopped ear.

Not until *A Peopled Landscape* (1963), however, after he had heard native English anew through American poetry (as well as Spanish and Russian), was he able to create a poetry where the chiming of self with world could come fully in its own without any resemblance to verse like this:

> The force that through the green fuse drives the flower
> Drives my green age; that blasts the roots of trees
> Is my destroyer.
> And I am dumb to tell the crooked rose
> My youth is bent by the same wintry fever.

Compulsive resonances without articulated relation—Thomas's qualities are those of the backward-moving romanticism that Tomlinson depicts in *Antecedents* (1960). Leading the poets of the 1940s like a latter-day Rimbaud, Thomas provides "The force / That through the green dark, drove them / Muffled dissatisfactions." They return, as Tomlinson sees, to "the forsaken garden"—to a place of potential growth, of verdurous relation—or rather, as one sees in Thomas, to a place of nostalgias and would-be innocence. One thinks of the "young and easy" fusions of *Fern Hill,* or of the merely dreamed kinships of creatures and place in the poem *In Country Sleep,* "the rooks / Cawing from their black bethels soaring." It is, for example, lack of relation genuinely astir between poet and landscape in *A Winter's Tale* that makes Thomas jig and shake things: "The carved limbs in the rock / Leap, as to trumpets. Calligraphy of the old / Leaves is dancing."

By contrast, the "calligraphy of present pleasure" that Tomlinson saw through a different artist, John Constable, is one that would have to be attentively *read*. Learning to construe signs and textures, to find light through the "green dark," he would also, in the 1950s, come nearer to his own purposes when considering Rilke's sense of objective being in a Duino elegy: how "the presences about one (house, bridge, fountain, gate, jug, fruit-tree, window, to use Rilke's phrase) become all the more charged with their own potency, exist the more sharply and incontrovertibly in themselves."[40] Without Hopkins's Christianity or Thomas's sham holiness, those "presences" intimate the secular yet religious quality embodied in the simple solidities about which Tomlinson wrote when he first entered Italy in 1950:

> The commonest objects
> Take presence from light. I instance
> Only bowl and water-jug, white porcelain
> Gross with the poverty of utility.
> It gathers sun, it rounds to a richness
> This double light, this scape with its
> Blazing undulations, its sky
> Dissolving the islands, hallows
> The least washed stones, moon-pocked and mountainous.[41]

In this previously unpublished fragment of verse Tomlinson is seeking the kind of balance by which the later art is poised. A religious fullness ("presence," "grace," "hallows") is set against, and kept in check by, the unsymbolic plainness of "commonest objects." In the same way, the "poverty of utility" counterweighs the riches of sunlight. (One remembers Ruskin's praise for Homeric "utility.") But domestic plain containment of potentially overpowering luxuriance is not just limitation but also balanced reception: the means by which one habitably gathers in and takes the measure of profusion without being an overemptied or an arrogant self.

It is the receiving yet shaping relation—the little container defining the newly clarified richness of the luminous solidities—that is later portrayed by Tomlinson in *The Ruin (Seeing is Believing)*. This time, however, the "presence" invited in has more to do with a Poundian "radiant world," with Roman *Lares* and gods of household, than a Christian deity:

> The laric world where the bowl glistens with presence
> Gracing the table on which it unfolds itself.

Conversely, Tomlinson's other revision of earlier lines in *The Ruin* speaks of a weakened "presence," where humanity has failed to inhabit place with any receiving openness or style. Now, in his sharper judgement, a decaying door in an abandoned house "could accuse / By this scant presence its clustering neighbours / Gross with the poverty of utility." It is, one realizes, the kind of moral perception relating to the world, or obfuscation of it, that gains new edge in *The Necklace* and *Seeing is Believing*. Ruskin's call for fidelity to fact remains a powerful example. But now also, with the poetry of Wallace Stevens and Marianne Moore, Tomlinson is to find his own way of proceeding from instances to plenitude—from engagement with the singular thing to a lit plurality.

2

"Thus Men Make a Mountain"

I

American poetry offered Tomlinson's developing art a vital sense of distance. Land and language—English as well as American—could be seen with an objectivity that leads to fresh relation. In the verse of Stevens, Moore, and Williams in particular, Tomlinson was taught the necessity of a poet's waking up to the strange otherness of place—all that one must negotiate with and not assume. For "bodied over against one" (to use Tomlinson's words in *The Necklace,* taken from Martin Buber),[1] America's immensity, geographical variety, and resistance to would-be settlers have historically forced on its literature the need to find accommodation with it and *in* it. The problem has been to discover the terms of truce, the civil means, by which both writer and people inhabit such alien ground and become its natives, grasping its "animal" concreteness. For Tomlinson also, the stimulus was crucial in his own reaching out toward the tangible, pluralistic world.

But in being open to such possibilities, Tomlinson had to keep a balance. The American sense of the immediate moment could slide into loose impermanence, just as the delight in multiplicity could turn into the kind of relativism where distinct things have a flat sameness of value: all densities and resistances softened and disembodied by the idealizing mind. Yet where Tomlinson can encounter a clear, American sparseness in looking at the world—purified of distraction rather than body—he has a literary means of reaching further toward concreteness. Therefore Stevens's poetic detachment (successor to the heightened mental consciousness Lawrence saw in the nineteenth-century American writers) is to provide the cool aeration of style that brings about the more engaged objectivity of *The Necklace*. Through this encounter, Tomlinson's verse-form is significantly clarified. Pared down to an irreducibly exact quality of line, phrase, and syllable, it achieves the discipline by which further progress is made, particularly when the fuller-bodied wit and flexibility of a different American

2: "Thus Men Make a Mountain"

poetry, Marianne Moore's, has its effect on the art of *Seeing is Believing.*

Throughout Tomlinson's engagement with American verse, however, there was a steadying factor, "the sheet anchor," as he says, "of having read Ruskin."[2] Indeed it was his Ruskinian sense of duty owed to the "truths" of elemental experience that was a counterweight to the potential aesthetic lightness of Stevens. Certainly, Tomlinson's interests as author of *The Necklace* coincide more with Stevens in his early *Harmonium* poems (1915–23) than with the later imaginer of Supreme Fictions. For, just as Frost in *North of Boston* (1914) escapes his previous Shelleyan ego, and Williams after *The Tempers* (1913) abandons his Keatsian or Pre-Raphaelite modes, Stevens most noticeably emancipates himself in *Harmonium* from a disabling romanticism. His hero Crispin, in *The Comedian as the Letter C*, journeys in purification from being an expansive self, an "insatiable egotist," to making his home, with compact bareness, out of the "quotidian" and the neighborly close: "Crispin dwelt in the land and dwelling there / Slid from his continent by slow recess / To things within his actual eye." It is the adjustment to proportion out of excess—the world housed yet housing the sensibility—that, one remembers, was the theme of Tomlinson's lines about the gathered sun in Italy: "I instance only / Bowl and water-jug . . . ." The gathering-in, the mutual relation of container and nature, is also Stevens's interest in *Anecdote of the Jar* together with a particularly American sense of the world as resistant wilderness when he considers how a jar is placed on a hill in Tennessee:

> The wilderness rose up to it,
> And sprawled around, no longer wild.
> The jar was round upon the ground
> And tall and of a port in air.
>
> It took dominion everywhere.
> The jar was gray and bare.
> It did not give of bird or bush,
> Like nothing else in Tennessee.

Artefact and nature, mutually clarifying, define each other's space. What "sprawled around" now reveals, in rhyming spread, what "was round upon the ground." Equally, rising up to the land, as the land to it, the jar, which "in air . . . took dominion everywhere," is, by the same rhyming partnership, seen only as "gray and bare"—its unverdured barrenness implying the fecund world round it, just as that world can be said in the final line to have its unique singularities revealed ("Like nothing else in Tennessee") by means of the singular jar. There is more emphasis on ordered relation than Tomlinson needs. But the American's cool, compact focus—drawing charged possibility into a bounded arena—is as important to his developing poetry of instances as Stevens's fantastical "anecdotes." *Earthy Anecdote*, for example, where a bristling firecat makes swerving bucks open a space of order round it, suggests one centering of forces. Another is seen in *Valley Candle*:

> My candle burned alone in an immense valley.
> Beams of the huge night converged upon it,
> Until the wind blew.
> Then beams of the huge night
> Converged upon its image,
> Until the wind blew.

The last line, repeating the third with expanded implication, has a characteristic transparency and elasticity. For nature, concentrated in upon the little human light, is then issued out, fully realized, by means of it. "Until the wind blew"—when first stated, seeming to snuff out all focus—is, by the end, revelation of the force lit up by our image-making, and henceforth vitally partnered by us.

In Stevens's *Six Significant Landscapes,* such a small point of concentration is playfully diversified. There can be choices, alternatives, flexibility; and in *Landscape I,* there is the freedom to consider—for instance—an individual who unegotistically fits into nature's stillness or movement:

> An old man sits
> In the shadow of a pine tree
> In China.
> He sees larkspur,
> Blue and white,
> At the edge of the shadow,
> Move in the wind.
> His beard moves in the wind.
> The pine tree moves in the wind.
> Thus water flows
> Over weeds.

Such uninsistence, however, means an absence of verbal pressure. Stevens is not concerned, like Tomlinson, with the way that a poet goes step-by-step through the process of establishing relation with wind and water as resistant substance. Instead, he verbally levels down the difference between solidities—the human being and nature—to a transparency, an easy apposition: "His beard moves in the wind. / The pine tree moves in the wind." Yet the clarity of style, for all the thinness, has the wit that plays against egotism in *Landscape III*:

> I measure myself
> Against a tall tree.
> I find that I am much taller,
> For I reach right up to the sun,
> With my eye;
> And I reach to the shore of the sea
> With my ear.
> Nevertheless, I dislike
> The way the ants crawl
> In and out of my shadow.

The flying mind is thus grounded, comically troubled with the indeterminate movement of the actual world, just as, in the sixth of his "significant landscapes," Stevens pits against rationalists, with their "square hats" and "square rooms," the amazing geometry ("Cones, waving lines, ellipses") of nature's ignored forms.

Thus, shifting easily between segmented versions, Stevens reveals how plurality and variations can open out from a single, containing theme. It is that flexing style to which Tomlinson responds with meditative agility in *The Art of Poetry,* where, he suggests, one can choose between entering dark fact or blocking the way with one's ego:

> The light makes white holes through the black foliage
> Or mist hides everything that is not itself.

Another poem, *Observation of Facts,* is also poised between alternatives. Either one mentally domesticates things—imposing mythically "a sort of chintz curtain" between one's self and a tree—or one truly dwells in the world by relationship:

> The tree stands: or does not stand:
> As I draw, or remove the curtain.

Thus, despite Stevens's theoretical air, his poetry strengthens Tomlinson's deftness in suggesting, without romantic insistence, a solidity of varied footings: "Those facets of copiousness which I proposed." It is a multiplicity, civilly suggested, that Tomlinson had seen in one of the first poems by Stevens that he read, *Thirteen Ways of Looking at a Blackbird.* Here, significantly, there is a dark-bodied sense of fact that ballasts the light chaste coolness of the poem's divisions. It is as if here, in particular, that Stevens's analyzing, segmenting mind saw the need for an "animal" constancy, a blackbird concreteness, which he must touch if all is not to collapse into white, divisive abstraction:

> I was of three minds,
> Like a tree
> In which there are three blackbirds.

Again, the transparent, almost bodiless style is at work. But Stevens must now counterbalance the thinness and the indeterminateness with the parallel blackbirds. In the same way, his perception of time's eery ambiguity is kept firm, weighted down, in section 13:

> It was evening all afternoon.
> It was snowing.
> And it was going to snow.
> The blackbird sat
> In the cedar-limbs.

The blackbird's shadow over an icicle-filled window in section 6 gives a dark backing, an enlivened assurance, behind a fearful coldness, so that an undefined "mood" can trace in it "An indecipherable cause." Blackness is the promise of a chaos contained, a plenitude made enterable, in section 9:

> When the blackbird flew out of sight,
> It marked the edge
> Of one of many circles.

In section 1, the blackbird is very much Stevens's lively counterpoise to the mind's white, bleak vision of multiplicity:

> Among twenty snowy mountains,
> The only moving thing
> Was the eye of the blackbird.

In Tomlinson's *Nine Variations in a Chinese Winter Setting*, where he imitates and diverges from Stevens's poem, the contraries within each instance possess a different identity. Not having to set blackness against abstraction, he can play reason and sensuous delight, substance and airiness, against each other in the kind of taut pairings shown by "variations" like the following:

2: "Thus Men Make a Mountain"

V
Pine-scent
In snow-clearness
Is not more exactly counterpointed
Than the creak of trodden snow
Against a flute.

VI
The outline of the water-dragon
Is not embroidered with so intricate a thread
As that with which the flute
Defines the tangible borders of a mood.

The flute in the poem very much occupies a similar place to that of Stevens's blackbird. Yet the flute recurs as the instrument of a proposed art—of a music the meditative passion of which need not be drowned inside the sensory world, but which, rising out of that world but dancing with it, can be emotionally and intellectually adaptive to all its changes. Tomlinson's negatives ("not more . . . Than," "not . . . so intricate . . . As") guard a positive freedom: a space inside exactness to consider the fresh but unlush aroma of "Pine-scent," as well as a flute sound, each matched and grounded by a walkable terrain of "snow-clearness" and "trodden snow."

The play of energized meaning, stylistically taut as it "Defines the tangible borders of a mood," has a physical edge that Tomlinson does not find in Stevens's work. However much the Englishman values reason, it does not have, as one sees in his comparable poem *Flute Music*, the American's kind of ordering. For "a flute / Governs the land, its winter and its silence" not with Stevensian "dominion," but with the sense of possibility, the springy discipline, by which a circumscribed "bound of passion" can bound forth, "reason's song / Riding the ungovernable wave." Yet Stevens's art, by its attack on rigidity of view, opens the way for Tomlinson's wider register. *Flute Music* does not have to be caught by a tragically romantic narrowness in which the only music is "A weeping among broken gods"—the elegiacal surrender to a "Red glow across olive twilight." Now there can be a greater span of feeling, mind, and color as the flute "moves with equal certainty / Through a register of palm-greens and flesh-rose."

There can also be the freedom, as in Tomlinson's *Suggestions for the Improvement of a Sunset*, to venture into distortion and thereby come back, newly steadied, to a genuine sense of time and space. For what deranges vision—the absolutism of a sunset "Drawing all light into its centre"—is challenged by a poem that goes on to suggest variety:

> Six points of vantage provide us with six sunsets.
>
> The sea partakes of the sky. It is less
> Itself than the least pool which, if threatened,
> Prizes lucidity.
>
> The pond is lime-green, an enemy
> Of gold, bearing no change but shadow.
>
> Seen from above, the house would resemble
> A violin, abandoned, and lost in its own darkness;
>
> Diminished, through the wrong end of a glass,
> A dice ambushed by lowering greens;
>
> Accorded its true proportions,
> The stone would give back the light
> Which, all day, it has absorbed.
>
> The after-glow, broken by leaves and windows,
> Confirms green's triumph against yellow.

In this choice of possible vantage points (such as a pool that *might* be threatened, or a house, disproportioned, that "*would* resemble" other things), one also has leave to consider the very opposite. There need be no drama of clash and distortion if the singular actuality of things is observed. For, letting them be, while guarding against their possible violation and attack, one comes to an alert peace where facts prise open their light for us within density. So, with a sense of value, one may "prize" dark lucidity in pool, pond, and house, and, saving the house from a violently reductive vision, so that it is not "ambushed by lowering greens," one sees that such color rightly grounds—rather than diminishes—human dwelling in the verdant world. The manmade and the natural, glass and vegetation, also light up a continuity against sunset endings. With "The after-glow, broken by leaves and windows," there are inlets upon a living onwardness.

The human presence coexists with a changing world. But Tomlinson's way of presenting the relation without diminishing the solidity of either shows how he increasingly differs from Stevens. It is a divergence that is revealingly evident in the American's poem *The Wind Shifts*, where the nonhuman is compared throughout to the human and only avoids the Pathetic Fallacy in such closeness by Stevens's suggesting the changeability of the collective human temperament that fits, without imposition, into an alike wind. Self and not-self slide together frictionless:

2: "Thus Men Make a Mountain"

This is how the wind shifts:
Like the thoughts of an old human,
Who still thinks eagerly
And despairingly.
The wind shifts like this:
Like a human without illusions,
Who still feels irrational things within her.
The wind shifts like this:
Like humans approaching proudly,
Like humans approaching angrily.
This is how the wind shifts:
Like a human, heavy and heavy,
Who does not care.

With Tomlinson, in *Sea Change*, his sense of an element's very resistance—its watery difficulty—forbids such relations. There is always a gap that has to be recognized between the sea and statements about it, between its illuminable darkness and our lit minds. "To define the sea—," he says at the start, and then breaks off in recognition of an elusiveness that constantly requires adaptive speech:

We change our opinions
With the changing light.

Light struggles with colour:
A quincunx
Of five stones, a white
Opal threatened by emeralds.

The sea is uneasy marble.

The sea is green silk.

The sea is blue mud, churned
By the insistence of wind.

Beneath dawn a sardonyx may be cut from it
In white layers laced with a carnelian orange,
A leek- or apple-green chalcedony
Hewn in the cold light.

Illustration is white wine
Floating in a saucer of ground glass
On a pedestal of cut glass:

A static instance, therefore untrue.

When statement is a fixed cutout from the flowing whole, it aptly belongs on a pedestal. But the poem's isolated instances point also to value—to language as individual propositions that emerge from paper's blankness (as if out of the sea they briefly utter) and then give way to silence, before another statement is tried, only to vanish in its turn. There is a virtue, the poem suggests, in calling the struggle of light with color on the sea "A quincunx / Of five stones," because that speaks for the density beneath change—as distinct from the ornamentality, the wrong kind of elegance, into which change is rigidified as the image of "Opal threatened by emeralds."

Yet as words slip awry, they also briefly grip. One can say "the sea is uneasy marble," and perceive immediately the hard-seeming swell of the wave like unsettled stone, even while the statement's "uneasy" accuracy also becomes evident—as also with the "green silk" comparison, or "blue mud," churned up as unstable the moment it is uttered. In a similar way, the "sardonyx" image singles out a hard, distinct moment of light and water, only to become overlusciously static, from "carnelian orange" to "white wine." Nature is to be devoured neither here nor in the later *Cézanne at Aix,* when Tomlinson says the mountain is "Immobile like fruit," then instantly shows it to be "Unlike, also," not "a component of the delicious."

Yet in touching that later art in *Sea Change* (event and statement held in nimble parallel; the reader adjusted to the flexible pace), Tomlinson has the basis for a maturity that more distinctly sets him apart from Stevens's poetic accords. He has little in common with the ideal congruity between the human "maker," or articulator, and the sea in Stevens's *The Idea of Order at Key West* (1934): "She measured to the hour its solitude . . . And when she sang, the sea, / Whatever self it had, became the self / That was her song, for she was the maker."

There is much indeed to separate Tomlinson's unmagisterial kind of "making" from Stevens's prescriptions, particularly *The Snow Man* with its abstract dissolving of self and scene:

> One must have a mind of winter
> To regard the frost and the boughs
> Of the pine-trees crusted with snow

Thinned down to a snowman, or an invisible man, one's bareness may vibrate with wind and world:

> For the listener, who listens in the snow,
> And, nothing himself, beholds
> Nothing that is not there and the nothing that is.

Avoiding egotistic excess at the cost of a depersonalized self and an empty otherness, Stevens provokes Tomlinson's correction in *The Art of Poetry* about the *being* of facts: "The fact being, that when the truth is not good enough / We exaggerate." The solidity of matter, and how we speak of it, is crucial:

> Proportions
>
> Matter. It is difficult to get them right.
> There must be nothing
> Superfluous, nothing which is not elegant
> And nothing which is if it is merely that.
>
> This green twilight has violet borders.
>
> Yellow butterflies
> Nervously transferring themselves
> From scarlet to bronze flowers
> Disappear as the evening appears.

Tomlinson's "nothings," unlike those of the *Snow Man*, define a vibrant positive, the hardy "elegance" and fullness by which, as he says in *Observation of Facts*, "The room flowers once one has introduced / Mental fibre beneath its elegance, / A rough pot or two." Such is the definiteness by which, after his words on proportion in *The Art of Poetry*, theory is immediately tested. "This green twilight"—specifically *this*, now—"has violet borders": a section extracted from shimmering time whose verbal edge defines the tremulous life of color inside it. As if in deliberate contrast to Stevens's bleak landscape in *The Snow Man*, the last four lines enclose and concentrate that summer vividness even further—the nervous flicker and metamorphosis of butterflies lighting up change and constancy, vanishing and arrival, elusive reality and containing form.

Tomlinson's practical yet delicate sense of the means by which a verbal habitation can be built on changing ground has, one remembers, a very distinct geographical basis: "I think it was Liguria and Tuscany and then Gloucestershire taught me the way men could be at home in a landscape."[3] As one sees in a poem about the Ligurian coast, *The Return* (1987), written over thirty years after *Sea Change* ("Grey seas, uneasily marbling, scourged the cliff"), the early description of the sea as "uneasy marble" belongs as much to an actual Italy as all the other instances that are compiled as a new whole out of broken speech in the last poem of *The Necklace*, *Fiascherino*. Indeed, with its view of a sea in dawn light, the poem shows how Tomlinson has begun to build his idiom out of cleansed, pared-down verbal units. All the clear fragments, breakages, and Stevens-like "variations" provide the articulated parts of this poetic "necklace"—the suppleness, by which his art can move more confidently with an ever-shifting nature. So, although it looks as if Tomlinson has returned to conventional stanzas in *Fiascherino,* he has actually created structures of separable pieces—segments whose firm or tentative phrasing springily suggests the way in which consciousness keeps its balance amidst flow. Thus the first two lines could almost be spaced out in the manner that Tomlinson later developed from Williams:

>   Over an ash-fawn beach
>   fronting a sea
>   which keeps
>   Rolling and unrolling
>   lifting . . . .

Put together again, however, the opening of *Fiascherino* presents the appearance of endless flux, an unrelenting movement that consciousness cannot penetrate:

>   Over an ash-fawn beach fronting a sea which keeps
>   Rolling and unrolling, lifting
>   The green fringes from submerged rocks
>   On its way in, and, on its way out
>   Dropping them again, the light
>
>   Squanders itself . . . .

Yet as time goes on, the observer from the cliff top finds a way into the flux. It can be broken open, meaning salvable from squandered light, when, in the final two stanzas, the sun's force is refracted into the new "low room" that appears—the meeting point between illimitable reality and the mind's need for bounds:

>   Content with our portion,
>
>   Where, we ask ourselves, is the end of all this
>   Variety that follows us? Glare
>   Pierces muslin; its broken rays
>   Hovering in trembling filaments
>   Glance on the ceiling with no more substance
>
>   Than a bee's wing. Thickening, these
>   Hang down over the pink walls

> In green bars, and, flickering between them,
>   A moving fan of two colours,
> The sea unrolls and rolls itself into the low room.

Since one's need to localize is met by an irreducible yet containable nature (our human "Where . . . ?" rhymingly answered by the sun's broken "Glare"), the sea no longer seems an alien mechanism. Fanlike it opens to us, submittingly "unrolls and rolls itself." Yet fanlike it also closes, with that mystery and revelation, flickering vitality and form, that has been seen throughout *The Necklace*. It is the play of reality's changing body against the confines of our image-making, that makes the airy yet solid "trembling filaments" seem about to vanish (to glance "on the ceiling with no more substance") only to hold steady. They remain, in diaphanous yet definite image, as "a bee's wing," and when light unexaggeratedly thickens, the "pink walls / In green bars" go on to build even further the truth of this imaginary "room" where the mind inhabits and is inhabited by the flowing world. To this confine, the sea, vigorously elegant, "A moving fan of two colours," enters as our guest, a "presence" disclosed, as with the bowl "Gracing the table on which it unfolds itself" in *Seeing is Believing*.

The art of that new book carries on from *Fiascherino* its feeling for bounded form and openness where acceptance of the flux, and resistance to it, make up the tempered, trembling balance of the human standpoint. It is the need for a located "Where" that again, in the other Italian setting of *Northern Spring (Seeing is Believing)* brings Tomlinson to seek a stable footing in the midst of flux:

> Where should one look
> In the profusion of possibilities? One conceives
>   Placing before them a square house
> Washed in the coolness of lime, a hub
> For the scattered deployment, to define
>   In pure white from its verdant ground
> The variegated excess which threatens it.

The imagining of such a cool counterpoise may derive in part from Stevens, but the "square house," with its angularity and clear embodiment of human form-shaping, reveals now the greater importance of Marianne Moore. For hers is the poetry where consciousness sets down its structured shapes amidst profusion with a peculiarly bold tact. They are verbal bounds of habitation, walls that define the enlivened moral sense, which in Tomlinson's poetry, after Moore, flexes awake with a new nimbleness.

II

In *The Necklace* Tomlinson had suggested that "Six points of vantage provide us with six sunsets." Yet, remembering the poem's concern for sensuous fact, one sees not so much a Stevensian kind of anatomizing as a physical and intellectual curiosity that resembles Moore's when she considers "an artichoke in six varieties of blue" and "the snipe-legged hieroglyphic in three parts" (*When I Buy Pictures*, 1921). Hers is a delight, zoological and botanical, in the strange animal quality of diverse fact and the equally strange adjustment of consciousness needed to take its measure. Thus, no sooner has one read the title of *The Mind Is an Enchanting Thing* (1944) than one's view is corrected. The enchanter is also "an enchanted thing," multiple in singleness, "like the glaze on a / katydid-wing / subdivided by sun / till the nettings are legion." But if that is a reminder of the "trembling filaments" like "a bee's wing" in *Fiascherino*, it also suggests, very precisely, the shared qualities of the two poets: each having, as Tomlinson says of Moore, a "Ruskinian open-ness to the creative universe in looking at the surfaces that it offers one."[4]

It is an openness, however, that is combined with Moore's very individual way of showing enclosures, as the mind unarrogantly makes and remakes structures to greet that universe. She has a quick, instinctive sympathy with its creatures, but she will not level down the contours of human mind, the stanzaic shapings of the poetry, however protrusively eccentric they may seem, so that consciousness can slide more easily with things. Instead, the mind's enclosures have to be seen in the process of making kinship with the unenclosed, the irregularity of the nonhuman. It is the exposed risk of creating congruence between orderly verbal habitations and nature's fluidity. Where, as in *The Steeple-Jack* (1932), "habitation" also means a place of community, a town on an American coast, the peril of reconciling civilized structures and moral consciousness with a sea that might wreck such orderings, provides its quiet exhilaration:

> Dürer would have seen a reason for living
>   in a town like this, with eight stranded whales
> to look at; with the sweet sea air coming into your house
>   on a fine day, from water etched
>   with waves as formal as the scales
> on a fish.

> One by one in two's and three's, the seagulls keep
>   flying back and forth over the town clock,
> or sailing around the lighthouse without moving their wings—
> rising steadily with a slight
>   quiver of the body—or flock
> mewing where
>
> a sea the purple of the peacock's neck is
>   paled to greenish azure as Dürer changed
> the pine green of the Tyrol to peacock blue and guinea
> gray . . . .

Significantly Moore invokes a European artist to shock into blithe awakening a particularly American sense of need. A conscious adjustment has to be made, tutored by risk. One "reason for living / in a town like this" is its stability and moral sureness founded on awareness of possible disaster ("eight stranded whales"). As has been observed, Moore blends one account—of Dürer's 1520 journey to see a stranded whale in Zeeland—with a newspaper report of eight whales beached off the eastern United States.[5] But she does it to create an expression of reasoned order that is flexibly peculiar enough to bind with, and to be justified by, the facts it accommodates. For at the very moment when the mind's artistry sees "water etched / with waves," it is saved from the appearance of overhuman imposition by the actuality of nature's own patterning, "as formal as the scales / on a fish."

Also the town clock no more obtrudes than the seagulls' beating of time, "One by one in two's and three's." Nor does a church soar too righteously if a steeplejack places danger signs by it, bringing pretensions back to earth when he "lets / down a rope as a spider spins a thread." It is the human and animal neighborhood for which Moore has prepared by means of Dürer, the artist who in his 1494 painting of the Tyrol presented natural perspective through illusion, turning foreground green into "peacock blue and guinea / gray," just as nature itself changes "a sea the purple of the peacock's neck . . . to greenish azure." So also here the animal body of nature's coloring bulks out of Moore's fact-adhering syntax: an incongruity that strangely makes congruence with the now extraordinary reasonableness of her style.

The "intermingling of human and natural attributes" in *The Steeple-Jack*, together with its "harmony of civilisation and nature," are noted by Tomlinson in a 1957 review of Moore's work.[6] But as a poet he carries forward a sense of vitalizing danger that underlies any such balancings. *The Littleton Whale* (1981), with its tale of a stranded leviathan and a Gloucestershire village, has more feeling for the potential ruin of habitable certainties than *The Steeple-Jack*. But, waking up out of disaster surpassed, the poem shares Moore's concern for what a community may reside upon and hold in common when the tide washes up "a whole house / with blue slates on it into Littleton Pill / and that house was a whale...."

Much earlier, however, *The Steeple-Jack* seems to possess for Tomlinson—from a Ruskinese point of view—an endangered yet invigorated sense of constancy. After all, it was of Ruskin that Moore and Tomlinson spoke most when they first met at her Brooklyn home in 1960: "She recalled going as a young woman with her mother to see Ruskin's house at Coniston, her mind's eye still retaining the memory of a peacock's feather he had owned and of a water-color of the Tyrol he had painted."[7] Indeed the recollection of such a housed variety is so strong that Tomlinson's poem *Over Brooklyn Bridge* (1963) seems, in its own remembering of *The Steeple-Jack*, to give Ruskin the position occupied by Dürer—where reason coexists with the pleasure of sensuous, changing fact:

>   Goodbye
> Miss Moore
>   I hope
>   the peacock's feather you once saw
>   at the house of Ruskin
>   has kept its variegations.

That hope has the buoyant courtesy, the shared internationalism, of a European speaking to an American in the dexterous lineation of another American, Williams. But, treading in space, as it were, the tone and form of Tomlinson's poem make envisaged risk a more agile experience than was necessary for Moore in *The Steeple-Jack*. "It could not be dangerous," she said, "to be living / in a town like this, of simple people, / who have a steeple-jack placing danger-signs by the church." But her Christian distrust of pride becomes Tomlinson's secular distrust of overweening rigidity. Early in his poem he is placing his own danger signs against the work of those who would glorify machine power in hammerblow assertion, like futuristic Mayakowsky quoted in his tribute to Brooklyn Bridge: "in the place / of style, an austere / disposition of bolts."[8] Stylistically, and therefore morally, Tomlinson's conception of bridge building—and the way people meet in speech—must be different, because for him strength comes out of admitted "weaknesses"—openings to hesitancy that invigorate the modest, definite comity of statement and habitation. Thus when Moore says, "I do not live in town / I live in Brooklyn," the vulnerability in her fear as to his possible dislike of the place is assuaged by

2: "Thus Men Make a Mountain"   53

Tomlinson's positiveness: "I liked Brooklyn / with its survival / of wooden houses." His opinion firmly but uncomplacently resides on a footing of words that must be felt out in space—a sureness that can only come from hesitation:

>   And what I liked
>   about the bridge
>   was the uncertainty
>   the way
>   the naked steel
>   would not go naked
>   but must wear
>   its piers of stone—
>   as the book says
>   "stylistically
>   its weakest feature."
>   I like
>   such weaknesses, the pull
>   the stone base
>   gives to the armature.
>   I live
>   in a place of stone
>   if it's still there
>   by the time I've sailed to it.

"I live" (as with "I like") is a definiteness planted in space and open to undoing (particularly to the real threat, Tomlinson suggests in the last lines, offered by the Cuban missile crisis of 1962).[9] Yet the vulnerable word keeps steady. The pull of the "stone base" against excess transcendence allows Tomlinson to cut through solidity and see into fact's opaque being, just as a suspension bridge in verse is opened out as an articulate structure of airy weight.

It is the interplay of transparency and concreteness, openness and closure, movement and stillness that makes Tomlinson particularly ready to learn the lessons not only of *The Steeple-Jack*, but also of Moore's earlier poem *The Fish* (1918). For here indeed stony fact has its darkness lit and swum through—once one perceives that the static-seeming title is actually on the move:

>   THE FISH
>
>   wade
>   through black jade.

As the poem continues, Moore keeps one's experience of reading the page tightly commensurate with the act of looking down through water. For both ways accept the unsteadying illusion—whether the sea's refraction, or lineation's odd bending and joins—that lands one back upon a refreshed, precise sense of substance, minus the excess of the fantasy vision. Thus the overluxuriance of "black jade"—an expensive medium for fish merely to "wade / through"—is abandoned in one's mind at seeing the sudden plain rightness of statement as it catches an undersea movement across rocks. One is not imprisoned by exorbitant human literateness anymore than by the strict syllabic rigidity of each stanza. Such an exaggerated-seeming human formalism encloses so much remarkable fluidity and is so tutored by it—opening and shutting as meaning runs from stanza to stanza—that reason precisely matches the watery strangeness it reveals:

THE FISH

wade
through black jade.
    Of the crow-blue mussel-shells, one keeps
    adjusting the ash-heaps;
        opening and shutting itself like

an
injured fan.
    The barnacles which encrust the side
    of the wave, cannot hide
        there for the submerged shafts of the

sun,
split like spun
    glass, move themselves with spotlight swiftness
    into the crevices—
        in and out, illuminating

the
turquoise sea
    of bodies . . . .

The reader has to move through a sentence's circuitous start ("Of the crow-blue mussel shells . . ."), with its "crow" camouflage, its coagulating assonance ("mus*sel*-shells"), in order to spy amidst opacity the live singleness of a creature who is "adjusting the ash heaps." Such undersea decorum, however, implies the strange patterned motion of a mussel's being, rather than an over-tidy human metaphor. It is a "fan" (one recalls the "moving fan of two colours" in *Fiascherino*), but, surrealistically, it is "injured," escaping the excess of the simile but touching the precision: the quivering vulnerability, the living flesh, beneath the hard shell and encrusted appearance. Closed, barnacled forms in nature are thus delicately seen into by the opening and shutting form of stanza that reminds one of human manufacture ("spun / glass") at the same moment that it partakes of the asymmetrical, cubistic world it lights up—"sun, / split like spun / glass."

The Fish, one now sees more clearly, has a vital bearing not only upon *Fiascherino,* with its broken sunrays, but also on the way Tomlinson holds the balance between self and nonhuman otherness in certain poems of *Seeing is Believing.* Flow within human fixture—or a "square" confine riding upon openness—make up the interplay of a poem like *Glass Grain,* where the sun shines through a window into a room. "The glare goes down," says the first sentence, speaking not just of sunset, but of the universe's fierce energy coming to earth and human encounter. The intensity remains, but met now by one's recognitions:

> The glare goes down. The metal of a molten pane
> Cast on the wall with red light burning through,
> Holds in its firm, disordered square, the shifting strands
> The glass conceals, till (splitting sun) it dances
> Lanterns in lanes of light its own streaked image.
> Like combed-down hair. Like weathered wood . . . .

As with Moore, the comparisons stay nonliteral. The sun is not "combed-down hair" but only visually unravelled by such likenings and refractions. The split sun can therefore run with the flow and grain of earthly things, as they with it, while both sides of this pairing keep their own distinct bodies. So there is a solidity felt out—a weight rather than bodiless paradox—in the contraries brought together in Tomlinson's language, as the window frame "Holds in its firm, disordered square, the shifting strands."

It is the firm disorder, which, in another poem, *Night-Piece: the Near and the Far,* both unsettles and reestablishes. For breakage gives back a whole—an earthly habitation in the sky as light penetrates cloud:

> Fissured, lit by the moon behind
> Prizing from black an ore of undertones,
> Over the houseless space, a hearth spills down.

The senses verify a homing point, but as if with the speed of Constable instantly noting in his sketchbook the sky's sudden shifts. It is perception of a center, a constancy in change that in *Winter Encounters* observes the "ceaseless pairings" of the English landscape and a civility built on movement:

> The house reposes, squarely upon its acre
>   Yet with softened angles, the responsive stone
> Changeful beneath the changing light:
>   There is a riding-forth, a voyage impending . . . .

Elsewhere in *Seeing is Believing,* the very title of a poem has its "square" repose, only to ride forth on the quick realization that the title is actually the first line. As with *The Fish* and after, one sees

ROSE-HIPS

Weather the frost

and

REFLECTIONS

Like liquid shadows.

Similarly, in *Paring the Apple,* one reads its first two lines as immobile categorizations fixed apart by "and":

> There are portraits and still-lifes.

> And there is paring the apple.

But by the third line—"And then ? Paring it slowly . . ."—the "And" has the reader on the move, out of flat addition into a possible round solidity. One grasps it verbally—or with a knife—by the surface falsity of art—a "peel" cut away from the real body, a skeletal version that, in *not* being the thing itself, is the counterfeit that carefully recreates its actuality:

> And then? Paring it slowly,
> From under cool-yellow
> Cold-white emerging. And . . . ?

2: "Thus Men Make a Mountain"

> The spring of concentric peel
> Unwinding off white,
> The blade hidden, dividing.

As Tomlinson says in his Constable poem, "The artist lies / For the improvement of truth. Believe him." Yet in improving the way one understands, and rebuilds through breakage, a "truth" that has such Ruskinian resonance, Tomlinson can still draw upon Moore's example. She, in a poem's opening, touches a whole country by fragmenting it from a title's generality into particulars:

ENGLAND

> with its baby rivers and little towns . . . .

But he, moving from title into poem, takes purchase on an ocean:

THE ATLANTIC

> Launched into an opposing wind, hangs
>   Grappled . . . .

Singled out as an instance—a wave hitting a shore—the Atlantic "hangs / Grappled" by the mind as well as the wind. For with its action broken open, its separate phases revealed, one grips, hovers with, then travels along a huge continuity. Impetus and understanding have come together in Tomlinson's verse-line with a whole new confidence, drawing strength not only from his ventures into Stevens and Moore, but also from his perception, long before, of Pound's breaking of the line into the unit, the facet: "Lithe turning of water, / sinews of Poseidon." Now those "talismanic fragments"[10] from Pound lead Tomlinson forward, through a poem that begins with an ocean yet comes to realized earth:

THE ATLANTIC

> Launched into an opposing wind, hangs
>   Grappled beneath the onrush,
> And there, lifts, curling in spume,
>   Unlocks, drops from that hold
> Over and shoreward. The beach receives it,
>   A whitening line, collapsing
> Powdering-off down its broken length;
>   Then, curded, shallow, heavy

> With clustering bubbles, it nears
> In a slow sheet that must climb
> Relinquishing its power, upward
> Across tilted sand. Unravelled now
> And the shore, under its lucid pane,
> Clear to the sight, it is spent:
> The sun rocks there, as the netted ripple
> Into whose skeins the motion threads it
> Glances athwart a bed, honey-combed
> By heaving stones. Neither survives the instant
> But is caught back, and leaves, like the after-image
> Released from the floor of a now different mind,
> A quick gold, dyeing the uncovering beach
> With sunglaze. That which we were,
> Confronted by all that we are not,
> Grasps in subservience its replenishment.

As with the "molten pane" of *Glass Grain*, the Atlantic's "lucid pane" lets one see into a terrain of relation: into the "quick gold" lit up when sun enters earth through water. Here, at the meeting of the elements, one comes to the energized ground where otherness faces self: "That which we were, / Confronted by all that we are not." In that encounter lies the tempering of the ego, the moral realization woken up by the poet's unmoralistic following through of an Atlantic tempered by wave and beach, as it "hangs / Grappled . . . lifts . . . Unlocks, drops . . . Unravelled . . . uncovering. . . ." Brought to earth, and "Relinquishing its power," the sea nevertheless takes on the energy of new relation, as it climbs sand, uncovers space, and (like the "nettings" by a katydid's wings in Moore's poem) catches the sun to ground with its "netted ripple."

Of all the poems in *Seeing is Believing*, *The Atlantic* most vividly reminds one of Hopkins in the journals, when he follows, instant after instant, the poise, crash, and spread of breakers. His was a delight in analyzing action that arose from a century in which the camera had made possible a new precision—as with the "chronophotography" of Étienne-Jules Marey in the 1880s, where the motion of birds' wings—or galloping horse, or gymnast's leap—could be recorded in all its divisible, consecutive parts and then printed together as a multiple whole in one photograph. Yet, as *The Atlantic* suggests, the breakup of action as a means of depicting movement through time and space has not only technical but moral implications for the art that uses it. Chronophotography like Marey's (or that of his American contemporary Muybridge) was, after all, a major stimulus for the brutalism of certain futurist artworks like Boccioni's sculpture, *Unique Forms of*

2: "Thus Men Make a Mountain"   59

Continuity in Space (1913). Here, for example, the artist seems to have cinematically dissected a walker's movement, then crammed all the separately revealed steps into one visual simultaneity—a faceless superman, bulging with time and space, his stride ever-impending.

It is the kind of Promethean willfulness acclaimed by Mayakowsky's futurism that, one recalls, was decisively answered by the tone and structure of Tomlinson's *Over Brooklyn Bridge*. One crosses space and time in that poem not by depersonalized force—man as the twentieth-century giant of the machine—but by the resilient strength of acknowledged "weaknesses," the modesty of human scale from which genuine action can vitally derive. One may grasp in subservience a replenishment, but Tomlinson suggests no mere selfless humility. He mitigates assertion, cuts down excess claims to mastery, in order to act from a springy energy of relation. Again one sees the closeness of the art to Ruskin, as when he observes Turner's waterfall leaping over the edge, the "hopeless abandonment of its ponderous power to the air"[11]—a yielding, a "prostration," that has the strength of the giver not the abjectness of the defeated.

In his sympathy with such a position, Tomlinson is set apart, as has been seen, from Hopkins's kind of Christian self-surrender. But he is to be distinguished also from the humbling ethic of the later (though not earlier) Moore. For her, the "presbyter," or salamander, of *His Shield* (1943) offers "a formula safer than / an armorer's: the power of relinquishing / what one would keep; that is freedom." She also observes the implicit lesson of willing service taught by the captive beasts of *Elephants* (1943). Obedient to those he carries in religious processions, the Indian elephant is "a life prisoner but reconciled ... His straight trunk seems to say: when / what we hoped for came to nothing, we revived." Yet, extending a foreleg to let his human rider climb on to him (so that he "expounds the brotherhood / of creatures to man the encroacher"), this elephant seems different from his counterpart in *Black Earth* (1918). Moore's Protestant consciousness shapes the moral significance of a poem she later retitled *Melancthon*, but the elephant of *Black Earth* expounds no brotherhood of creatures. Instead, it voices its own indomitable but unarrogant being—animal in its tough-skinned darkness of fact:

>   this piece of black glass through which no
> light
>
> can filter—cut
> into checkers by rut
>   upon rut of unpreventable experience—

With its "back... full of the history of power" ("encrusted layers of old experience, of old knowledge," as Tomlinson describes its armored hide[12]), the elephant has all the temptation to personal pride weighed down by the past. But it has its own individuality—a "spiritual poise," says Moore—weathered into being, into strong presentness, by the history it carries on its back:

> The sediment of the river which
> encrusts my joints, makes me very grey but I am used
>
> to it, it may
> remain there; do away
>   with it and I am myself done away with, for the
>   patina of circumstance can but enrich what was
>
> there to begin
> with.

The "patina of circumstance" and Tomlinson's 1957 discussion of the poem, clearly connect with his essay on the plays of Isaac Rosenberg, "Fate and the Image of Music" (written 1957, but not published until 1974) where he examines Rosenberg's concern with the individual's attitude to inherited fate—to the "fiendish persistence of the coil of circumstances"[13] that may be actively grasped and turned into positive destiny. The Nubian in Rosenberg's *The Amulet* is significantly regarded by Tomlinson as a captive who is also free inside his own self-discipline: a "primitive giant in this context of total acceptance"[14] who submits not from romantic sick melancholy but from measured contemplation.

This is "black earth" morally illuminated in a way that suggests the relation of the individual to a whole greater than the self, but through which the self is fully realized—a perception that brings Tomlinson back, via Moore's poem, to Eliot's "Tradition and the Individual Talent," in which he regards the elephant's skin as symbolizing "the protective power of both personal insights and traditional wisdom."[15] At the basic level of the verse-line in *Black Earth,* one observes the special truth of this for Tomlinson, as he individually finds a way in to the modernist tradition of Pound and Moore through the cleansed, verbal fragments that find their order within a constraining whole. He notably admires Moore's use of the "syllabic lay-out to take cognizance of the humbler components of language,"[16] as with the dexterous spacing between words, and the finite clarity of "it" in

2: "Thus Men Make a Mountain" 61

> 					I am used
> to it, it may
> remain there; do away
> 		with it and I am myself done away with....

Immediately evident is the significance of such an example for *Cézanne at Aix,* where Tomlinson shows the meeting of self and a nature that takes body not in a hard-skinned animal, but in a mountain's resistant stone. Unbroken, dense otherness is penetrated, made realizable, by art's breakage—by a human consciousness that can discriminate without distortion:

> 				it is not
> Posed. It is. Untaught
> Unalterable....

Yet Tomlinson shares with Moore and Rosenberg a sense of animal being inside stonelike fact: an innateness that the self must reach toward and articulate. Rosenberg's play *Moses* shows the realization that comes to the eponymous hero of the captive Israelites: "Startlingly, / As a mountain side / Wakes aware of its other side, / When from a cave a leopard comes . . . Sprang an intelligence."[17] For Tomlinson, this is "the inanimate mountain rousing suddenly into consciousness"[18] as well as Moses's mind discovering his own instinctive powers. It is also, one sees, the moment when fate's stony fixity is transformed into a more supple destiny and hence offers a standard by which Tomlinson judges evasion of such possibilities in a later poem, *Ariadne and the Minotaur* (1972). Here Ariadne, fearing to traverse the labyrinth and find her animal-human relative, the minotaur, will not enter the "dark stone" from which "the bestial warmth / would rise to meet her." It is a betrayal, a refusal to articulate, a "put-by destiny" with murderous result. But in *Seeing is Believing,* with *Oxen: Ploughing at Fiesole,* there is no evasion. Man and animals cleave together a ground of relation. When the beasts seem to "speak," in a way that recalls *Elephants* or *Black Earth,* it becomes clear how supremely Tomlinson has made the effect his own. This is to lie "For the improvement of truth" with a special mastery:

> The heads, impenetrable
> And the slow bulk
> Soundless and stooping,
> A white darkness—burdened
> Only by sun, and not

> By the matchwood yoke—
> They groove in ease
> The meadow through which they pace
> Tractable. It is as if
> Fresh from the escape,
> They consent to submission,
> The debris of captivity
> Still clinging there
> Unnoticed behind those backs:
> 'But we submit'—the tenor
> Unambiguous in that stride
> Of even confidence—
> 'Giving and not conceding
> Your premises. Work
> Is necessary, therefore—'
> (With an unsevered motion
> Holding the pauses
> Between stride and stride)
> 'We will be useful
> But we will not be swift: now
> Follow us for your improvement
> And at our pace.' This calm
> Bred from this strength, and the reality
> Broaching no such discussion,
> The man will follow, each
> As the other's servant
> Content to remain content.

Man falls in step with the beasts. So also the reader, from the poem's outset, must adjust to the pace of "The heads, impenetrable" and an opaque "slow bulk." One cannot rush or articulate this "Soundless" mystery, and it is not until one passes through the "white darkness" of line 4 that the density is lightened, in both senses. Then, with the verse-line unclenching, one begins to see past opacity into a ground (as it is now spaciously revealed) where the animals "groove in ease / The meadow through which they pace / Tractable." In that last word, a tract's weight is landed upon, but its heaviness is flexibly alleviated. Humanity—and the reader—are led by the oxen, as it were, toward an eased relation with the earth: to an accommodation with it, and therefore upon it, where beasts and man inhabit the world in equity. For these "Tractable" animals, bowed to their real master, the sun, and aristocratically stooping to necessary tasks with humanity, embody the terms of mutual relation and habitation, where none dominates place or is dominated. As with the Atlantic wave, the oxen are tempered but with a spiritual poise that makes them neither slaves nor rulers—

their stride outpacing the notion that they are governed by humanity's "matchwood yoke" ("debris of captivity," as if smashed already or easily breakable), yet suggesting an inward power that is so strong it can afford to abjure violence, leaving the yoke intact, a periphery.

These animals teach courtesy, as they "consent to submission . . . 'Giving and not conceding / Your premises.'" But the poet's tact meets the oxen precisely as he voices what he acknowledges as voiceless ("the reality / Broaching no such discussion") while deferring to the animals' "unsevered motion" by his careful verbal severances. The creatures are not humanly imposed on by one's speech because one must go at their unspeaking yet articulable pace—waiting for them to complete their unhurried statement, from "Work / Is necessary, therefore—," over the pause to "We will be useful . . . ." Animal deliberation and syntax's hesitation go in harness together. Reasoning, "therefore," rightly accompanies nonreasoning sureness, just as the man follows the oxen, "each / As the other's servant."

Flawlessly sustained, the poem matches form to fact, human to animal, without a single moment of imbalance either side. Tomlinson, one sees, has done without Moore's stanzaic symmetries, but he has taken note of the way her formalism can suggest both confine and a wider fullness—how one can retain literate consciousness at the same moment that one is reaching through enclosure (and the flat page of reading) into a fuller-bodied sense of space and animal being. So one can be a reader of page and world without being a cerebral egotist, but also without forgetting that one uses rational forms (word, phrase, lineation) to move via literariness into the sensuously tangible, and back again. It is Moore's specially American heightening of this effect that brings together mind and concreteness, human and animal, transparent and opaque, as a key set of partnerships for Tomlinson in such poems as *The Steeple-Jack, The Fish,* and *Black Earth.* But one needs to observe that there is a further Moore poem, *An Octopus,* that suggests those qualities of a profuse and diverse America that are important for Tomlinson in seeing his direction as a distinctly English poet. Finding that, it becomes clear, also involves his further realization of Ruskin's significance for him.

III

An Octopus (1924), with its depiction of the glaciers on Mount Rainier, in the state of Washington, was written by the kind of poet— as Tomlinson describes Moore—"for whom there is no war between science and poetry, and for whom fact has its proper plenitude."[19]

Echoing there his own poem, *The Farmer's Wife* (1963), Tomlinson might almost be speaking about the factuality gathered with such wide-ranging zoological pleasure in *An Octopus,* for Moore draws not only from such remarkably differing sources as Cardinal Newman, the National Parks Service regulations, Ruskin, the *Illustrated London News,* and *The Saints' Everlasting Rest,* but also from the many contrasting terrains of North America. In that last respect, Moore's poem, with its annotations, is nearer to the democratic inclusiveness of *Leaves of Grass* than the allusive Europeanism of *The Waste Land,* since Moore, student in biology at Bryn Mawr, admirer of Bacon, W. H. Hudson, and John Dewey, has a distinct American lineage behind her belief in the "reconciliation of the attitudes of science and contemplative aesthetic appreciation."[20] One thinks of Crèvecoeur, Audubon, and Thoreau who supplied Agassiz, the Harvard naturalist, with specimens, as well as Clarence King, the Ruskinian and geologist taught by Agassiz, who became United States surveyor of the Rockies and discoverer of the glaciers on Mount Shasta.

For Tomlinson, one way into such an America—whether the Mount Rainier glaciers seen by Moore, or a New Mexican mountain—lay through a picture. In *Some Americans* he tells of receiving for his nineteenth birthday in 1946 *An Illustrated Handbook of Art History,* which included a reproduction of Georgia O'Keeffe's painting, *The Mountain.* Although its colors had been changed to monochrome, the picture was a valuable translation. As a means of grasping by form the energy of stone, it

> entered one's meditations. In it, all the sinews of the mountain stood revealed. It seemed to have heaved upward and fallen sideways like a sleeper who has just turned over. And yet it was not in any way personified. The colors, reduced uniformly to grey ... could have been those of ice or fire. What the printing could not eliminate was the firm articulation of the musculature, the rock-thrust, the held declivities, the sense of an even light bringing the whole to bear.[21]

Later he came to associate *The Mountain* with *An Octopus*

> where an entire mountain mass is "gone over," with its octopus of ice on top "'Creeping slowly as with meditated stealth, / its arms seeming to approach from all directions.'" So evidently it was ice color the grey reproduction had suggested. Wrong again, but the wrongness scarcely injured the picture of the landscape it essentialized although both were the color of fire. The form rode in the mind unimpaired until it was to blaze back at me from the outside at a first sight of the Sangre de Cristo Mountains abrupt above the New Mexican desert.[22]

The process is strikingly similar to that in his poem *The White Van* where nature's colors are momentarily translated to a monochrome that equips the mind to reenter rich profusion. But Tomlinson's experience with *The Mountain* has further significance. He is also describing the manner in which his own sensibility, born to Stoke's "grey-black," meets the "gray" of American abstracting consciousness (fortuitously recreated in a version of a picture) in order to reach through its helpful surface to the world's vivid body: that which eludes the purely reductive mind, but which reveals itself to one of analytical reverence. It is there, beyond Stevens's *Snow Man* abstractings and beyond the "white, abstract end" of Ahab's quest for the white whale (as described by Lawrence). For with Moore's "octopus," the mind, as it looks at the page's stillness, finds itself moving into the animal-like texture of an American landscape, with all its colors and surprises. Therefore,

AN OCTOPUS

of ice. Deceptively reserved and flat

is a literary deception and a truth. It is an obvious metaphor, a flat paper collage of quotations and observations. Yet, acting as the *readable* surface of a solid, a slow-moving glacier, the human words can tentacularly reach out through acknowledged illusion (and the literalness of the imagination she implies in another poem[23]) to real ground and real animals. Thus, gathering "an octopus of ice" (from the *National Parks Portfolio*) and "twenty-eight rivers of ice" (from Clifton Johnson's travel book, *What to See in America*, 1919),[24] she piles up a factual, thick immensity, while allowing one to see through its literariness of surface—the paper animal that is flexible enough to reveal the contours and odd variety of a mountain:

> it lies "in grandeur and in mass"
> beneath a sea of shifting snow-dunes;
> dots of cyclamen-red and maroon on its clearly defined pseudo-podia
> made of glass that will bend—a much needed invention—
> comprising twenty-eight ice-fields from fifty to five hundred feet
>   thick,
> of unimagined delicacy.

A biological sense of fact ("clearly defined pseudo-podia") lets one accept the falsity of an image ("false feet," indeed) so that one's consciousness may find footing in actuality. This counterfeit yet truth-finding "octopus" can thus suggest a way into nature's density, as one adjusts to its adjustment: its turning towards our human need with "glass that will bend." So also we, with Moore and the changing "octopus," bend towards the variable qualities of nature and share its contrasts. Scientific fact (as gleaned from Moore's reading of an article about the octopus in the London *Graphic*) underlies her moral sense of the contraries within the human—the power that necessarily goes with a sensitiveness and vulnerability. So the timid octopus, she reads, in "the wonderful anemone-starred pools" of the Channel Islands, can "pick a periwinkle out of a crack," yet "crush a larger prey with the grip of a small python":[25]

> "Picking periwinkles from the cracks"
> or killing prey with the concentric crushing rigor of the python,
> it hovers forward "spider fashion
> on its arms" misleadingly like lace;
> its "ghostly pallor changing
> to the green metallic tinge of an anemone-starred pool."

The last line's "metal" significantly shows hard-edged factuality intrinsic to a tenderness. The language of delicacy is not oversoft—nor is the *Graphic's* description of "anemone-starred pools" too aesthetically defenseless a view of the frightened octopus's refuge—when Moore adds words from *The Illustrated London News* on the "Lesser Octopus": "The delicate green metallic tinge is due to the irodocysts below the layer of the colour cells."[26] Yet the governing firmness that holds together the poet's contraries in a characteristic moral balance of the stern and the pliable, toughness and timidity, hard surface and humbler vulnerability, originates here from Ruskin. For the anthologizing Moore of the collective *Octopus* draws on a passage from Ruskin's own anthology, *Frondes Agrestes* (1874), which he arranged from selections out of *Modern Painters* chosen by "The Younger Lady of the Thwaite, Coniston." In the Alps, he describes

> companies of pines ... in quiet multitudes, each like the shadow of the one beside it—upright, fixed, spectral, as troops of ghosts standing on the walls of Hades ... yet with such iron will, that the rock itself looks bent and shattered beside them,—fragile, weak, inconsistent, compared to their dark energy of delicate life.[27]

Looking back at the previous lines of the poem, one sees why the ice mass is sensitive enough to bend, and also why the sensitive "ghostly pallor" is stiffened by a "metallic tinge." For "iron will," in this Ruskinian vision, is modified by "delicacy," just as, modifying, it is a vein of hard metal inside the potentially fragile:

> The fir-trees, in "the magnitude of their root systems,"
> rise aloof from these maneuvers "creepy to behold,"
> austere specimens of our American royal families,
> "each like the shadow of the one beside it.
> The rock seems frail compared with their dark energy of life,"
> its vermilion and onyx and manganese-blue interior expensiveness
> left at the mercy of the weather;
> "stained transversely by iron where the water drips down,"
> recognized by its plants and its animals.

European pines, transplanted to the land of equality ("each like the shadow of the one beside it") bring a royalty, an upraised rigor, to their new setting. Their hold on the soil is "the magnitude of their root systems" (as quoted from the Scottish-American conservationist of the western forests, John Muir),[28] where "magnitude," in the light of Ruskin's indomitable "quiet multitudes," rises beyond mere size to suggest the moral significance that might be learnt from such tenacity.

There is a similar Ruskinian effect at work on Moore's use of quotations when she takes phrases from another travel book, W. D. Wilcox's *The Rockies of Canada* (1903). The latter, describing the region of Alberta near lakes Louise and Agnes, that Moore visited in 1923, the same year as her first visit to Mount Rainier, speaks of Canadian cliffs "disposed in horizontal layers of a hard and shiny quartz sandstone, stained red and orange, transversely by iron, and vertically banded purple and black, where oozing waters drip from the trees above."[29] Transferred to an American setting, and applied to Ruskin's "weak" Alpine rock, Wilcox's words are changed, on the one hand, to emphasise moral frailty—the inordinate delight in worldly treasure, heaped up with adjectival "expensiveness"—while, on the other hand, the words also suggest a weathered moral strength that cuts athwart weakness, so that it is "stained transversely by iron where the water drips down." By this ethic, nature, disdaining the values placed on its jewels by human greed and vanity, leaves them carelessly in the rain: a splendid power of relinquishment that is armored against pride and the errors of an overbeautifying aesthetic.

One remembers the "jade" merely waded through in *The Fish*. When an underlay of rock matters more for its hard being than for any luxuriant price put upon it, there are solid grounds to make relations with the singularity of its animals. Thus, shunning sentimental anthropomorphism, Moore sees "thoughtful beavers / making drains which seem the work of careful men with shovels." This is the kind of animal-human habitation that, in the passage immediately following, is stonily vigilant against whimsy and excess. But to define it precisely, by a witty rigor, Moore subtly edits the descriptions of a varied North America that she finds in Wilcox and Johnson.

There is profusion of a markedly luxurious kind in the latter's account of the "gorgeous palace of bears," the "concealed" caves in Oregon that are "pendent with calcium gems, pillared in alabaster, and tapestried in crystal."[30] When Moore also reads his description of a petrified forest in Arizona, with its bridge of "jasper and agate," its trees "tumbled together as if whole quarries of marble and onyx had been dynamited,"[31] she has an image of jeweled splendors that have been amazingly—yet rightly—dashed in ruins by a nature that works on very different principles. The bears of the poem are therefore remarkably unnoticing inhabitants of a vainly irrelevant luxury. What matters is the stony armor of their homes, the mineralogical camouflage of which they are part (their "den" syntactically hidden by Moore), not the glitter of palatial finery that she amasses from Wilcox's description of Lake Louise's colors ("those faint but exquisite hues seen in topaz, transparent quartz, or tourmaline crystals")[32] only to blow it apart. The reader thus moves, as it were, towards the firmer stone, the harder metal, of resilient animal being:

>   of the bears inspecting unexpectedly
> ant-hills and berry-bushes.
> Composed of calcium gems and alabaster pillars,
> topaz, tourmaline crystals and amethyst quartz,
> their den is somewhere else, concealed in the confusion
> of "blue forests thrown together with marble and jasper and agate
> as if whole quarries had been dynamited."
> And farther up, in stag-at-bay position
> as a scintillating fragment of these terrible stalagmites,
> stands the goat,
> its eye fixed on the waterfall which never seems to fall—

As with the "gold- / defending dragon" in *The Plumet Basilisk* (1932)—the lizard of a country where Indians threw away riches into Lake Guatavita—there is, beyond abandonable luxury, the greater animal treasure: hard-edged singularity and delicacy of being. There is the "scintillating fragment," the goat, verbally chipped off from the mountain's "stalagmites," who is as much a solid outgrowth of Rainier as the rest of the poem's "American menagerie": like "the mountain guide evolving from the trapper," "the nine-striped chipmunk," the water ouzel, the white-tailed ptarmigan, "the eleven eagles of the west," and "the spotted ponies with glass eyes." These small Indian horses with their colorless retinas (and great stamina, as Wilcox reports[33]) seem in Moore's poem to have evolved their eyes from what they see as well as what they eat—"frosty grass . . . and rapid draughts of ice-water." Followed through, into their syntactical and geographical terrain, these "hard to discern" ponies have the hidden stillness yet potentially mobile being in which the reader participates from the beginning to the end of the poem. There, at the last, the "glassy octopus" has the still yet flexible surface by which one sees into a ground, a movement of meaning—of the animal that takes us by surprise in an avalanche, "launched like a waterfall," that never seems to fall.

The "scintillating fragment" by which one regrasps the whole could almost be a talisman for Tomlinson in *Seeing Is Believing*. It has the lit solidity, the Ruskinian sense of particular fact, that suggests why Tomlinson's poems *Frondes Agrestes: On Re-reading Ruskin* and *Geneva Restored* implicitly look towards Moore. Certainly he observes a continuity for his own poetry after *An Octopus* by noting the remarks on the pine by Ruskin in *Frondes Agrestes*, which follow those used by Moore. The tree, says Ruskin, has a "green and full *roundness*. It stands compact, like one of its own cones."[34] For him, it is not the wild, "ragged" pine of untruthful art, since it casts, in self-containment, "only a pyramidal shadow."[35] As Tomlinson can also observe, a few pages later in *Frondes*, Ruskin's eye for the precise, for the unexcessively compact, holds steady against his tendency to blazing effusion. Sunlight need not overwhelm language when he describes the effect on the rainy foliage of the Roman Campagna:

> I cannot call it colour,—it was conflagration. Purple, and crimson, and scarlet, like the curtains of God's Tabernacle, the rejoicing trees sank into the valley in showers of light, every separate leaf quivering with buoyant and burning life; each, as it turned to reflect, or to transmit the sunbeam, first a torch and then an emerald.[36]

That change in the leaf to "emerald" is for Tomlinson, in his own *Frondes Agrestes,* a luminously concrete instance of Ruskin who, moment by moment, matches his language to a shifting, temporal world. Indeed the very form of Tomlinson's poem, with its collection of such instances, reflects the form of Ruskin's *Frondes,* itself a compact anthologized version, a revelation in miniature, of *Modern Painters,* with its multitude of gathered instances. It is appropriate, therefore, that Ruskin's openness to a pluralistic world should be celebrated by Tomlinson's *Frondes Agrestes,* when, remembering Moore's "anthology of transit,"[37] the poet goes from event to event:

A leaf, catching the sun, transmits it:
'First a torch, then an emerald.'

'Compact, like one of its own cones':
The round tree with the pyramid shadow.

First the felicities, then
The feelings to appraise them:

Despite "the curtains of God's Tabernacle," Ruskin effectively looks at a universe governed by the sun: by the force that comes to earth in *Seeing is Believing* through the ocean wave, through a glass pane, through the oxen's "white darkness," and now through the small leaf—or the "frons," the leaf, of Tomlinson's trim verse-line. For in measuring up to sun, then trees, with Ruskin's aperçus, Tomlinson touches a whole through a fragment. As in *Cézanne at Aix,* he enacts another's tight fidelity to objective being by his own close alignment of style—in this, to Ruskin's unblurred acuity of vision that is to be celebrated despite its possessor's deviations. The poem, in fact, acknowledges a loss when Ruskin says that "Intense clearness" in nature being "a *notable* thing," we are meant, "in all probability," to enjoy the effects of mist.[38] In such a mood, Ruskin's dislike of artists who project a savage melancholy upon landscape can go to its own extreme. So he smoothes the jagged as he imagines nature taking "wonderful pains" to harmonize broken rock, so that moss gathers "over it in little brown bosses," making it seem "clothed with a soft dark leopard skin."[39] This is no sharp-edged sense of animal being (no more than shown by the stylistic attire of Dylan Thomas when seen satirically in Tomlinson's *Antecedents,* "dressed / In the skin of a Welsh lion"). But the poet stays patient, ready to wait out all the blurring and softening, until Ruskin recovers a new focus:

> Light, being in its untempered state,
> A rarity, we are (says the sage) meant
> To enjoy 'most probably' the effects of mist.
>
> Nature's difficulties, her thought
> Over dints and bosses, her attempts
> To beautify with a leopard-skin of moss
> The rocks she has already sculpted,
> All disclose her purposes—the thrush's bill,
> The shark's teeth, are not his story.
>
> Sublimity is. One awaits its passing,
> Organ voice dissolving among cloud wrack.

> The climber returns. He brings
> Sword-shaped, its narrowing strip
> Fluted and green, the single grass-blade, or
> Gathered up into its own translucence
> Where there is no shade save colour, the unsymbolic rose.

Not until Ruskin descends from the realms of overhumanizing romanticism (where only symbolic roses break in flower) does he reenter a ground where his botanist's eye is again in action: "Gather a single blade of grass, and examine for a minute quietly its narrow sword-shaped strip of fluted green."[40] Fact once more is seen to have its proper plenitude. Dark opacity, acknowledged, contains its own unsuperfluous light. As with the pine, casting no excess shadow, so in the rose there is *"no shadow, except what is composed of colour. All its shadows are fuller in colour than its lights, owing to the translucency and reflective power of the leaves."*[41] It is a perception to which Tomlinson pays tribute by gathering it up into his own verse-line where Ruskin's accuracy is translated into new justness. Moore deliberately lets her quotations bulk out of her verse in all their strange contingency, but Tomlinson draws on Ruskin to display an exact measure: the precise weighing of a writer's words against the thing they describe. Thus the lengthening list—

> Sword-shaped, its narrowing strip / Fluted and green

—is exactly met and balanced by the small fact of

> the single grass-blade

In the same way, the poem's last two lines enact Ruskinian containment of overflow. All those words, from "Gathered up" to "colour," are themselves gathered up, held in precise poise, by the sufficiency of "the unsymbolic rose."

The factual standpoint holds. But in *Geneva Restored*, the other specifically Ruskinian poem of *Seeing is Believing*, such a standpoint is a place to walk and live in, a town whose architecture and "sociality" closely adhere to a mountain, the Salève over Geneva. What Tomlinson sees, by means of Ruskin's autobiographical *Praeterita* with its memories of Geneva, is a people's capacity to create a habitation from rock—from the hard, unexaggerated factuality that underlies their civil values and Ruskin's own vision. It is characteristic that *Praeterita* finds a base in neglected stone: "I don't think anybody who goes to Geneva ever sees the Salève ... and the Salève, unless you carefully peer into it, and make out what it is, pretends to be nothing—a long, low swell like the South Downs."[42] Such is the mountainous heave beneath the network of human dwellings and cultivation, as

> the upper terraces look across . . . to the open southern country, rising in steady slope of garden, orchard, and vineyard—sprinkled with pretty farmhouses and bits of chateau, like a sea-shore with shells; rising always steeper and steeper, till the air gets rosy in the distance . . . and the great walnut-trees have become dots, and the farmsteads, minikin . . . and then, instant—above vineyard, above farmstead, above field and wood, leaps up the Salève cliff, two thousand feet into the air.[43]

Recalling Geneva as he first knew it in the 1830s, Ruskin finds constancy (the "same inaccessible sort of family dignity" retained by houses around cathedral and college) as well as a town that intimately fits its setting: "on its height of pebble-gravel knit almost into rock." It was "this bird's-nest of a place" that, to Ruskin's mind, was historically "the centre of religious and social thought, and of physical beauty, to all living Europe!"—the Geneva, that is, of Calvin, Rousseau, Byron, Saussure the geologist, and Turner. At such a point in *Praeterita*, however, one sees Tomlinson necessarily having to demur from Ruskin's overextended claims about the town's dominance, just as he does in *Frondes Agrestes*, when Ruskin climbs into the mists of sublimity. With *Geneva Restored*, the poet grounds his sense of the place's enduring significance—central, concrete, unexaggerated—on the more factually precise and local observations of Ruskin. A geological footnote in *Praeterita* is a starting point. For the cliffs of Salève are made of "an extremely compact limestone, in which the compressed faulted veins are of marble indeed." And this is one solid reason for living in a town like this:

> Limestone, faulted with marble; the lengthening swell
> Under the terraces, the farms in miniature, until
> With its sheer, last leap, the Salève becomes
> The Salève, juts naked, the cliff which nobody sees
> Because it pretends to be nothing, and has shaken off
> Its seashore litter of house-dots. Beneath that,
> This—compact, as the other is sudden, and with an inaccessible
> Family dignity: close roofs on a gravel height,
> Building knit into rock; the bird's nest of a place
> Rich in protestant pieties, in heroic half-truths
> That was Ruskin's. Guard and rebuild it.

Having compacted Ruskin's language back to the rock of its perception, in tribute to what is unsuperfluously *seen*, Tomlinson suggests fidelity to a close-knit relationship between people and place. One may guard and rebuild that, with a religious steadiness that avoids the clamor as well as the piety of Ruskin's unhappy Protestantism. *Geneva Restored,* therefore, continues at a wary distance from the extremism in *Praeterita* that damns the Genevan liberals for terracing the town "with their polypous knots of houses, communal with 'London, Paris, and New York.' Beneath which, and on the esplanades of the modern casino, New York and London now live—no more the Genevese." They have broken away, insists Ruskin, from their old "Genevese" center into the cosmopolitanism, the uprooted modernity of a nineteenth-century Europe in its wars. France, Germany, Italy, bound around nothing, must be decried for "their pieties, and their prides, their arts and their insanities, their wraths and slaughters, springing and flowering, building and fortifying, foaming and thundering round this inconceivable point of patience."

At such a point, however, one escapes from Ruskin's noisy distress and comes back with him to quiet focus. As Tomlinson suggests, one returns to the calmer, meditative excitement, factually enclosed, which lets the Salève become again, in sheer clarity, the Salève (just as Mont Ste. Victoire, kept faith with by Cézanne, can be, in Tomlinson's parallel fidelity, something that "is not / Posed" but "is"). Ruskin himself moves within such confines when he meditates on "A little canton, four miles square, and which did not wish to be six miles square!" For these are the strict boundaries of place and historical time that contain a perpetual eternal possibility—the relationship that a civil people may solidly remake with their setting. Indeed, such airy yet concrete potentiality is suggested by Tomlinson in language that draws not only on Ruskin but also on Elizur Wright, the American translator of La Fontaine's *Fables*. In the preface to the 1841 edition of his translation, Wright says, "Human nature, when fresh from the hand of God, was full of poetry. Its sociality could not be pent within the bounds of the actual."[44] Yet those bounds define the factual as well as the spiritual reality that Tomlinson's poem goes on to defend:

> Guard and rebuild it. We are in the time
> (The eternity rather) before the esplanades, New York
> Bear-ridden and the casino unbuilt, Paris and London
> Remain at Paris and London, and four miles square
> A canton of resined air that will not be six
> Refreshes a sociality that will not be pent
> In the actual. Round this inconceivable
> Point of patience, men travel on foot.

2: "Thus Men Make a Mountain"

Men walking inside the bounds of their space, not a long-vanished Europe revolving round it—that is the continuously present value that Tomlinson brings from this restoration of Geneva and this reencounter with Ruskin. For in the poetry after *Seeing is Believing* the "inconceivable / Point of patience" is to take on a newly conceived form where, moment by moment in a verse-line or a terrain, humanity is bound to a center, neither inflated in significance nor letting itself be reduced to nothing. There is, for example, the daily tenacity of the grape farmers in *The Compact: At Volterra* (1972), who "pit their patience against the dust's vacuity." There is the quietly meditated grip of the Hopi Indians on a more resistant land (*Arizona Desert*, 1966): "Here, to be, / is to sound / patience deviously." Yet here also, at the surface of words, not just soil, one *hears* the way a human presence, with its unexorbitant being, keeps its rhyme with a place, as "be" keeps a footing "devious-ly." It is the tact of an art—the verse-line having to earn its hold, like habitation justified—that Tomlinson has extraordinarily sharpened through American poetry and Ruskin and then applied to American ground itself. The adobe houses of the Indians on top of the Arizona mesas are therefore not so far, after all, from a Genevan "bird's nest of a place":

> Villages
> from mud and stone
> parch back
> to the dust they humanize
> and mean
> marriage, a loving lease
> on sand, sun, rock and
> Hopi
> means peace.

As with *Oxen: Ploughing at Fiesole,* the poem's disclosure, fragment by fragment, not only slows the reader to a meditative pace, but also offers the equivalent of a land that must be carefully cultivated. The sentence on the page, broken into pieces, is an explicit reminder of the need by human consciousness to recompose meanings, make legibility, from a world that is not paper: one not to be tyrannized by one's "readings" nor allowed, on the other hand, to swallow one up. With such objectivity granted, a parallel is possible between the Indians' patient building in solidities and a building with words. Thus "Villages" juts from blank paper, as much as it comes "from mud and stone." But even as the curt phrasing seems like human assertion in the desert (and a verbally sparse terrain), the "Villages ... parch back / to the dust." Scaled down, however, they cause the reader to

2: "Thus Men Make a Mountain"

make the kind of adjustment that was necessary in *Fiascherino* where sunrays that "Glance on the ceiling with no more substance / Than a bee's wing" are nevertheless "Thickening." As one reads, piece by piece, "Villages . . . parch back / to the dust they *humanize*," where the last word, cleansed of arrogant suggestion, carries, irreducibly, the meaning of relation to a place: "marriage, a loving lease / on sand, sun, rock and . . . ." Although "lease" means no permanent possession, the human seems to expand again. Like Indian villages, the poetic word seems to be spreading out with "sun, rock, and . . . ," but, with surprise, one is returned to the unexcessive—to the compactness of a people's name, "Hopi." Where the reader seeks meaning, and the Indian villages embody it, "Hopi" brings language and habitation together, as it "means peace," chimes with "lease," and self-containedly holds its place on mesa and verse-line.

Arizona Desert, in fact, like *Ute Mountain* from the same volume (*American Scenes,* 1966) demonstrates Tomlinson's impressive advance from the art of *Seeing is Believing,* on the basis of all that was achieved there. The necessary constraints of a poem such as *Cézanne at Aix* have brought their own freedom. Now, after Moore, and particularly after the effect of Williams's verse has been absorbed, Tomlinson can depict the way one may unpossessively grasp a place or take hold of a mountain mass in one's mind, without having to ward off the wrong meaning of "humanize" with negatives: "Unlike . . . not / Posed . . . Untaught / Unalterable . . . a presence / Which does not present itself." *Ute Mountain,* with its recreation of the human yet stony mass adjacent to the ancient Indian pueblo of Mesa Verde in Colorado, has sureness of a different kind:

> 'When I am gone'
> the old chief said
> 'if you need me, call me',
> and down he lay, became stone.
>
> They were giants then
> (as you may see),
> and we
> are not the shadows of such men.
>
> The long splayed Indian hair
> spread ravelling out
> behind the rocky head
> in groins, ravines;

> petered across the desert plain
> through Colorado,
> transmitting force
> in a single undulant unbroken line
>
> from toe to hair-tip: there
> profiled, inclined away from one
> are features, foreshortened, and the high
> blade of the cheekbone.
>
> Reading it so, the eye
> can take the entire great
> straddle of mountain-mass
> passing down elbows, knees and feet.
>
> 'If you need me, call me.'
> His singularity dominates the plain
> as we call to our aid his image:
> thus men make a mountain.

"We call to our aid . . . ," for the Ute legend serves a practical human need, here and now, quite distinct from a mythic past and biblical mystery ("They were giants then"). Separate from that, one can accept a present closeness, "as you may see," between the eye's image and reality's mass—a partnership between a complex mountain immensity and human consciousness, agile in mind and senses. But Tomlinson sustains the kinship by his avoidance of humanizing myths in American literature. He does not follow the example of Williams's *Paterson I* (1946) where, in *The Delineaments of the Giants,* the poet traces the huge sleeping bulk of Paterson himself and his "stone ear," together with a female giant: "The Park's her head . . . her monstrous hair . . . scattered about into / the back country." This requires belief without the earned and proven seeing of *Ute Mountain.*

What Tomlinson ravels out in his poem—stanza opening on stanza in elongated flow—is the articulation of American terrain, a marriage with it by speech, that Williams hears too disparately ("What common language to unravel?") in the roar of the Passaic River. *Ute Mountain,* in its swift correspondence between form and fact, follows through, Ruskin-like, the lines of geological energy across the plain and the page's white space,

> in a single undulant unbroken line
> from toe to hair-tip:

Here the fragmenting yet unifying quality of the art is even more nimbly revealed. A mountain, broken open in speech to have its "unbroken line" uttered, and its plurality of detail grasped by one "singular" image, is both usefully human in shape yet at the same moment distinctly nonhuman in fact. Set apart, nonintimate, the mountain is "profiled, inclined away from one . . . ." But in that distancing lies the grounds for the nearness one can have: the recognition of the foreshortened features, "the high / blade of the cheekbone" that, like Ruskin's "Sword-shaped . . . single grass-blade," is the incisive particularity by which one's realization pierces back into the whole without rupture. It is a "reading" where one has leave neither to dissolve one's consciousness nor mentally overpower what is seen. Such is Tomlinson's balance of suggestion that "the eye / can take the entire great / straddle of mountain-mass" with a grip that verbally respects its weight, its stony otherness, yet can feel, in the mass "passing down elbows, knees and feet," the tremor of its energy in one's own body. It is mutual relation voiced in the kind of poetry that strains after no Prometheanism or the would-be vanishing of the self as an American native in the Stevens mode. Tomlinson is giving back to America, with renewed intelligence, what America—particularly Williams's unmythic poetry, as one now sees—has given him as an Englishman and a European: the means of inhabiting a land, the terms by which men boldly make a mountain.

3

In the Tutelary Spirit

>   man
> In an exterior, tutelary spirit
>   Of his own inheritance, speaks
> To celebrate . . . .
>
> Charles Tomlinson, *Movements* (1973)

I

To inhabit a land is also to be vigilant. Throughout Tomlinson's poetry one sees either the individual or a people reclaiming kinship with a ground by an act of wakened alertness—a centering on place, a coming to focus, that resists modern dislocations and a wastrel sense of space. "Guard and defend" (the call of *Geneva Restored*) speaks, indeed, for the "tutelary" kind of guardianship that appears in the poems. But this is not the spirit of protection one associates with a land's deities or sacred icons. Instead, Tomlinson's non-Christian yet religious impulse is to express it in a variety of secular forms. By chastening the ego, by cleansing the will, one makes ready to receive again the powers or "presences" that exist, often forgotten, in place and home. Giving room to them, or a "house," is after all the capacity to make welcome, at its most alert, which Tomlinson first sharpened through Moore's poetry.

Just as the figure of the "house" recurs in *Seeing is Believing*, so in the books that follow, where Williams rather than Moore is the influence (*A Peopled Landscape*, 1963; *American Scenes*, 1966), it is the image of a tree that also comes to the fore. Firm in its ground yet resiliently climbing, the "tree" is like a sign of the emboldened dexterity that Tomlinson sees via Williams—the patience to elicit, step-by-step, the animate being of a place, as if it were a plant that subtly battles into view out of devastations and neglect. Now more clearly, Williams's New Jersey, with its hard urbanism and pastoral quickening, leads Tomlinson back in the poetry to the Stoke townscape, to take its measure as never before, and unsentimentally divine here—as also in poems of Italy and Mexico—the openings through which the powers of a place enter once more to repossess a ground and its people.

Tomlinson speaks with new flexibility for such recoveries because he has adapted Williams's short-line form of the interwar years, as well as the three-ply line from *The Desert Music* (1954) and *Journey to Love* (1955). But it was his own poetry in *Seeing is Believing* (largely completed by 1956 before he had read Williams seriously and first used the three-ply form in 1957) that was the unwitting preparation for what he gained through the new influence. As has been seen, *Cézanne at Aix* points the way forward. But so also, in a more Rilkean sense, does *Château de Muzot*. For at Muzot (the Swiss house where Rilke completed the *Duino Elegies* and *Sonnets to Orpheus*), the chaste relation between artist and objective nature leads Tomlinson, in his own parallel enactment, to speak of a "tightly-rosetted" moss that firmly clusters upon stone yet has a hardy openness as it "Accepts from all weathers / What it receives."

The perception of weathered strength is one that Tomlinson is to take further in his developing art. In the same way, a letter by Rilke, written in 1925, articulates tutelary feelings that are echoed directly in another *Seeing is Believing* poem, *The Ruin*, yet even there are looked beyond. For Tomlinson instinctively reaches towards the localizing energy that, as Williams shows, can combat barrenness—especially the American kind decried by Rilke in the course of his letter:

> Nature, the things we move about among and use, are provisional and perishable; but, so long as we are here, they are *our* possession and our friendship; sharers of our trouble and gladness, just as they have been the confidants of our ancestors . . . . Even for our grandparents a "House," a "Well," a familiar tower, their very dress, their cloak, was infinitely more, infinitely more intimate: almost everything a vessel in which they found and stored humanity. Now there come crowding over from America, empty, indifferent things, pseudo-things, *dummy-life* . . . . A house, in the American understanding, an American apple or vine, has *nothing* in common with the house, the fruit, the grape into which the hope and meditation of our forefathers has entered. . . . The lively, experienced things that *share our lives* are coming to an end and cannot be replaced. *We are perhaps the last to have still known such things.* On us rests the responsibility, not merely of preserving their *memory* (that would be little and unreliable), but their humane and laral worth. ("Laral" in the sense of household gods.)[1]

Although Tomlinson in *The Ruin* similarly observes how the "laral" (or "laric") world is shut out, his emphasis removes him a little beyond Rilkean finality. A sense of incoming possibility is here, despite the fact that

> our houses
> Are no longer ourselves; they dare not
> Enter our hopes as the guests of meditation
> To reanimate, warmed by this contact,
> The laric world where the bowl glistens with presence
> Gracing the table on which it unfolds itself.

Even as one reads, such religious "grace" or "presence" is turning into a secular graciousness—literally brought home by a household object as it "unfolds itself" in the present. The bowl is not quite Rilke's vessel of the past "into which the hope and meditation of our forefathers has entered." For here, now, in unfolding *thisness* ("warmed by this contact") it signifies the possibility of the opposite—the way by which, in daily openings-out, human beings may let houses "Enter our hopes as the guests of meditation." The language of other poems in *Seeing is Believing* similarly makes clear an attentive hospitality to such guests who, like the stones "waiting on presence" (*In Defence of Metaphysics*), are "inhuman / In a human dependence." Revitalizing our sense of courtesy and civility at its deepest, the world's manifold "presences" call on us to measure up to them with a proper answer or invitation. "Let it stand / A stone guest / In an unhospitable land," says Tomlinson in *Aqueduct,* where the socially welcome and the elemental resound together in the image of grasped flow—a conduit of water.

Human beings are channels too, as is seen in poems after *Seeing is Believing*. But unlike the Shelleyan idea of the self as a vessel—the ego ecstatically flooded by demoniac powers—there is modesty, self-bounding, a stability in the flux. People are seen as conveyors of the "laric world," or unpretentious custodians of it, by their very lack of an insistent ego or speech, their silence a testimony to the unseen, yet to be uttered land of presences that is embodied through them. So there is the "tutelary of that upland field," the Staffordshire laborer of *The Hand at Callow Hill Farm* (1963), whose silence has a quality in common with the "inarticulate philosopher," the boy who is leading a bull in *History* (1963), "the guardian / Of a continuity he cannot see." There are also the "Philosophers / Of the common run," the men who silently ruminate (*Bridges*, 1974) above the roar of the motorway. They are, in their way, very similar to what they lean upon—

bridges into the greater silence and the presences of an England waiting for access, "As though the quiet, rebegotten as they lean, survived / Through them alone, its stewards and sustainers." Caught by the circumstances of their era, bounded by harsh fact, they nevertheless guard, and make visible, the possibilities that lie beyond the immediately desolate. In this respect, they are like the salvagers of *The Way In* (1974). Pushing their pram through a waste scene—the streets of a British city, in the process of being demolished and rebuilt—they have a "pale / Absorption staring past this time / And dusty space we occupy together." In Tomlinson's tact of suggestion, it is a look that "Gazes the new blocks down": sign of the unspoken desire that cuts through degraded externals ("what they are looking at they do not see") and keeps guard over the civility, the true homeliness, which *can* be there for a people beyond debris and failure.

One recalls the want expressed in another British place of flux—the railway restaurant of *Terminal Tramps* (1969)—where a mad woman, from the midst of her confusion, finds clarity of need: "I expect / a civil answer." The female salvager of *The Way In* also embodies an expectation:

> She is our lady of the nameless metals, of things
>   No hand has made, and no machine
> Has cut to a nicety that takes the mark
>   Of clean intention—at best, the guardian
> Of all that our daily contact stales and fades,
>   Rusty cages and lampless lampshades.

She is "lady" of what is *not* there, in Tomlinson's strict adherence to the fact of a wasted townscape. But, simultaneously, she is guardian of all those metals yet to be named, things yet to be manually made or "cut to a nicety" by a machine—the still unarticulated relation with materials, the "clean intention" persisting as a possibility. In the poem's balance of fact and potency, there is no place for idealistic hope, only for a resourcefulness made deeper, tougher, and nimbler by the dereliction it must outgo.

Tomlinson's keen sense of the stream that runs below a desert surface—or of buried energies that could remake a civil place from urban destruction—brings him close to Williams. But he draws especially near, with a shared tutelary concern, in the *Seeing is Believing* poem, *On the Hall at Stowey*. Here, in the rural setting of a ruined country house on a Somerset estate (not Coleridge's Nether Stowey, however[2]), Tomlinson sees how stone walls depend on humanity "To measure the love, to assess its object, / That trusts for continuance to the mason's hands." But in a major respect, the "continuance" of Stowey's meaning lies with the poet, as he makes his way at the beginning through strange terrain:

> Walking by map, I chose unwonted ground,
> A crooked, questionable path which led
> Beyond the margin, then delivered me
> At a turn.

Choosing yet also chosen, decisive yet also submissive, the poet moves via the "questionable path" (and "doubtful light") toward the old hall, as if in these opening stanzas he were learning to adjust—stylistically and morally—to the conflicting qualities of energy and tempering, pride and modesty, firmness and flexibility, that, over centuries, have shaped this place. With remarkable closeness, the syntax follows the modified way in which Stowey has become what it is:

> The doubtful light, more of a mist than light
> Floating at hedge-height through the sodden fields
> Had yielded, or a final glare
> Burst there, rather, to concentrate
> Sharp saffron, as the ebbing year—
> Or so it seemed, for the dye deepened—poured
> All of its yellow strength through the way I went:

Self-correcting as it goes (yet by that, winning the right to define a strength), Tomlinson's style moves in a kind of agile sympathy with the house itself. What "Had yielded" (like the tall "house line" in stanza 3, tied to the earth, with its own submissive pride, "under a nest of barns") can also be said, with keener resurgence, to have "Burst there, rather, to concentrate / Sharp saffron." There is to be no tragic predictability, no high, nostalgic overview. The step-by-step movement forward—or groundlevel tracking where one cannot see the whole thing but gathers fresh acuity at each turn and corner—enables Tomlinson to swerve into apparent digression ("the ebbing year— / Or so it seemed, for the dye deepened") as a way forward, with assonance and alliteration ("seemed ... dye deepened") to an exactly forceful clarity. So "the ebbing year ... poured / All of its yellow strength through the way I went," the poet's stride keeping pace with that tempered yet powerful light emerging out of blur, which the style enacts in a later stanza. There the poet encounters walls,

> All stone. I had passed these last, unwarrantable
> Symbols of—no; let me define, rather

> The thing they were not, all that we cannot be,
>   By the description, simply of that which merits it:
> Stone. Why must (as it does at each turn)
>   Each day, the mean rob us of patience, distract us
> Before even its opposite?—before stone, which
>   Cut, piled, mortared, is patience's presence.

As with Ruskin's "unsymbolic rose" or *The Castle* in *Seeing is Believing* ("It is a real one—no more symbolic / Than you or I"), the object has its own sufficiency. This "Stone," not to be passed by or symbolically surpassed, calls the walker to attend, and the verse-line to acknowledge, its objective concreteness. But the stanza's last sentence, with its broken phrases, can only rearrive at solidity through the experience of nagging impediment, of petty banalizings that, in being suffered, sharpen response: "Why must . . . at each turn) / Each day, the mean rob us . . . distract us . . . ?" Traversing such contours, the sensibility comes back—with stylistic surprise yet inuring rightness—to a whole regained: to the shaped and gathered recomposure that lets calmness inhabit, in the way that stone "Cut, piled, mortared, is patience's presence."

In the sixth stanza, such patience is seen to extend across a larger tract of time. What one experiences earlier in the poem as a verse style that weathers adversity, as it doubles back on itself, then goes forward again, now becomes one's education in the vigor of those who farmed Stowey over centuries, and in the fruits which modified its architecture. *At Holwell Farm* (*Seeing is Believing*) shows provender in stone as a reflection: "Pears by the wall and stone as ripe as pears." But the door at Stowey answers more extraordinarily to its lands and crops:

> Five centuries—here were (at the least) five—
>   In linked love, eager excrescence
> Where the door, arched, crowned with acanthus,
>   Aimed at a civil elegance, but hit
> This sturdier compromise, neither Greek, Gothic
>   Nor Strawberry, clumped from the arching-point
> And swathing down, like a fist of wheat,
>   The unconscious emblem for the house's worth.

A land's fruit harvested by hand—an abundance gathered and contained across centuries—has been stylistically regrasped by an emblem "swathing down, like a fist of wheat." This is no conventional adornment, but a compact energizing in stone of the relationship between people and their land over time—a constancy amidst change and deviation. "Five centuries—here were (at the least) five"—Tomlinson's breakage of line yet confirming solidity (as he lands on the factual weight of the last "five") again points to the sureness working its way through modification, and back to earth, which the emblem's style itself underwent. The "linked love, eager excrescence" (the close bond of people over generations with their place, as heard in the tight, alliterative matching) found overstrained expression in the mode that initially sought loftiness ("arched, crowned with acanthus, / Aimed at a civil elegance.") Descending from such style (and from the throat-constricting hard *c*'s and unaspirated syllables with which Tomlinson suggests it), the architecture found its "civil elegance" nearer the ground—just as the poet aspirately frees the breath to show the way Stowey "hit / This sturdier compromise, neither Greek, Gothic, / Nor Strawberry." Since "Strawberry" (wittily minus its "Hill") was too luscious an architectural fruit for this place of wheat, the door-stone comes "swathing down" to earth: sign of a fecundity that is held in temperate bounds, not of a sensuous overflow that causes the mind to drowse. For although Tomlinson depicts across stanzas the movement of burgeoning, as the earth

> Out of the reddish dark still thrust up foison
> Through the browning-back of the exhausted year:
>
> Thrust through the unweeded yard, where earth and house
> Debated the terrain

eye and consciousness can match up to this plenitude. As with the door, an inscription lets one take the measure of—and "read"—this earth:

> My eye
> Caught in those flags a gravestone's fragment
>   Set by a careful century. The washed inscription
> Still keen, showed only a fragile stem
>   A stave, a broken circlet, as
> (Unintelligibly clear, craft in the sharp decrepitude)
>   A pothook grooved its firm memorial.

The words on the stone are broken, unintelligible, but that renders all the clearer a stylistic tradition that cuts through fragmentation with a keen, continuous edge. Grooving deep, the hand—which at Stowey is harvester, holder of the plough, and here is literate inscriber—touches both the finality of death and sharply felt life, "firm" in both senses. A whole culture of mind and senses, of vitality and self-tempering, is thus evinced and made the reader's experience as one traces "a fragile stem" and then is forced to pause (impeded by "a broken circlet" and the parenthesis), only to work patiently on through balk and blur (extracting sharp *"craft"* from faded "decrepitude") towards the won clarity of the pothook's "firm memorial."

It is one sign of that mutual relationship between people and setting that, as the poem now suggests, later generations have abandoned. Stowey's ruin has been accomplished by human negligence and by nature, which, having been left untutored and no longer our ally, destroys by "blind battery." In fact, the reader can observe how Tomlinson, to define the loss, draws on the concept of man's bold yet sensitive intervention in a landscape known to Pope and his age. "Consult the Genius of the Place," the landscaper is advised in the *Epistle to Burlington,* for, by audacity and tact, one makes a collaborator of nature, which thereby fully realizes itself: "Now breaks, or now directs, the intending lines; / Paints, as you plant, and, as you work, designs." The overbearing ego (Timon in the *Epistle*) is no more acceptable than is architectural inflation at Appleton House where, says Marvell, "Bodies measure out their Place," the self-disciplined man fitting into nature, as nature around him.

Yet Tomlinson's Stowey poem, as it speaks such relation anew, shows clearly that the genre, at its profoundest, is not "country house" verse but meditatively energetic pastoral, the poetry of close-knit moral habitation. It grieves at destructions, but without elegy. So, at the poem's end, when the walker finally turns away from Stowey, he is "Saddened, / Yet angered beyond sadness, where the road / Doubled upon itself." For this is the voice of endurance and flexibility—of the resilience learnt by the doubling back, the negotiation of impediments, the correcting of course, and the pressing onward along a more keenly defined continuity. Moreover, in adapting his own verse style to the contours (and stylistic fortunes) of Stowey, Tomlinson has allowed the facts of a place to shape the form of his poem with a versatility that looks toward Williams. At its deepest, such close matching is the tutelary verve that indicates the enrichment to come.

II

In his memoir, *Some Americans,* Tomlinson tells of visiting Williams for the first time in 1959. Going through New Jersey,

> I crossed that marshy flatland, the Meadows, between New York and Rutherford. Trucks were dumping their fill in the remaining spaces be-

tween suburban outcrops. Development was going forward here and there with no distinguishing center or direction. A touch of civility in the white Lutheran church whose scrupulously painted wooden structure dominated one settlement. Then: scattered filling stations, motels, wires, roads, presaging a future, perhaps. Suddenly a river with birds on it, a lost pastoral almost side by side with all this.[3]

The passage is not just a response to a scene but to Williams's own treatment of such a background in many poems, that "raw merging of American pastoral and urban squalor" (as Tomlinson describes it elsewhere[4]) in which human particularity wins back from the scattered and the unrealized a small center of repossession—the inlet through which the land reenters mind and dwelling. Yet, as *Ute Mountain* suggested, regaining touch with the currents of place is for Tomlinson not dependent on a mythical America, as in Williams's *Paterson,* or (for all its achievement) in the earlier narrative, *In the American Grain* (1925). The latter evokes an "Indian" continent, calling its explorers to answer its challenge and allure. But Williams's verse, as Tomlinson shows, offers an answer of a different kind—the reply, step-by-step, unexaggeratedly, to the cry of a more localized nativeness. Inside much smaller bounds, quickened and concentrated, one may then open out to immensities in right relation—neither attempting to swallow the vastness by fantasy nor trying to lose oneself within it. Williams, in fact, speaks most convincingly of all for "the still-unravished bride of silences" (as Lawrence described "Indian" America in his review of *In the American Grain*[5]) when he is at work in the relative confines of Rutherford, New Jersey—the ground that in the end is not so far from an England under threat.

The New Jersey Meadows (trucks "dumping their fill" on ground developed without "distinguishing center or direction") return one to the specifically English place, centerless, spoiled, and abandoned, in Tomlinson's poem, *From the Motorway* (1984): "Gulls flock in to feed from the waste / They are dumping, truck by truck." Nature, no longer a collaborator, has been left merely predatory in this nameless place without relation. Tomlinson's question ("How / Shall we have it back, a belonging shape?") shares the same sense of land failed by its people as Williams when he scathingly contemplates betrayal of ground in the 1923 poem that begins, "The pure products of America / go crazy." He views his compatriots, sunk in the tawdry and inarticulate before the great fact of their land, as having failed to see it or admit its modifying power into consciousness. "No one / to witness / and adjust," he says of a country whose "degraded prisoners" are shut off from pastoral "while the imagination strains / after deer / going by fields of goldenrod." It is a theme of American need that another American poet, George Oppen, carries on from Williams and voices, significantly, in the tutelary language of Tomlinson. For Oppen's long poem, *Of Being Numerous* (1969) quotes Williams by observing that "The pure products of America / go crazy" in the madness of the illimitable. Unable to "defend / Limitation," even if they want, the human "products" cannot enclose their sprawling sensibilities. A terrible distancing must overcome genuine relation between near and far if "we" have no neighborly principle to stand upon,

> And cannot defend
> The metaphysic
> On which rest
>
> The boundaries
> Of our distances.

The words directly echo Tomlinson's *In Defence of Metaphysics* (1960) where "Stones are like deaths. / They uncover limits." This recalling of verse that guards boundaries (and the solid otherness that waits to be admitted, "inhuman / In a human dependence") rightly connects Tomlinson with Williams and a similar purpose—the rediscovery of scale by means of limits that one observes, for instance, in the slow, careful movement of Williams's poem *View of a Lake* (1936). Seen by the side of a "recently blasted" rock and a railroad track, a human group in its stillness holds its ground (a definite "Where") against despoliation and the would-be rush of a different America:

> Where a
> waste of cinders
> slopes down to
>
> the railroad and
> the lake
> stand three children
>
> beside the weed-grown
> chassis
> of a wrecked car
>
> immobile in a line
> facing the water
> To the left a boy

> in falling off
> blue overalls
> Next to him a girl
>
> in a grimy frock
> And another boy
> They are intent
>
> watching something
> below—?

Like other watchers in Tomlinson's poetry, the children are firmly part of this age's circumstance. Indeed, as the verse-form brings the scene's desolate bits into view, the human figures seem clothed in the same lost dishevelment. Yet, by accepting the flat, impoverished facts, Williams has the basis on which to extricate—quietly, growingly, from beneath the fragmented surface—a vertebrate sense of fact and desire. The sinews of a more upright "intent" and sharpening attention begin to be felt as one moves across the disconnected bits (a railroad section sign, a service hut, a sheaf of wires, a frame house that looks "flayed") to a tree:

> Opposite
>
> remains a sycamore
> in leaf
> Intently fixed
>
> the three
> with straight backs
> ignore
>
> the stalled traffic
> all eyes
> toward the water

With clean counterpoise ("Opposite"), the sycamore "remains" tenaciously "in leaf"—a concentrated staying power amid the loose and broken that the children also match from within themselves, as their "*Intently* fixed" gaze and a tree "*in* leaf" move together on the same steady current. One hears the chime of "sycamore," indeed, as they "igno*re* / the stalled traffic" and converge "all eyes" on the greater flow beyond waste and deadlock.

View of a Lake has precisely the qualities of anchorage in solid fact and of extension—the lineal reaching-out, with no loss of balance—

that are to be so important for Tomlinson in Williams's poetry. But *Young Sycamore* (1927) shows even more boldly and eagerly how the American stretches the verse-line, to raise a tree from the ground:

> I must tell you
> this young tree
> whose round and firm trunk
> between the wet
>
> pavement and the gutter
> (where water
> is trickling) rises
> bodily
>
> into the air with
> one undulant
> thrust half its height—
> and then
>
> dividing and waning
> sending out
> young branches on
> all sides—
>
> hung with cocoons—
> it thins
> till nothing is left of it
> but two
>
> eccentric knotted
> twigs
> bending forward
> hornlike at the top

"This" specific tree, exactly wedged between pavement and gutter (or between stanza and stanza) has a "round and firm trunk" that must physically (and lineally) pivot its weight, balance its energy against the ground ("where water / is trickling"). For thus, without magnifying or subduing its vitality, it rises into the air with the full-poised impact of "bodily"—that "one undulant / thrust" where curving resilience transmits a force upwards, just as the adjectival short *u*'s push into and embody "thrust." So accurate is the gauging of resources by tree and poet that physical energy seems to branch and attenuate, "dividing and waning," without dissipation even as it "thins," and the reader has to stretch ("bending forward") to catch the last, small embodiments of the sycamore, as they split, piece by piece—or word by word—into "two—eccentric—knotted—twigs." Right up to the final, curving singularity ("hornlike at the top"), Williams keeps balance superbly, by a central tact, a treelike touch and hold.

There are other examples of a plant determining a poem's shape, as in Williams's *The Crimson Cyclamen* (1936). But this poem's connection with the visual arts and Williams's contemporaries (in this case, the painter Charles Demuth) is an important reminder of another dimension to *Young Sycamore*, its emergence from the sensibility of an age and documented ways of seeing, which also produced the work of the photographer Alfred Stieglitz. One recalls in particular, Stieglitz's eye for moments of centering or convergence as they arise in the American urban and industrial scene. There is his *Winter, Fifth Avenue* (1893) where the high branch of a tree curves in line with a cabhorse far below as it bends against a snowstorm. Or, in another photograph (*The Hand of Man*, 1902) there is the upward fume of a steam locomotive counterbalanced by the crisscross glisten of rails on which it runs. There is also *Spring Showers* (1902), which very probably, as Bram Dijkstra has argued, is a direct source for Williams's *Young Sycamore*. In Stieglitz's photograph of a New York scene (described by Dijkstra) one sees "an empty, wet expanse of sidewalk and street, gritty and shining with pebbles, sand, and rain. A young tree breaks out of the flat, stone surface, its thin trunk scattering into a microscopic tracery of branches and a spotted rhythm of cocoons. Next to it is an old, bent man with a huge broom, sweeping the gutter. In the distance are the towering buildings of the city, nearly obliterated by rain."[6] Although no human being appears in *Young Sycamore*, Stieglitz's work still retains an affinity with a later poem by Williams called *The Poor* (1938). Here, "in an unfenced / age," an old man "sweeps the sidewalk," defining a boundary, through which— all ten feet of it—there runs the wind that "has / overwhelmed the entire city." It is a moment of pinpointing and recovery of scale, that, together with *Young Sycamore* and *View of a Lake*, offers the possibilities that Tomlinson develops in *The Tree* (1974).

Based on a photograph, the poem is written with a fraternal sense of what Williams had achieved in relation to Stieglitz's work. But this time the urban factuality of *The Tree* came from a photograph sent him in 1973,[7] with its depiction of a working-class street in northern England that, although not Stoke, has distinct reminders of the place where he grew up. In the picture's foreground, a child with hooded coat works away with a shovel at the remains of snow on a pavement, while just behind him there is an older type of streetlamp

3: *In the Tutelary Spirit*   91

whose triangular helmet cuts sharply into a sky's winter whiteness. Across the street, above the dour, terraced houses, some chimneys (one industrial) are fading into the mist, while along the pavement, on the same side as the shoveller, other children are playing. A dog stands blackly in the road. All would be drearily uncentered—scatterings without connective energy—but for the intent effort of "this" digging child—the incisive little action that (like "this young tree" in *Young Sycamore*) has the specific, local particularity by which, consciously or unconsciously, the human being works toward a cleared and lightened solidity:

>   This child, shovelling away
>   what remains of snow—
>   a batter of ash and crystals—
>   knows nothing of the pattern
>   his bent back lifts
>   above his own reflection:
>   it climbs the street-lamp's stem
>   and cross-bar, branching
>   to take in all the lines
>   from gutter, gable, slates
>   and chimney-crowns to the high
>   pillar of a mill chimney
>   on a colourless damp sky:
>   there in its topmost air
>   and eyrie rears that tree
>   his bending sends up
>   from a treeless street, its roots
>   in the eye and in the net the shining
>   flagstones spread at his feet.

Bent over in play, the child takes on his back the weight of a playfully branching pastoral, but without burden or poetic imposition, for he (and, by extension, the poet) open out into its fullness an instinct for the whole that has its roots in grounded limit. Instead of fantasy, Tomlinson speaks for the modest, organic desire that must grapple with resistant fact in order to verify human want—clean space—every step of the way. So, not outflying concreteness, but nimbly footed in relation to it (to "make a *dance above* the fact," as Tomlinson sees in Williams's poetry[8]), *The Tree* can stretch and "take in" hard angularities, finding new grip and balance as it follows out the lines that go "from gutter, gable, slates / and chimney-crowns to the high / pillar of a mill chimney." But the imaginary tree can only repossess such hardness because the words not only climb but also root down—

so that "sends up" leaps off "bending," while "tree," as it "rears" through "eyrie," takes one back to "a treeless street," yet also to an interchange between ground and air, limits and possibilities. By not taking the counterfeit image as literal, one has the freedom to admit inside that "street" the "tree" that ineradicably grows there—like a fact of human desire whose sought branching and interknitting cannot make one ignore other facts, but which partners and opens out their darkness. Thus the roots of the "tree" are only "in the eye." Yet "in the net" (street angles held by an image without softening), there is an entire cleansed ground laid open before the child, like a gift's lit abundance: "the shining / flagstones spread at his feet."

This is to reach towards a pastoral inside the urban, without strain or imbalance. But the adaptation of the short-line American form also lets Tomlinson adventure more exactly than before in an animal or primal world—a daring of instinct and mind, one sees, that does not mean the betrayal of self-responsible consciousness. Wordsworth stretched the pentameter toward the same poise, at the borderline of human and nonhuman,

> when I have hung
> Above the raven's nest, by knots of grass
> And half-inch fissures in the slippery rock
> But ill sustained, and almost (so it seemed)
> Suspended by the blast that blew amain . . . .[9]

Yet for Tomlinson to speak his own kind of impetus and hesitancy, elasticity and firmness—to make newly present, in fact, the attentive reach of the English romantic tradition—he draws on a different lineage. Williams, not Wordsworth, is the immediate forebear of a poem such as *The Fox Gallery* (1969), but only thus does it achieve the Wordsworthian excitement and measured agility by which human understanding stretches out toward an animal seen from the upper story of the poet's house in Gloucestershire. "Fox fox" is the cry with which he wakes his wife, and, by a similar wakening of a married couple in *The Littleton Whale* (1981), an animal seems almost to enter habitation, or to *be* it, for "that house was a whale." In *The Fox Gallery*, people are roused by another entering force as

> the animal
> came on—not from side
> to side, but straight
> at the house and we craned
> to see more and more, the most
> we could of it and then

> watched it sheer off deterred
> by habitation, and saw
> how utterly the two worlds were
> disparate, as that perfect
> ideogram for agility
> and liquefaction flowed
> away from us rhythmical
> and flickering and
> that flare was final.

Housed inside language and consciousness, they nevertheless crane "to see more and more"—their impulse toward the animal held back by the walls of human form (or line endings) beyond which they try to stretch, elongating sight with *and* after *and*: "and then . . . and saw . . . and flickering . . . and / that flare." It is a conspicuous adding on: a coming awake, through the fox, of time in the moment-by-moment way that human beings must mentally conceive it, yet also the subverbal, seamless reality of time as lived. Fox and people head for each other, meet, as it were, through the habitation where named and nameless being come together in "the fox gallery." Yet Tomlinson must emphasize the very disparateness of human and animal in order to hit the exact terms of their real encounter. For the word-picture of the fox ("that perfect / ideogram for agility / and liquefaction") is both an example of human literateness outgone by the animal's wordless actuality, as it "flowed / away," and the very means by which that flow is uttered, as its vividness comes to occupy speech and habitation. So, even though the last *and*'s ("and flickering and") reach out to an emphatically vanishing fox ("and / that flare was final.") a continuity stays alight. The boundary of wall and language—unconfused with, yet open to presences outside it—has let animal fire come home, to enter as the guest of man and wife in a bond that marries back humanity to the nonhuman world.

In Tomlinson's earlier poem, *The Well* (1966), there is another bond discovered—between subterranean dark and a people's civil consciousness. But here, in the setting of a Mexican convent at Oaxaca, Williams's variable line is used to reach out beyond the self into the intuitive, because it also lets Tomlinson keep grip on mind and solidity. So, in the first lines, as an implicit presence rather than a personalized "I," he is not flowing away but

> Leaning on
> the parapet stone
> Listening down
> the long, dark

> sheath through which the standing
> shaft of water
> sends its echoings up....

"Leaning," "Listening"—the self in those participles feels out and delicately makes chime with a blind underlay of "stand*ing*" water and its "echo*ings*." Yet because "Listening down" is actually elided to three syllables, so that it keeps parallel with "Leaning on," a subtle link is kept between underground and surface consciousness. This remains true even as line 5 lengthens into exploratory descent. For its downward-probing elasticity is related back to a finiteness of understandable form—a "sheath" that fits exactly the echoing "shaft" and thus is the clothing, the channel, by which elemental, sensuous density comes into the consciousness, instead of being lost in the nakedly unrealized. Indeed, it is the "standing" steadiness of the water in the well—a constancy rather than flux—that is sounded out, given articulation, and brought back into the Mexican day:

> Catching, as it stirs
> the steady seethings
> that mount and mingle
> with surrounding sounds
> from the neighbouring
> barrack-yard: soldiery
> —heirs, no doubt
> of the gunnery that gashed
> these walls of tattered
> frescoes, the bullet-
> holes now socketed
> deeper by sunlight....

Now, as the well's "seethings" mingle with the "surround*ing*" and the "neighbour*ing*," one hears in the liquidity an infiltrating stamina, the supple strength that (heard in "Catching") carefully moves over the gashed surface left to this place by a revolutionary past, as the eye travels, in place and verse-line, across the abrupt linkages of hyphen, colon, and dash.

Yet there is a deeper continuity that one traces. Those sounds from the "barrack-yard: soldiery / —heirs, no doubt of the gunnery that gashed / these walls" are both "neighbouring" and neighborly. For the ear, drawing on the well's refreshment, tutors the eye to look through the broken externality, through the walls with their "bullet- / holes" (violence stilled by the line-break) and see, via the sun's well-like deepening, a more enduring civility. It is the moment in the poem when the individual mind (as signified in the capital letter presence of "Leaning," "Listening," and "Catching") becomes part of the communal consciousness. The individual self remains "Aware," but now it chimes with a wider awareness that is locally "there" and in relationship "their":

> and the bright gaps
> giving on to the square
> and there revealing
> strollers in khaki
> with their girls Aware
> of a well-like
> cool throughout
> the entire, clear
> sunlit ruin....

To be "Aware," in this newly spacious sense of leisured time, of civil soldiery and marriage, is also to rhyme with and yet go beyond loss—like "the brilliant cupids / above the cistern / that hold up / a baldachin of stone / which is not there." A past's excess is outlived, just as a people seem to have discovered a steadiness after history's fury and overflow. It is part of one's communal "Hearing" now:

> Hearing the tide
> of insurrection
> subside through time
> under the still-
> painted slogans
> *Hemos servido*
> *lealmente*
> *la revolución*

"We have loyally served the revolution." But in the stilling of old causes, the stillness of present feeling keeps loyal to a calmer, deeper *revolución*. History's fixed ruins are outpaced by the flow of a harmonizing, replenished time.

In one way, *The Well* suggests Tomlinson's difference from Williams—the need to bring into justifying consciousness, step-by-step, the communal spirit of place. Yet the poem also directs one back to all that Tomlinson has learnt from the American, especially an alertness to the given thing—the chanced-on person, object, or event that lets through the nativeness (as distinct from nationalism) of place. It is, for example, what Williams happens upon in *Pastoral* (1917) when he observes the oddly habitable way that poor people give access to the spirit of a less insistent America:

> I walk back streets
> admiring the houses
> of the very poor:
> roof out of line with sides
> the yards cluttered
> with old chicken wire, ashes,
> furniture gone wrong;
> the fences and outhouses
> built of barrel-staves
> and parts of boxes . . . .

The straight idea of American progress is flouted by these homemade asymmetries. Apart from the delight they give, however, there is little further realization.

In Williams's glad exactitude, however, lies Tomlinson's sense of opportunity. Significantly, he notes of Williams in *Pastoral* and his later poem, *The Poor* (1938), that "Instead of wishing simply to reform the poor ('It's the anarchy of poverty / delights me . . .'), he senses there is a point where the imagination, partaking of this anarchy, could dance with it, could 'lift' it to an answering form but a form fully responsive to the waywardness and inconclusiveness of daily realities."[10] It is Tomlinson's own sense of the wayward and disruptive that serves him well when he too, like Williams, begins to unclench a city's tight surfaces. But his "answering form" is intellectually sharper than the American's. As with the play of ripples in Tomlinson's 1969 poem, *Swimming Chenango Lake* ("each / Liquid variation answerable to the theme / It makes away from, plays before"), "answerable" denotes accountability to fact, but also the capacity for reply. For the nimble human consciousness, separate from what it dances with, undertakes a dialogue where it can "answer" fact—particularly the degraded, urban variety—with the language of possibilities.

It is the extent of that endeavor in Tomlinson's *Canal* (1963) and his tact in neither exaggerating nor understating the pastoral freshnesses that can be there—the quickening asymmetry delved for inside a town's hard symmetries—that shows how much his "answering form" partakes of Williams's unrushed gradualness. *Canal* looks back, for example, to the kind of patient, disclosing style that one sees in the American's *Spring and All* (1923):

> Now the grass, tomorrow
> the stiff curl of wildcarrot leaf
>
> One by one objects are defined—
> It quickens: clarity, outline of leaf

3: In the Tutelary Spirit

Piece by piece also, *Canal* travels a Stoke waterway, but Tomlinson brings to the poem his own distinctive qualities, as seen elsewhere in the sinuous, liquid strength of *The Well* and the alertness to animal being in *The Fox Gallery*. The "wandering," uninsistent motion of the birds on this canal ("Swans. I watch them . . .") sets the pace for the human observer, but also cleaves a way open. They "come unsteadying / the dusty, green / and curving arm / of water"; and, by their slight, rippling upset of the town's angularities reflected in the canal, the swans give one the means to cut through—very carefully—the dense samenesses of this place. The birds are like the oxen who lead man forward in Tomlinson's Fiesole poem. Here, however, that illuminating, animal presence is more implicit and intermittently glimpsed, as the poem's eye turns away after the first lines, to contemplate harder facts:

> Symmetrically punched
> now empty rivet-
> holes betray
> a sleeper fence:
> below its raggedness
> the waters darken
> and above it rear
> the saw-toothed houses
> which the swinging
> of the waters makes
> scarcely less regular
> in repetition. Swans
> are backed by these, as
> these are by
> a sky of silhouettes,
> all black and almost
> all, indefinite.
> A whitish smoke
> in drifting diagonals
> accents, divides
> the predominance of street
> and chimney lines . . . .

Instead of looking at this townscape en masse and predictably despairing of it as a wasteland, Tomlinson takes it piece by piece, tracks it in filmic close-up, as if only by staying this near to fact's hurtful edges can he feel his way to the unpredictable and assuaging. So there is fidelity in letting "Symmetrically punched" hit the eye alone at first. He is true to urban repetition's blunt insistence—and, in being so, rightly able to find a way through the seemingly opaque and fastened.

Thus one reads on to discover "now empty rivet- / holes" and the loosening barrier of a mere "sleeper fence," made from railway timbers, yet also sagging like a sleeper from the fixed and upright. So there is an easing of rigidities, but the eye must still contend with the "saw-toothed houses" whose self-mirroring suffers only slight disturbance ("scarcely less *regular* / in *repetition*") from the "swinging / of the waters." Nevertheless, the birds' gracious movement on the canal has rocked such fixities, and "Swans" come back into view and verse-line. Although the town's insistent sameness keeps pushing them from sight, their ripple further helps the eye in its loosening of riveted certainty. Thus, despite surface packed on surface, the self-chiming pattern (where swans are "backed by *these*, as / *these* are *by* / a *sky* of silhouettes, / *all* black and *almost all* . . .") leads surprisingly to the "indefinite." Homogeneity is broken into, and, with the sight of "A whitish smoke / in drifting diagonals," the swanlike disruption of the urban mathematic begins to tease out a hidden space and horizon:

> And, there, unseen
> among such angularities—
> a church, a black
> freestanding witness
> that a space of graves
> invisibly is also
> there. Only
> its clock identifies
> the tower between
> the accompaniment of stacks
> where everything
> repeats itself—
> the slag, the streets
> and water that repeats
> them all again
> and spreads them rippling
> out beneath
> the eye of the discriminating
> swans that seek
> for something else
> and the blank brink
> concludes them without conclusion.

One goes beyond endings. For the poem steadily makes it possible to cut through the blockage of the seen to what "invisibly *is* also / there"—towards a "space of graves," but also toward the *is* of present being, of living time and space, that the church's clock "Only" (yet tenaciously) is witness of. As it protrudes—and as one's eye refuses to let it be crowded out of sight—one is tutored by a rising, new vivacity that takes the measure of the weary insistencies where "everything rep*eats* itself— / the slag, the str*eets*, / and water that rep*eats* / them all again"—a chime danced beyond, and resisted, by a different tune, as water "repeats / them all again / and spreads them rippling / out beneath / the eye of the discriminating / swans." The judicious adjective given to the birds is a reminder of the poem's moral and visual exactness—seeking no easy romantic outflow, but taking the measure of inescapable boundaries. Only thus is the ripple of the new made visible out of the unseen, and only thus does one avoid being driven back on the self and its repetitious assertions. Quietly yet decisively, the human observer, via the swans, gives room and habitation to the pulse that could, with stronger beat, recivilize house and city.

Again, however, Tomlinson's tutelary care in such a poem (to persuade a vital otherness back inside human boundaries, yet claim no more than is precisely sayable) retains a kinship with the nongarrulous tact of Williams in prewar poems such as *Morning, A Bastard Peace, Autumn, To a Poor Old Woman,* or *Proletarian Portrait.* In these New Jersey scenes and others, the reader must adapt his pace and slow down to consider the way that people localize their ground as they work, walk, dig, eat, sweep, cut grass, play, or sit in the sun. None of this is to be philosophized. "No ideas but in things," says Williams, with a respect for fact that clearly has Tomlinson's agreement—if not a similar readiness—to let the sensuous, objective world unfold at the expense of the realizing consciousness. Taken far enough, as Tomlinson sees, this can be a surrender of the self to circumstance and (taken further still) a sliding into fatalism. It is the Englishman's resistance to flux—the sense of the undissolved, concrete world, and the integrity of the dancing awareness that plays in relation to it—that brings him closer, in moral intelligence, to Marianne Moore's art.

Yet ultimately Williams's poetry is his greater stimulus, because Moore's distinctive style, with its syllabic formalism, remains too individually or idiosyncratically hers to become the starting point for development that Williams offers—in lineation and in those sharable, extendable cadences that (as Tomlinson says in the uncollected poem, *Letter to Doctor Williams,* 1957) "will pass into the common idiom."[11] It is an idiom that underlies the moral verve and language of community—that England of greater spiritual density—in Tomlinson's *A Peopled Landscape.* There, in such poems as *Return to Hinton, Up at La Serra,* and *John Maydew,* one is to see the three-ply form rid of the sentimentality to which Williams can be liable, and working with the taut sinews of the best New Jersey poems. Through Williams, one also realizes, Tomlinson gains not just lineal flexibility, but also access to a tradition of factuality in American writing that more keenly defines his sense of native ground as a European and an Englishman.

III

The strength of such a tradition, working through Moore and Williams, has already taught Tomlinson vital new ways by which a poet can "ask the fact for the form."[12] Indeed, his use of this quotation (from Emerson's essay "Poetry and Imagination," ca. 1860) to describe Williams's art implies his whole acknowledgment of the Americans' longstanding concreteness in literature, right down to their feeling for the humblest object. As Tomlinson says in *The Poem as Initiation* (1967), "there is no occasion too small for the poet's celebration."[13] So Emerson's example in "The American Scholar" (1837)—as he tells over "The meal in the firkin; the milk in the pan; the ballad in the street"[14]—belongs, for Tomlinson, in his introduction to the *Selected Poems* of Williams, with the "list" poems of Whitman and Williams's *Paterson V,* where even a grocery list is brought into verse.

One recalls Tomlinson's early lines about "Bowl and water-jug" in a Ruskin-like instancing of the ordinary. It is clear, however, that his English temper and Ruskin's steadying example make such hospitality to fact the awakening of mind rather than a materialistic dulling. So "The commonest objects / Take presence from light"—everyday utensils, workingly allied with us yet cleansed of human ego, admitting a "grace" or unknown presence inside the confine that we can also enter, with newly sharpened realization. The common object is thus a meeting point between self and external otherness. Therefore it is appropriate that Tomlinson, having said that there is no occasion too small for the poet's celebration, should go on to cite Williams's red wheelbarrow and Wordsworth's "naked table," for in Williams's 1923 poem,

> so much depends
> upon
>
> a red wheel
> barrow
>
> glazed with rain
> water

> beside the white
> chickens

because of everything that, in color, solidity, wetness, texture, place, or animals, is lit up as wondrous fact by—*within*—the "barrow"; also because a human idiom, fragmented to reconstitute that clean-grasped world, must hover "upon—a—red—wheel—barrow." Much similarly depends upon another clean utensil in Wordsworth's *Prelude,* book 1: "the naked table, snow-white deal, / Cherry or maple," round which the cottagers play cards while, as Tomlinson describes it, "winter is raging outside—rain and frost and splitting ice."[15] Plain wood here is the starkly elemental brought inside—the very means by which human delight makes heated truce with freezing nature.

Significantly, it is the bracing interplay of domesticity and American winter, as in Emerson's poem, *The Snow Storm* (1847), that also affects Tomlinson. Emerson traces the way by which people and elements partake of each other's domain. The snow, "fierce artificer," makes its "frolic architecture," while human beings create from the blizzard's fury an energized sense of habitation: "the housemates sit / Around the radiant fireplace, enclosed / In a tumultuous privacy of storm."

Outer frenzy defining inner stability—a nearness won out of distances—is an idea that Tomlinson literally carries forward in the European scene of *Travelling* (1987) where a rainstorm dashes against the window of a train as "we swung through the daylight dark / And on, in a tumultuous privacy of storm." Tomlinson articulated this kind of balance previously in the English rural setting of *Winter Encounters:* "Calmness within the wind, the warmth in cold." But now, especially in the poems of the 1960s, he seems to draw more fully on that frost-keen quality, playful yet tough, that Williams's antecedents, such as Whittier, bring to their presentation of community and place. Whittier's winter idyl, *Snow-Bound* (1866) shares with Emerson's snow poem, a delight in a coldness pierced by human habitation, with people cutting a tunnel through the great drifts to make their Aladdin's cave and the outside snow letting the room's fire seem to burn inside it, "radiant with a mimic flame" or "warm hearth . . . blazing free." But even more importantly, in a poem that memorializes a vanished past on a Quaker homestead, Whittier too actively celebrates "the stir of hall and street, / The pulse of life that round us beat," to melt into the weakly wistful, for such verse, like the best of Williams in his localizings, demonstrates the kind of unnostalgic strength that the American tradition can offer an Englishman who is ready to parallel it with his own tenacity—the meditative stamina with which Tomlinson contemplates the forces in his own country that threaten place and meaning.

In *Return to Hinton,* from the standpoint of a Somerset farmhouse, Tomlinson considers an England of the late 1950s, where postwar affluence and its promises disguise a threat to older continuities. But in a poem subtitled "Written on the author's return to Hinton Blewett from the United States," there is to be no statutory elegy on vanishing rural ways. The mood, if unrancorous, is tougher—clear-eyed in its adaptation of the American verse-line to evoke the constancies, persistencies, and relationships, still astir in a ground long worked and cherished. There is a place's "presence" within these rooms and utensils, an airy openness inside weight and solidities that the three-ply line lifts into view as the poet's eye moves from the parlor of the farm towards the kitchen:

>   the mullions and flagged floor
>   of the kitchen
>   through an open door
>   witness a second
>   world in which
>   beside the hob
>   the enormous kettles'
>   blackened bellies ride—
>   as much the tokens of an order as
>   the burnished brass.

Like "the Bible / open at Genesis / on the parlour table," the view "through an open door" gives religious and secular "witness" to an order under threat from the "merely new"—the vistas of an imaginary future, of a political and economic utopia. In a language whose common idiom has been nourished by the Bible, the non-Christian poet wonders whether continuities will be passed on. Will her son (he asks the farmer's widow) "transmit / that more than bread / that leaves you undisquieted?" Yet her very composure—the "sadness without bitterness" of a woman who has "given / grief its due" and in bereavement closed her door on despair—is mark of the constancy she has earned, of her "won readiness" for a life beyond death and loss. Although, unlike the poet, such steadfastness is clothed in Christian Nonconformist terms ("a worn dress / of chapel gospel"), he has common cause with her as he undespairingly faces "death" of another kind. Ultimately, it is a greater perishing they stand against—she, unwitting tutelary, and he, conscious defender ("Our language is our land"):

3: *In the Tutelary Spirit*

>   Death's
>   not the enemy
>   of you nor of your kind:
>   a surer death
>   creeps after me
>   out of that generous
>   rich and nervous land
>   where, buried by
>   the soft oppression of prosperity
>   locality's mere grist
>   to build
>   the even bed
>   of roads that will not rest
>   until they lead
>   into a common future
>   rational
>   and secure
>   that we must speed
>   by means that are not either.

With "locality" under threat (to be steamrolled flat as "mere grist" by the highway builders who distance our nearnesses), Tomlinson brings the force of American experience to bear upon his own country's situation. So an English moral wit, incisively transforming Williams's cadences, refuses to sell off land and language for "a promised mess of pottage / that we may not taste." Thus futurizing abstractions are resisted by a land's idiomatic concreteness—the resources of native speech and secular experience, provendered by harvest and Bible. Words may be susceptible to corruption, bit by bit, but piece by piece also (as Tomlinson shows in the three-ply form where one can meditatively hover on separate words and phrases), language has the chance to rise clear of its own subversion and come into dancing attack. So, in the verse-line, Tomlinson catches the smoothing tones of the beguilers as they offer "*soft* . . . pro*sperity*," with its hidden and cushioned "*oppression*." Such "even bed" of future levelings will give no ease, because, as the next line shows, pushing on, this is a "bed / of roads that will not rest" until society is evened out

>   rational
>   and secure

—an imaginary balance, on page and in mental prospect, that Tomlinson undoes by a reminder of the willful speed by which it is sought. For, as one sees in the final lines—where the poet's reasonableness is bedded in no false security or illusory "rational" future—to stand upon the truly grounded, to speak for a verifiable past and present, has its own plain refreshment:

> For who has known
>   the seasons' sweet succession
>   and would still
> exchange them for a whim, a wish
>   or swim into
>   a mill-race for an unglimpsed fish?

Patience unfolds in the calm spacing-out and alliterative balance of "the seasons' sweet succession." But, in equally versatile enactment, Tomlinson evokes rushing impatience ("whim" and "wish" toppling into "swim" and drowning in pursuit of that "unglimpsed fish"), only to catch it all back inside a calmly sane question. Right to the last, the poem's style and adaptive demeanor are the embodiment of what it defends—an experience contained within speech, land, and centering place. It is the sureness not of dull ruralism or futurizing but of a measured resilience.

Return to Hinton, then, has the dexterous grip on what it values that Tomlinson foreshadowed in his Stowey poem. It also has what Williams calls in his *Autobiography* the "integrity of understanding to insure persistence, to give the mind its stay"[16]—the sinewy tenacity, verse-line pulling against verse-line, that the American shows in his own way with *The Pink Locust* (1955):

> I'm persistent as the pink locust,
>   once admitted
>   to the garden,
> you will not easily get rid of it.
>   Tear it from the ground,
>   if one hair-thin rootlet
> remain
>   it will come again.

As with his other poems on flowers and trees, Williams here escapes self-regard by looking carefully at the organically unfolded thing, the plant that, "once admitted / to the garden," moves from seeming controllable (in the balance of the line-break) to being the rampant growth that, in the following lengthy line, "you will not easily get rid of." The next sentence is adroitly broken, to catch the fury of human exasperation ("Tear it from the ground") and the delicate, fibrous thwarting of such force ("if one hair-thin rootlet / remain"). For "remain" hangs on its own—just—as a tiny nucleus from which spreads all that "will come again" in rhyming persistence. *The Pink Locust,* indeed, has the alacrity of word poised with word that one sees also in *To Daphne and Virginia* (1954):

>   There is, in the hard
>   give and take
>   of a man's life with
>   a woman
>   a thing which is not the stress itself
>   but beyond
>   and above
> that,
>   something that wants to rise
>   and shake itself
> free.

The mobile-like flotation of lines—the ever-changing balance of lengthy segment with smaller—avoids the emotional flaccidity to which the form can be liable. Instead, there is the toughly delicate interplay of marriage's "give and take," as one side ("of a man's life with") is verbally weighed against another ("a woman"). The reader must stretch through the next line's appropriately extended length to *"that,"* which—suspended alone—is above the conflict between man and woman, but which emerges out of it. Held in place, almost in midair above the contestants, with a Lawrentian sense of a marriage bond, it is "something that wants to rise / and shake itself / free," except that "free," sited and exact, keeps the "thing" poised in the discipline, not looseness, of liberty.

As has been seen, such keen balancing is Tomlinson's interest, especially where, in Williams's poem *The Orchestra* (1954), dissonance begets harmony. Tuning up, like birds at dawn, the orchestra raises its "sun," a keeping of equivalence between wordless nature and human art speech that brings the American very near to the Englishman's concerns:

>   The precise counterpart
>   of a cacophony of bird calls
>   lifting the sun almighty
>   into his sphere: wood-winds
>   clarinet and violins
>   sound a prolonged A!

                  . . . .

> Ah, ah and ah!
> > together, unattuned
> > > seeking a common tone.
> > Love is that common tone
> > > shall raise his fiery head
> > > > and sound his note.

Yet ultimately in the poem, the "love" raised up by this orchestral dawn has no rigor, in verse-line or feeling, to support it. When Williams declares, near the end, "My heart is / innocent. / And this the first / (and last) day of the world," one sees why Tomlinson observes that "a poem initially as fine as 'The Orchestra' runs aground on the most banal professions of innocence."[17]

Thus, however, much of the three-ply form and idea of attuned dissonance carries over into Tomlinson's own orchestral poem, *Ode to Arnold Schoenberg* (1963), it is the taut, unslackened Williams of a different poetry who is implicitly celebrated there. It is the man who, in his 1917 poem *Trees,* evokes the thrust and counterthrust of opposing forces ("Bent ... from straining / against the bitter horizontals of / a north wind"), just as he does in another poem of the same year, *Spring Strains,* where, in visual tension, the sun against a tree "Pulls the whole / counter-pulling mass upward" and "locks" the "ground in a terrific drag that is / loosening the very tap-roots!" It is this Williams, not the would-be "innocent," who leads Tomlinson in *The Way of a World* (1969) to hold in verbal simultaneity, both steadying and upheaval—the memory of a wind's "weightless anarchy" and the "counterpoise" of tree, bird, and seed. At once, in the same criss-cross pulsing, he touches

> > > the two
> > Gravities that root and uproot the trees.

Upset and anchorage in this treelike way also find expression (aptly via Williams's form) in the 1963 ode Tomlinson wrote after hearing the violin concerto by Schoenberg. Here music is a "double tree" because its dissonance fractures yet reconstitutes the sensory world afresh:

> > At its margin
> > > the river's double willow
> > > > that the wind
> > variously
> > > disrupts, effaces
> > > > and then restores

> in shivering planes:
>   it is
>   calm morning.

The concerto's "shivering planes" shiver to pieces at the same moment that they are bracing the listener back—layer by layer (or plane by plane, in Tomlinson's verse parallel)—to the "shivering," wintry invigoration of actuality regained. In recomposure after unrest, "it is / calm morning," the "it is" of concrete otherness and human perception rebonded once more, as shown earlier in Tomlinson's paralleling of Cézanne's art ("It is not / Posed. It is."). Only now, his use of Williams's form makes one aware of the wider, communal reality toward which the poem is moving:

>   Day. The bell-clang
>   goes down the air
> and, like a glance
>   grasping upon its single thread
>   a disparate scene,
> crosses and re-creates
>   the audible morning.
>   All meet at cockcrow
> when our common sounds
>   confirm our common bonds.
>   Meshed in meaning
> by what is natural
>   we are discontented
>   for what is more,
> until the thread
>   of an instrument pursue
>   a more than common meaning.

Music's clang ("Day") leads back, in its wakeful particularity, and regard for the singular, to the pluralistic world or "disparate scene." So also Schoenberg's "single thread," or thematic constancy, guides one through the teeming and labyrinthine to the space of the real that only art's imagining can define. Such music, for all its abstraction, brings one to a ground of relationship—between human beings and also between self and the natural world. We are, as it were, at the place inside the disparateness of the world's places, where "*our . . . sounds*" are interverified and, in being sounded out, closely "*confirm*" a "*common*" linkage. So, in this awakening—this cockcrow "audible morning" of encounter—there need be no human speakers yet, because this is the artistically defined standpoint for the actual, spoken ground of meeting that is to be heard in Tomlinson's Italian poem *Up at La*

Serra. But the Schoenberg ode, although musically reaching beyond community, still keeps in touch with it. It is as if Tomlinson's subject—a concerto written in the United States by an "exiled Jew"—has affinity with his concern to define his own European rootedness in the light of American experience. Thus even though Williams's lineation lets him reach out—so he is not imprisoned

> by what is natural

but seeks

> for what is more,

he can retain the air-borne poise of

> a more than common meaning.

because he is still held, kept in balance, by the "common" ground of nature and community where we are "Meshed in meaning."

In *Up at La Serra,* such a spacious consciousness (rising out of an actual community, yet circling back to clarify it) belongs to an individual. Paolo Bertolani, a young poet in a town of unemployment on the Ligurian coast, just after a communist victory at the elections in the early 1950s, is portrayed by Tomlinson as striving towards the larger realization that only the artist in Paolo, as distinct from political dreamer, can begin to grasp. Set apart from La Serra at the poem's opening, as he watches the sea from the cliff, he has the detachment to observe in "the shadow-run / the sway of necessity down there / at the cliff-base"—the compulsion of circumstance, the endless demand for work and money that grips the town, like the *"Soldi, soldi"* cry seemingly heard in the very tide-beat. He knows the deprivations stored up for a man like him who has "no more to offer / than a sheaf of verse / in the style of Quasimodo." Yet Paolo at first lacks sufficient conscious knowledge to contest what seems to him—oversubjectively rapt and hypnotized—the power of fate. The (seeming) voice of the waves floods too powerfully and symbolically upon him, a monotonous rhythm that would drag down the consciousness and subtler harmonies he has begun to find on the heights. It is the wave-cry that seems to get inside La Serra and Paolo's language of civil welcome:

> Come in
> by the arch

3: *In the Tutelary Spirit*

       under the campanile parrocchiale
and the exasperation of the water
    followed you
        its *Soldi, soldi*
unpicking the hill-top peace
    insistently.

However, with line poised against line ("Come in . . . by the arch"), one also hears a less insistent tune—the neighborly rhyme ("under the campanil*e* parrochial*e*"), with a hilltop sense of space, that Paolo would bring back into his native town if his mind were not forced to chime with a narrower social music ("*Soldi, soldi* . . . insistently"). Yet Paolo's calling as a poet suggests the terms of resistance. His art, it seems, will not be that of the isolated aesthete but of one who guards the deeper linkages between people and place:

       Came the moment,
he would tell it
    in a poem
        without rancour, a lucid
testament above his name
    Paolo
        Bertolani
—Ciao, Paolo!
    —Ciao
        Giorgino!
He would put them
    all in it—
        Giorgino going
over the hill
    to look for labour;
        the grinder
of knives and scissors
    waiting to come up, until
        someone would hoist his wheel
on to a back, already
    hooped to take it,
        so you thought
the weight must crack
    curvature. And then:
        Beppino and Beppino
friends
    who had in common
        nothing except their names and friendship;
and the sister of the one
    who played the accordion

and under all
the *Soldi, soldi.*
  sacra conversazione
    del mare—
della madre.

Tomlinson's poem spaciously sets out a name ("*Paolo . . . Bertolani*") in foretaste of the "lucid / testament," the peopled poem of clear consciousness without personal egotism that the young man strives toward. Right away his individualizing lights up and becomes part of the language of daily encounter ("—*Ciao, Paolo! / —Ciao / Giorgino!*"), the lively comity of a people that resists downpulling fatalism. So in the poem that Paolo will write, his inclusion of Giorgino seeking work "over the hill" and the knife-grinder "waiting to come up" suggests no descent into bitterness, but a narrative of hardship faced squarely and risen against by individuality or fellowship. The knife-grinder trustfully waits for someone to "hoist his wheel" on his back, and Paolo as poet answers to his condition. For what Tomlinson lineally follows is the young man's vigorous, unsentimental sympathy as he bends with the grinder's "hooped" plight—measures the almost crushing weight that threatens to "crack . . . curvature"—so that he may raise up, without exaggeration, the singularity of a man who is *not* destroyed. It is an eye for the distinctness of people, set apart yet bound together in friendly space, that singles out Beppino from Beppino and carefully identifies "the sister of the one / who played the accordion." Against such individualizing music of community (where "one" chimes with "accordi*on*"), there plays a darker, more insidious harmony—the downpulling, symmetrizing force of "*Soldi, soldi, / sacra conversazione / del mare*." But now, in meditating a poem of risen place (<u>Up</u> *at La Serra*) Paolo gains a certain mental freedom the moment that he recognizes inside the *mare* the demanding call of *La Madre*—that matriarchal power of La Serra that unconsciously dominates the minds of the town's young men.

As Paolo sees, they have an "air of stupefaction," although, as Tomlinson suggests, Paolo, for all his hilltop clarifying of mind, still struggles on beneath a certain self-deception. His healthy communal feeling has not yet escaped its political expression by the kind of Italian communism that is psychologically close to a *Madre*-dominated Catholicism. Thus "Mao / blessing the tractors" (in a wall calendar) lives, not too incongruously, alongside a *Madonna di Foligno*. Indeed, Paolo the would-be communist is restlessly driven towards political and religious cohesions: "He believed / that God was a hypothesis, / that the

3: *In the Tutelary Spirit*

party would bring in / a synthesis, that he / would edit the local paper for them . . . ."

Yet with calmer ambition, as the writer who seeks to bring La Serra alive in a poem (a peopled present that almost recalls the portraits of a past community in *Snow-Bound,* and before that, *The Deserted Village*), Paolo combats more profoundly the voice of *mare* or *Madre*. It is as if Tomlinson is remembering through him the other novice poet depicted by Whitman in *Out of the Cradle Endlessly Rocking*. Roused to his vocation by Paumanok's shore, Whitman as a child hears the whisper of the sea, the "savage old mother," calling "Death, death, death, death, death":

> The undertone, the savage old mother incessantly crying,
> To the boy's soul's questions sullenly timing, some drowned secret hissing,
> To the outsetting bard.

For the "outsetting bard" of La Serra, the deathly lure is not an American-style immersion of mind in ocean or nativeness. It is the prostitution of young men's energies by economic necessity and the sway of their "puttanna-madonna." Working at La Spezia, or left idle, or hacking wood, or chasing crickets for the mad Englishwoman, or laboring on the Milanese dentist's villa, or getting ready for the tourist season—they are subtly betrayed by a darkness, as extensive, it seems, as the shadow of the harlot's mother, "lengthened-out behind her," on the day of communist triumph at the election. Yet, by the end of the poem Paolo is no longer ready to grant such blackness its overmetaphoric power. Now his art seems more like a counterpoise to history and circumstance, as one looks with him beyond the mingling of political dreams, matriarchy, and commercialism—beyond

> treason so readily compounded
>   by the promiscuous stir
> on the iridescent sliding water.
>   He had sought
>   the clear air of the cliff.
> —Salve, Giorgino
>   —Salve
>   Paolo, have you
> heard
>   that we have won the election?
>   —I am writing
> a poem about it:
>   it will begin

> *here, with the cliff and with the sea*
> *following its morning shadow in.*

What was hailed earlier as a communist apocalypse (the "Day / which began all reckonings") begins to seem less immediate than actual, lived time, the day-by-day encounter of friend greeting friend and of the sea breaking on the shore. One can almost follow the transition at work in Paolo's mind as the verse-line moves from Giorgino's excited news of the election to a calmer, deliberating reply:

> *—I am writing*
> *a poem about it:*

The "it" of politics is making way for the "it" of a less delusive new starting point that will solidly *"begin / here"*—in the clarifying space of relation between sea and cliff, self and actuality. The dark subjectivism that previously ruled his watching of the sea ("The shadow / ran before it lengthening / and a wave went over") is placed now, like another fatalistic overflow (the "lengthened-out" shadow of the putt-anna-madonna) in the light of proportion. Precisely itself again, the sea once more belongs to nature's process, *"following its morning shadow in,"* and, as in other poems, teaching a way back to time's rhythms that the human observer can follow in his turn—traveler on a motion deeper than illusion or disillusionment.

Of all Tomlinson's poems of the 1960s, *Up at La Serra* is the most significantly connective. Through Paolo's tutelary individuality, as well as through the recreation of a town's whole ethos, Tomlinson traces a way from early work like *Fiascherino* and *Geneva Restored* (each with its own cliff-based consciousness) to later historical and political poems such as *Assassin* (1969), *Machiavelli in Exile* (1972), and *Charlotte Corday* and *For Danton* (both 1978). Individuals of such poems are more dangerously dispossessed or more severely enduring the consequences of their actions than Paolo, but, whatever their greater adversities (as described later in chapter 6), they reach out towards a similar unfateful pulse—that Wordsworthian sense of a still yet traveling humanity within the cosmos that one "Lucy" poem evokes: "No motion has she now . . . Rolled round in earth's diurnal course." It is this scene also—and the English tradition—that Tomlinson again touches, by means of Williams and his three-ply form, in *Sea Poem*. Written in 1957 and collected in *A Peopled Landscape*, (1963), this is the first poem by Tomlinson to imitate explicitly the layout of the American's verse. Here, significantly, is an echo of Wordsworth's *Resolution and Independence* where, like Paolo on the cliff (or Danton on the bridge over the river near his native town), another motionless figure signals an ever-rolling universe:

>   each
>   shift
>   with its separate whisper, each whisper
>   a breath of that singleness
>   that "moves together
>   if it moves at all" . . . .

Where the whole is seen via the part and the part reverberates within the whole, the Wordsworthian quotation gains further resonance inside Tomlinson's new verse-tune. It speaks of the tremulous balance between self and world, local and universal, besides offering resistance to mere flux and fatalism—as Wordsworth sees in the consoling strength of the leech-gatherer on the lonely moor:

> Upon the margin of that moorish flood
> Motionless as a cloud the old Man stood,
> That heareth not the loud winds when they call;
> And moveth all together, if it move at all.

The old man in his still, tutelary poise also has kinship with the crouched and balanced figure who gives his name to *John Maydew or The Allotment,* the most personally individualized of the Stoke poems in *A Peopled Landscape.* Here Tomlinson presents a disguised portrait of his father as seen in his vegetable allotment on the hill above Etruria Vale and the Shelton Bar-Iron Steelworks. Maydew, in this scene of industrial despoliation and green assuagement, also brings to mind one of Williams's intent figures. But this man—imagined as a worker in the steel mill and unlike Tomlinson's actual father[18]—bears more explicitly the marks of his country's history than the people seen briefly in the short New Jersey poems. He is also (as is discovered in the first part of the poem before he himself appears) one who shares in the resiliences of locality, however small his allotted portion:

>   Ranges
>   of clinker heaps
>   go orange now:
>   through cooler air
>   an acrid drift
>   seeps upwards
>   from the valley mills;
>   the spoiled and staled

>   distances invade
>   these closer comities
>   of vegetable shade,
>   glass-houses, rows
>   and trellises of red-
>   ly flowering beans.
>   This
>   is a paradise
>   where you may smell
>   the cinders
>   of quotidian hell beneath you;
>   here grow
>   their green reprieves
>   for those
>   who labour, linger in
>   their watch-chained waistcoats
>   rolled-back sleeves—
>   the ineradicable
>   peasant in the dispossessed
>   and half-tamed Englishman.
>   By day, he makes
>   a burrow of necessity
>   from which
>   at evening, he emerges
>   here.

The "spoiled and staled / distances" may threaten, but against them are set the carefully tended nearnesses of "here." The very word in that last line—firmly sited, precisely allotted—is like a measure of the small bounds dug and cultivated, in leisurely refreshment, by working people during the weeknights and weekends. The verse itself, layer upon layer, evokes the sense of realized earth—*here*—in the hillside pastoral's unrushed, stalwart pace: "here grow / their green reprieves / for those / who labour, linger." This England of bounds made habitable and civil ("these closer comities / of vegetable shade, / glass-houses, rows / and trellises") makes its stay against a different England's burning diffuseness because it knows its enemy. "This / is a paradise"—and unsentimentally so—because here "you may smell . . . quotidian hell" and value the more keenly the temperate satisfactions won in the face of fire and waste, slag and cinder. Indeed, in a poem where the verse-line lets one feel out the tough, adjectival grip in each syllable of "in-er-ad-ic-able" (and where "*peasant*" forcefully runs through "the dis*p*ossessed . . . Englishman"), "Th*is* / *is* a parad*is*e" also because it touches the *is* of present being, the resonance that one hears in "trell-*is*es," where language stays close to the earth of particularity and continuity—as opposed to the alienating, the distancing, and the overweening. "This / is" (like "*these* closer comities" and "*those* / who labour") grasps the definite, without excess claim, in a way that resembles the adverb in "red- / ly flowering beans" as it curls round, tendril-like, from one line to the next, getting hold not in overluscious redness, but in cool tenacity.

There is, in fact, a tempering of fire throughout the poem—both in the clinker heaps going orange under "cooler air," and in Maydew, as the reader now comes upon him. For the bitterness of the exiled countryman—the man who came "unwitting" from the Great War "in all the pride / of ribbons and a scar / to forty years / of mean amends"—is being mitigated at the moment that he is seen. Squatting to feed with worms a toad whose eyes are "as dimly faithless / as the going years," he balances in relation to loss and replenishment:

> The valley gazes up
> > through kindling eyes
> as, unregarded at his back
> > its hollows deepen
> > > with the black, extending shadows
> and the sounds of day
> > explore its coming cavities,
> > > the night's
> refreshed recesses.
> > Tomorrow
> > > he must feed its will,
> his interrupted pastoral
> > take heart into
> > > those close
> and gritty certainties that lie
> > a glowing ruse
> > > all washed in hesitations now.
> He eyes the toad
> > beating
> > > in the assuagement
> of his truce.

As with the swans of *Canal*, the animal pulse suggests a more equable tune than bitterness and devastation. Through the creature, as it were, Maydew takes the measure of different "eyes"—the "kindling" furnaces of his workday life—now seen at a tempered level where truce can reign between man and valley. "Tomorrow / he must feed its will," not as a slave, but with his own self-mastery, going down the hill only in the way he stoops to feed a toad on his allotment, bent close to earth, nurture, and continuities. It is his reinvigorated sense of the latter that he (like Paolo returning to La Serra) will bring back from height to wasteland: "his interrupted pastoral / take heart into / those close / and gritty certainties." Such, indeed, is the leveling-up of man to desolation that Maydew's taking of heart also suggests a counterattack upon the industrial distancings—the diffuseness brought into a core of graspable nearness and thisness, of "those close / and gritty certainties" that hurtfully grate, but need not overpower us. So, against embitterment, keeping the balance of possibility amidst waste, John Maydew squats by the toad.

The sense of animal being is vital here—a pulse beyond the self from which one may draw new will to cut through inertia or staleness. It is the piercing of impediment that is seen in Tomlinson's later poem, *Foxes' Moon* (1974). Here again, as in the Maydew poem, it is "Night over England's interrupted pastoral." Foxes enter towns with a stealth that cleaves through the worn, urban idea of place—through "The white displacement of a daily view / Uninterrupted." If human sleepers could wake to such a vision, they might have the welcoming openness of the people in *The Fox Gallery*—or of the poet, as self-described, fishing in Staffordshire's canals and rivers: "Silently ... willing the fish to appear—or not willing, just letting the fish drift up, luring them in a peculiar will-lessness into one's mental orbit."[19] In an angling sense, it brings to consciousness, from beyond the ego, the possibilities that Tomlinson also suggests in *Poem for My Father* (1984) about the man who was John Maydew's original:

> I bring to countryside my father's sense
> Of an exile ended when he fished his way
> Along the stained canal and out between
> The first farms, the uninterrupted green,
> To find once more the Suffolk he had known
> Before the Somme. Yet there was not one tree
> Unconscious of that name and aftermath
> Nor is there now. For everything we see
> Teaches the time that we are living in,
> Whose piecemeal speech the vocables of Eden
> Pace in reminder of the full perfection,
> As oaks above these waters keep their gold
> Against the autumn long past other trees
> Poised between paradise and history.

To "fish" one's instinctive way back to a wholeness goes alongside the need to walk the ground with one's intelligence. *Poem for My Father,* therefore, with its implicit stride out from Stoke by the side of the canal, is one masterful result of all that Tomlinson has taught himself and learnt from American verse about poetry's ability to pace through the localized, conscious terms by which one wins back ground from history's wastings. In this poem, the reader travels from Tomlinson's remembrance of his own "exile" father to the exiling memory itself of the Great War that bars the way to "Suffolk" and "uninterrupted green" with the "Somme," no longer the name of an actual river, but rather a murderous climacteric. Suffering its consequences—time reduced to its historical "aftermath" in a kind of determinism—we endure a Fall, where "everything we see / Teaches the time we are living in"—a déjà vu mentality projected by us on tree or world, then read back in staleness on ourselves. Self-echoingly the syllables ("we *see* / Teaches . . . we") resound with "*piecemeal* speech." Yet "Eden" and its "vocables" can also be heard, in parallel stride with the smallness—a potential, untragic language of the greater memory as they "Pace in reminder of the full perfection." One has dexterously moved from "Somme" abstraction, back to the actuality of *this* canal and "these waters," where particular oaks, keeping pace with the fallen sense of time, raise up the "gold" of their gleaming time against autumnal fate.

So here, resisting downfall, yet not soaring to an easy transcendence, the poem is "Poised between paradise and history." Its final line implicitly recalls another "exile" of the Great War besides Tomlinson's father. Ivor Gurney, poet and composer, (1890–1937) was one for whom his particular England—his native Gloucestershire and Cotswolds—became for him a sane centering point in war and troubled peace. His countryside, says P. J. Kavanagh in the preface to his 1982 collection of Gurney's poems, "is an ideal imaginative landscape, poised between the past and a dreamed-of, liberated future, between History and Paradise."[20] Yet now, in turning to Gurney, one sees that no loosely fanciful "ideal" brings Tomlinson to admire a poet who, like himself, found in American verse the quickening of his English instinct for locality and continuities. For Gurney at his finest has emancipated himself from Georgianism of style and feeling. He provides, in fact, the kind of sharply concrete idiom that is in itself a new vantage point, the means by which one may reevaluate the more familiar Anglo-American link between Edward Thomas and Robert Frost. If that casts light on Tomlinson's own relations with American poetry, so equally it can be said that Tomlinson illuminates Gurney's achievement and all they share—a lineage in action.

4

Between Paradise and History

I

Lineage means place. For Gurney especially, it meant the county town with its surrounding landscape where he grew up at the turn of the century. His Gloucester, pre-1914, was the old Roman city of river, canal, docks, and cathedral—a place of music, with its Three Choirs Festival, where Gurney and his friend, Herbert Howells (another future composer), heard some of Elgar's and Vaughan Williams's most recent work. But it was only after war had distanced Gurney from the region that it took on its deeper significance across time. Then it most revealed itself as a landscape of historic constancies, settlements, shapings, and civilizings—the peculiarly cherished and individualized group of locations that northern France brought to mind at almost every turn. Through war he saw again, but more eagerly, such villages as Maisemore, Framilode, Frampton, Dymock, and Minsterworth, hills such as Cooper's, Crickley, and Cranham, and the spaces of the Gloucestershire plain and Severn Estuary where he had once sailed with Will Harvey, another friend.

Today's Gloucestershire is divided by a motorway running southwest to Devon and northwest to the Midlands and Stoke. The England Gurney knew, and its presences, seem almost a world away. Yet for Tomlinson—the Midlander who has lived in Gloucestershire since the 1960s—a relation persists:

> Driving north, I catch the hillshapes, Gurney,
>   Whose drops and rises—Cotswold and Malvern
> In their cantilena above the plains—
>   Sustained your melody: your melody sustains
> Them, now—Edens that lay
>   Either side of this interminable roadway.
> You would recognise them still, but the lanes
>   Of lights that fill the lowlands, brim
> To the Severn and glow into the heights.

> You can regain the gate: the angel with the sword
> Illuminates the paths to let you see
> That night is never to be restored
> To Eden and England spangled in bright chains.

For Ivor Gurney belongs with *Poem for My Father* (both in *Notes from New York*, 1984). This time, however, the debarring light comes from motorway rather than from the mind. One is shut out of Eden, but, as before in Tomlinson's art, one sees the need to grapple with impediment and find thereby the terms on which unfanciful wholeness might reemerge here and now. It is thus, without mystic transcendence, but with a strong sense of contoured fact, that the artist earns the right once more to the nimble mutuality of a dance where the "fallen" world and rising delight go together, where nature and Eden move together in the fall-yet-rise pattern of Cotswolds and Malverns—where also Gurney's art, retraced by Tomlinson's, has the music of grasped substance and chiming relation, as when the hills "In their cantilena"—pronounced "cantil*ay*na"—"above the p*lains*— / Sust*ai*ned your melody." This, in further chime (for Gurney's shade, if not for us), is to "*regain* the *gate*" to Eden.

Yet Tomlinson's response to Gurney's work as nontranscendental, disciplined by the factuality of terrain, points toward a poet who at his best, during his lifetime, could have no easy access to "Eden" or any paradise of his imagining. In a 1917–19 poem, he may see English landscape as an inducement to rhapsody, "a beating at Heaven gate" and a "flood of tide that bears strongly home," but, by this time, a balk had been put upon his exultancies by service in France (summer 1916 to autumn 1917, during which he was gassed, wounded, and suffered breakdown prior to his discharge in 1918). The result is not an ironic poetry like Owen's or Sassoon's, for, however much he felt cheated by his motherland in doing her "strange service," as he called it, it was a new sobriety of vision that entered the poetry—perception of an England whose contours are regained *through* France when, in *Near Vermand* (1919–20),[1] he is, as sentinel, physically pinned down, "Lying flat on my belly shivering in clutch-frost." Alert at all levels ("Head cleared ... the cold bringing me sane," as he says in another wartime poem), his are the cold, clear observations of a man on guard:

> Looking eastward over the low ridge; March scurried its blast
> At our senses, no use either dying or struggling.
> Low woods to left—(Cotswold her spinnies if ever)—
> Showed through snow flurries and the clearer star weather,
> And nothing but chill and wonder lived in mind; nothing
> But loathing and fine beauty, and wet loathed clothing.

"*Loathed clothing*"—words meshed tightly together, as clothing to the uncomfortable skin itself—is an example of language earning its keep in a Tomlinsonian sense. But despite the snow-keen acuteness of observation that Gurney shares with the other poet, he has his own distinctive manner: snapshot terseness ("Looking eastward ... Low woods to left") as well as the stylistic partnering of "beauty" and the abhorrent. Indeed, Gurney's readiness to bring war's pains and energies to the service of once golden words like "joy," "glory," "wonder," and "noble" suggests how much the battlefield not only disciplined his tendency towards old raptures, but also how such discipline helped him articulate the more durable and subtle sense of the civilized lying inside his particular kind of Georgianism.

By "Georgian," and Gurney's admiration for poets such as John Masefield, Wilfrid Gibson, and Lascelles Abercrombie in Edward Marsh's anthologies (1910–22), as well as those never published there (Hilaire Belloc and Edward Thomas), one means more than a taste for enfeebled, late-romantic pastoral. Lawrence, although later rejecting Marsh's acquiescence in outworn poetic currency, originally applauded the first *Georgian Poetry* in 1912 (and especially the Masefield sea poem, *Biography*, also admired by Gurney) for an energy that had left behind nineteenth-century fatalism—"like a big breath taken when we are waking up after a night of oppressive dreams."[2] In the event, as one sees with Belloc, the vigor could only go a limited distance, for in a poem like *The South Country*, Belloc offers merely a robust kind of snug, cottager-pastoralism when he calls on men of the Weald to sing Sussex songs with him in a house of deep thatch. This "Myth of England" (as Tomlinson observes via the critic John Holloway[3]) is one that narrows Britain's historical and geographical variety to a "South Country" milieu, sufficient to provide Edward Thomas with the title of his 1909 book and to lead Gurney in a 1915 poem to imagine his friends gathered, Cotswold-style, in "creeper clad old houses / Of beautiful grey stone." Yet, in the end, Gurney meant more by habitation than the cosily picturesque, just as he went beyond Belloc's hearty version of the comradely to find a more enduring communal strength in the settlers of land and place.

He came to such realization through war. But, as Tomlinson has noted in his article "Ivor Gurney's 'Best Poems'" (1986),[4] there were other forces, in music and poetry, that were also sharpening his purpose. Tomlinson refers in particular to Gurney's letter of May 1915, written while he was training with the Gloucestershire regiment before he went to France. There he speaks of longing to hear again Vaughan Williams's *Sea Symphony* whose first performance he had attended two years earlier in London. By September 1915 he is telling a correspondent that Whitman, whose *Sea Drift* poems provided the words of the choral symphony, is "my latest rediscovery, and he has taken me like a flood."[5] But not just a flood, for, instead of being encouraged by Whitman's lengthy line and sonorities towards effusion in his own verse, Gurney has learnt a steadying power from the American—the vocal means by which he can take a larger yet carefully paced breath. Energy's wave, as one sees in Gurney's *The Sea Borders* (1919–22), now has a bulwark against it:

> I musician have wrestled with the stuff in making,
> And wrought a square thing out of my stubborn mind—
> And gathered a huge surge of spirit as the great barriers bind
> The whole Atlantic at them by Devon or west Ireland.

Such lines almost recall Gurney's letter of February 1915 to his old sailing companion, Will Harvey, about the sea and "the hard friendly life of that wrestle with that most untameable, unknowable element of God."[6] In the poem it is a fight with shaping resistances—up against the necessary "great barriers" that war provided in another form, for then the barrier that concentrated Gurney's energies was the untranscendable physical circumstance of frontline existence, with its terrors, tedium, and deadlock. He had not been long in France before he is telling a correspondent (June 1916) that after all "this grey petty monotony" he "will gather all the overstrength of spirit, so hardly earned and force it, coax it, lead it to the service of Joy for ever."[7] "Joy," so readily overused elsewhere in the poetry ("such joy in peace," "joy yet greater made"), now has purposeful vehemence put at its disposal, and the gathered spirit of the verse, like the gathering of "overstrength," suggests the tightened resolve that, without excess or flagging, looks toward Whitman's example.

Gurney found special sustenance in *This Compost,* a poem by Whitman that he admired so much in the trenches that he wanted to set it to music, for the poem taught a width of stride yet also a temperateness—how to pace oneself in a wasteland; how to find a slow, calmer, inner beat:

> It grows such sweet things out of such corruptions,
> It turns harmless and stainless on its axis, with such endless successions of diseas'd corpses,
> It distills such exquisite winds out of such infused fetor,
> It renews with such unwitting looks its prodigal, annual, sumptuous crops,
> It gives such divine materials to men, and accepts such leavings from them at last.

By this kind of extendable yet anchored lineation (long before a similar quality in Williams's verse was translated into Tomlinson's), Gurney came nearer the documented, instanced factuality that had largely gone from English verse since Wordsworth, apart from "Ruskinese" Hopkins. But Whitman could offer both the singing of facts (as with the particularized ships given their meditative rhythm in *Crossing Brooklyn Ferry*) and the stillness inside movement, the coherence drawn into tightness out of disparate pieces, as in *Sparkles from the Wheel*—the pause as a knife grinder and pavement audience stand inside an ever-sharpening moment with its frictional grip of part on part: "The low hoarse purr of the whirling stone, the light-pressed blade." It was by such instancings that Gurney came more directly into contact with his own talent for holding the disparate or chaotic together, a skill that he learned to bring into the poetry from his prose. Thus in a letter of February 1916, written while still training in England, Gurney shows a keen eye for the incongruities of hut life: "reading Shakespeare and composing in a continual and profane noise."[8] His infinitive clauses also catch in snapshot the separate particularities of discomfort: "to feed on the first thing that comes along . . . to sleep on bare boards . . . rising at midnight to stoke fires, or fulfill the needs of nature."[9] All this may seem a long way from the noble vistas hailed by Whitman in *Song of the Open Road:*

> To see nothing anywhere but what you may reach it and pass it,
> To conceive no time, however distant, but what you may reach it and pass it,
> To look up or down no road but it stretches and waits for you,
>   however long but it stretches and waits for you,

Yet scaled down and applied to immediate experience, as with *Signallers* (1922–25), Whitman's line wakes up in Gurney's an English voice that holds together comic delight and high seriousness. As David Jones would discover much later (*In Parenthesis,* 1937), there can be an idiom in which army slang and the language of the exquisite cohabit:

> To be signallers and to be relieved two hours
> Before the common infantry—and to come down
> Hurriedly to where estaminet's friendliest doors
> Opened—where before the vulgar brawling common crew
> Could take the seats for tired backs, or take the wine
> Best suited for palates searching for delicate flavours
> (Or pretty tints) to take from the mind trench ways and strain,
> Though it be on tick, with delicately wangled sly favours.
> Then having obtained grace from the lady of the inn—

4: Between Paradise and History 123

> How good to sit still and sip with all-appreciative lip,
> (After the grease and skilly of line-cookhouse tea)
> The cool darkling texture of the heavenly dew
> Of wine—to smoke as one pleased in a house of courtesy—

This savoring of the civilized owes less to Belloc's drinking songs and his verses in *Courtesy* than to a more toughly-earned sense of a people outgoing history's would-be brutalizations—a feeling for the continuities of courtesy that anticipates Tomlinson. It does so by a self-regulation in pace and register where Gurney, no longer leaping at heaven in the old way, can enjoy, in unrushed appreciation, "The cool darkling texture of the heavenly dew / Of wine." This is a verve that alights on each pieced-out privilege ("To be signallers . . . to be relieved . . . to come down") and, with short *i*'s, teases open in careful monosyllables each relished moment: "to sit still and sip with all-appreciative lip." Connoisseurship stays friends, unpreciously, with what is "common" in its best communally shared sense, so that delicacy gains wiry strength (fresh credit, in fact) out of slang's persuasion, "Though it be on tick, with delicately wangled sly favours." It is like the impishness that energizes decorum, the laughter behind the straight face of "innocent" in the poem's final line, when the outdone infantry arrives to find "those apparently / Innocent signallers drinking, on tick, at last beer."

Such a line, fragmented, slowed by short *i*'s and delayed in comic impact right up to the last syllable ("beer"!), has the kind of narrative control applied by Gurney's prose to the battlefront itself. The style in which he writes in summer 1917 from a trench behind a blockhouse has the tense, nervous hilarity of a man who must itemize everything seen, heard, and read into succinct, containable bits: "Fritzes shells; One sunset; two sunrises; 'Bible in Spain'; The tale of the cutting up of the KRRs in 1914 . . . of the first gas attacks . . . of the man who walked in his sleep to Fritz, slept well, woke, realised, and bolted; Thirst; Gas; Shrapnel; *Very* H.E."[10] Shut inside terse punctuation and limited to initials, the explosive implications of "*Very* H.E." are muted by a frenetic nonchalance—painfully indicative of the cost to Gurney of preserving some sane demeanor through it all. When transferred from prose to verse, as in the poem *The Silent One* (1919–22), such fragmenting and agitation are the pressure upon—yet comprise the terms of—an extraordinary steadiness. One can hear the resonance of Whitman, as in the latter's *Kosmos*—

> Who includes diversity and is Nature,
> Who is the amplitude of the earth

—but now it belongs to poetry of a more difficult inclusiveness:

> Who died on the wires, and hung there, one of two—
> Who for his hours of life had chattered through
> Infinite lovely chatter of Bucks accent:
> Yet faced unbroken wires; stepped over, and went
> A noble fool, faithful to his stripes—and ended.
> But I weak, hungry, and willing only for the chance
> Of line—to fight in the line, lay down under unbroken
> Wires, and saw the flashes and kept unshaken,
> Till the politest voice—a finicking accent, said:
> 'Do you think you might crawl through there: there's a hole.'
> Darkness, shot at: I smiled, as politely replied—
> 'I'm afraid not, Sir.' There was no hole no way to be seen
> Nothing but chance of death, after tearing of clothes.
> Kept flat, and watched the darkness, hearing bullets whizzing—
> And thought of music—and swore deep heart's deep oaths
> (Polite to God) and retreated and came on again,
> Again retreated—and a second time faced the screen.

It is a Chaplinesque sequence of bad nerves and quick recomposure, but in all this shifting surface or running to stand still, Gurney holds on to a balance. Only a tensely adroit vigor (by a man who knows his exact ground and the barrier he cannot step over in word or action) is able to bring together, without ironic clash, the fixity of the comrade "Who died on the wires" and the live fluency of the same person "Who ... chattered" so recently—all with a battlefield sense of decorum as to what is fittingly quick or vaingloriously dead, so that "Infinite lovely," refused transcendence, must coexist with sprightly "chatter." By the same strange poise, Gurney is no more flippant about the NCO who did go stepping over sensible limits ("noble fool, faithful to his stripes") than he is oversardonic about the officer ("the politest voice—a finicking accent") who invites him to join the foolhardy. The "finicking" may be instantly rebuked by curt fact ("Darkness, shot at"), but the gentleman is answered by the strenuously upheld courtesy of his subordinate, one whose own fine manners have been earned out of harassed self-command ("Polite to God," even as he swears). Barriers of trench or statement are not to be surpassed; in that, one sees how much goes to the making of civility's live speech as distinct from the language of deathly obedience.

The practical nature of the civil is also shown by Gurney's poem *First Time In* (1919–20), with its memory of the occasion in June 1916 when he and fellow novices were given instruction in survival at the front by a group of Welsh soldiers. What they learnt were "all

necessary / Commonsense workmanlike cautions of salutary / Wisdom
... Calm thought discovered in mind and body shaking." Moreover,
a sense of shared human value was defined by danger, as when "one
took us courteously / Where a sheet lifted, and gold light cautiously /
Streamed." Later in the poem, when talk with the hospitable Welsh-
men is said to have brought memories of Cotswold's summer air after
sunset ("streams of gold"), Gurney is obviously moving away from
the caution applied to golden eloquence by wartime need. Yet when
he is not emotionally wandering (as in the postscript he added after
the war about disappointed soldiers "Who looked for the golden Age
to come friendly again"), he can grapple more surely with a persistent,
tangible sense of the civilized, with materials to be worked, skills to
be mastered, and knowledge to be inherited from a tradition. Then
he is much closer to his vision of a Flanders landscape, shaped and
crafted with care, in a letter of July 1917: "a flat land of continual
cultivation ... where one may see windmills with the old new delight
and pride in man's cunning and masterful mind; where churches are
a landmark, and houses loom large, a country ... almost entirely of
man's fashioning. A Scarlatti, early Mozartish atmosphere."[11]

"Cunning," as inherited and applied knowledge, directs us to a later
poem like *The Lock Keeper* (1919–22) where Gurney celebrates man's
"Cunning of practice, the finding, doing, the getting ... A net of craft
of eye, heart, kenning and hand." But such "doing" and "getting" have
a concrete meaning most of all for him when music supplies a re-
minding standard—when the practicality of tradition implies not a
Belloc, but a Byrd or a Bach, and when any Georgian hunger for lost
pastorals is supplanted by a delight in continuing, intricate craft, as
in the poem *Hedger* (1922–25). Here the mastery of Bach ("Father of
all makers" in another poem) is verified by Gurney's sight of a deft
English hedge-maker at work:

> To me the A Major Concerto has been dearer
> Than ever before, because I saw one weave
> Wonderful patterns of bright green, never clearer
> Of April; whose hand nothing at all did deceive
> Of laying right
> The stakes of bright
> Green lopped-off spear-shaped, and stuck notched, crooked-up;

Bach and the weave of a hedge; Scarlatti and Flanders: the poet
who makes such connections also foreshadows Bunting's suggestion
in *Briggflatts* of stars and lakes echoing the "condensed" music of
Scarlatti. But in *Hedger* (significantly centered on the making of a

barrier, the resistance he cannot overleap, like war's impassable wire), Gurney shows his own individuality as a poet by the way that he takes on some of the hedger's daring discipline—catching by rhyme the furls of feeling, twining them into a verse-line that may lengthen but not overflow. Indeed, aesthetic looseness in the breathy, run-on vowels ("dearer . . . weave . . . bright green, never clearer") changes to tight verbal grip the moment he seizes the hedger's physical *doing* as fact to be proven along the line by his own chopping off "bright" from "Green" and by his syllabic singling-out of each part while, hedgelike, the separate pieces stay in alignment, interknit: "lopped-off spear-shaped, and stuck notched, crooked-up."

By such close work Gurney enters a tradition and further extends the comradeship he first knew in the war years to a longer sense of artistic community—as when, in a postwar poem, he tells of finding Byrd's music on a stall in a London street and how he felt the thrill of standing "in company of" Jonson's "great friends." It is the friendship that is important in separate poems on Townshend and Chapman, but especially so in *Looking There* (1919–22) when Jonson's artistry itself acts as a counterbalance to Gurney's troubled mind: "the great surge and sway / Of 'Cataline' shall me safe from the dangerous way / Of thinking of too much beauty by an evil snatch." At that point, Gurney seems to verify with remarkable precision Tomlinson's insight in *Poetry and Metamorphosis* with regard to Eliot and others:

> one grasps anew the way "the individual talent" comes into possession of an exact knowledge of its own situation—becomes capable of uttering it, stating it—by opening itself to the great past instances, losing and finding identity through the encounter in a metamorphosis of self. What the individual talent loses is the unnerving, unnerved sense of naked homelessness and lonely complaint. What is found is that human woes, though specific to oneself in the uniqueness of one's situation, are no longer homeless or condemned to formless outcry.[12]

As Gurney shows in his celebratory poems on Whitman, Thoreau, and Irving from 1922 to 1925, as well as in *Portraits* from the same period (Washington, Jefferson, Jackson, and Lee: makers of a country through "freedom's struggle, and the settling"), the search for a stability beyond the homeless state is continued via America. Thus in *Felling a Tree* (1919–22), his adaptation of Whitman's verse-line is a poetic means of entering a wider England, both in the "struggle and the settling." For though he battles to fell a Gloucestershire ash, there is also a settled, cultivated peace to be won through the fight—like the meditative pause after the first blows, which in turn leads back to intensified effort, as if he is cutting a way into past, present, and beyond:

> Rested—and took a thought and struck onward again,
> Who had frozen by Chaulnes out of all caring of pain—
> Learnt Roman fortitude at Laventie or Ypres,
> Saw bright edge bury dull in the beautiful wood,
> Touched splinters so wonderful—half through and soon to come down
> From that ledge of rock under harebell, the yellow flower—the pinewood's crown.
> Four inches more—and I should hear the crash and great thunder
> Of an ash Crickley had loved for a century, and kept her own.
> Thoughts of soldier and musician gathered to me
> The desire of conquest ran in my blood, went through me—
> There was a battle in my spirit and my blood shared it,
> Maisemore—and Gloucester—bred me, and Cotswold reared it,
> This great tree standing nobly in the July's day full light
> Nearly to fall—my courage broke—and gathered—my breath feared it,
> My heart—and again I struck, again the splinters and steel glinters
> Dazzled my eyes—and the pain and the desperation and near victory
> Carried me onwards—

Tomlinson remarks that "One of the surprising things about Gurney's attachment to Whitman was that it did not lead to mere superfluity. The piled-up, almost laborious effects of 'Felling a Tree' serve the theme of the poem itself."[13] Exactly so; because in not taking over Whitman's garrulity or indiscriminate embrace of the world, Gurney builds up, without flagging, the cumulative presence of history—what he sees in his separate poem on Whitman as the "makings of generations" that the American fails to honor. So the exhilarated Englishman whose patient verse-line allows him to stop, to breathe, and then to go on again, takes the measure of the unhurried powers that across time have been the making of him and tree: "Maisemore—and Gloucester—bred me, and Cotswold reared it, / This great tree." Out of this he recovers scale and proportion, for, like Whitman in his Lincoln elegy ("from this bush in the dooryard / With delicate-color'd blossoms"), Gurney keenly notes the tiny issuing point—that which "From that ledge of rock under harebell" connects the small, grounded particularity of the tree to its size through time. Minute by minute in the present ("Four inches more . . . Nearly to fall"), growth in the past, piece by piece, is physically here: "the crash and great thunder / Of an ash Crickley had loved for a century." But this soldier of "Roman fortitude," who asked in a July 1917 letter, "Who will dare talk of the glory of Waterloo or Trafalgar again?" means a different "glory" when the boughs of this "Trafalgar" tree come down:

> The last desperate onslaught—took the two inches of too steady
> Trunk—on the rock edge it lurched, threatening my labouring life
> (Nearly on me). Like Trafalgar's own sails imperiously moving to defeat
> Across the wide sky unexpected glided and the high bank's pines and fell straight
> Lower and lower till the crashing of the fellow trees made strife.
> The thud of earth, and the full tree lying low in state,
> With all its glory of life and sap quick in the veins . . .
> Such beauty, for the farm fires and heat against chilly rains,
> Golden glows in the kitchen from what a century made great . . . .

He will not forsake the language of the "golden" and of "beauty," and yet the tree's resistance—its contained fire—has made him gauge precisely the vocal energy needed to meet it, as he "*took the two* inches of *too* steady / Trunk." It is as if Gurney knows how many stored powers must also be drawn on to pay for the "golden" and yield "heat against chilly rains."

In another poem from the same period, *Of the Sea*,[14] he tells over the resources of the past even more fully. The Whitmanian line ("Cornwall surges round Zennor like the true delight / Of earth all savage with a force enemy to man") lets him recount not only the sea zest gathered in by the Britain it hits against, but the writers who enabled him to "read" that power—Hardy in *The Dynasts,* the Coleridge of *The Ancient Mariner,* and Walt Whitman with his "haunted sea." One looks ahead to the "sharpness of brine and sea breeze"—"a moral terrain where you must confront nature"[15]—which was to be so important for Tomlinson when he ventured into American poetry and its vision of the sea: Pound's "Lithe turning of water," Moore's *The Fish* and *The Steeple-Jack,* Crane's *Voyages,* and Stevens's Crispin poem of the ocean. Yet, sea or land, Gurney like Tomlinson could find in the American example a dimension beyond the self and its individual griefs that, in a different way, was also available to Edward Thomas.

Although Gurney compared himself to Thomas, killed at Arras in 1917 ("he had the same sickness of mind I have—the impossibility of serenity for any but the shortest space"[16]), the steadiness that Gurney did achieve lay in his opening-out, after discipline, to large perspectives and continuities. But Thomas's achievement only became possible by his narrowing down—ridding his poetry of all that he had intellectually acquired, as literary pilgrim, from writers on the English countryside, but which he had not directly proved for himself on the senses. A bounded factuality became his arena, and, though it was more confined than Gurney's, he reached it—a concreteness more real to him than his own evanescent self—by a similar restraint upon the ego and by an American stimulus that in his case was provided by Robert Frost. It was the latter's *North of Boston* (1914), with its New Hampshire cadences, that helped bring him to a refreshed Englishness of speech and verse-line. But unlike Gurney, the influence took effect on a poet whose most important theme was not closeness to a heartland but adjustment to dispossession—to severance from a past or future England, and the possibility of finding a ground in verse, however small, however briefly affirmable, that he might stand inside.

II

One does not forget, of course, the larger spaces of English rurality and tradition that Thomas, the London Welshman growing up in suburban Wandsworth during the 1880s, so passionately yearned for when he read Richard Jefferies and his books on Wiltshire woodlore. What matters, though, is not unattainable earth but graspable limit. "Here was a man," says Tomlinson,

> born into a period lacking cultural centrality, who strove towards it in both prose and verse. He matured in the nineties and his poetry coincided with the Georgians.... [He was] a man who had had the stabilising vision of the England of traditions and crafts, of Jefferies and Cobbett, of Sturt's *Wheelwright's Shop*, the England that shaped such poems as *The Manor Farm, The Barn, Lob, Cockcrow, Haymaking*. He experienced perhaps the final phase of that England. But *in it*, he was never *of* it. His feeling for Nature—a nature wooed into the spiritual orbit of England by centuries of local civilization—was strangely undermined by the scepticism which Thomas also inherited.[17]

He goes on to cite Middleton Murry's 1919 review of Thomas's poems, with its comment: "He knows his beauty is beautiful, and his home no home at all." Indeed, one is reminded of Thomas's self-distrust and seeming displacement in a poem such as *Wind and Mist* (1915), where a speaker, standing outside an unpeopled house swept bare of illusion, tells how "the wind and I / Between us shared the world." (In *The New House* of the same year, the poet is alone, suddenly aged and fated, in a homeless place.) Yet a more chilling dislocation is presented in *Haymaking* (1915) where Thomas, for all his celebration of a country scene, with its laborers and team horses, must in the end set the whole moment at an eerie distance when everything becomes a cold pastoral lost in immensity: "This morning time, with a great age untold, / Older than Clare and Cowper, Morland and Crome . . . All of us gone out of the reach of change— / Immortal in a picture of an old grange." This is no scene of traditional crafts in action, as with Gurney's *Hedger*. The utterable, onward past has been overarched by a vast silence—the anonymity behind history and names.

Thomas, however, knew tradition in a more immediate sense: not as a ghostly, distanced rurality, but as an inheritance of literary possibilities close at hand. One especially sees it at work when he is able to recover for poetry the flexed, muscular particularity, adept at shifting with thought's motion, that Wordsworth possessed, that *he* instinctively had, and that was brought back to realization by his contact with Frost's idiom, the American verse-speech preserving the drama of sinewy statement that had once existed more fully in English poetry. So, when one considers again the wind of *Wind and Mist,* with the shifting, unpredictable voice of its main speaker, it is not only a desolate blast that is heard, but also the sound of solidities being vigorously spoken for: "flint and clay and childbirth" as distinct from cloud-castle dreams. It is the noise of concreteness, of syntax's unexpected thrusts and counterblows, whose volume must seemingly be increased by Thomas as a guarantee of firm ground and not-self against his own self's poetic drift towards silence, void, and doom. Sound as key to substance (the felt, immediate England he *can* touch) makes its significant appearance in the Farnham, Surrey, part of his book, *In Pursuit of Spring* (1914), which led him, at Frost's encouragement, to venture from prose to poetry. Farnham for Thomas is associated with the countryman Fred Bettesworth and the books written about him by George Bourne (Sturt). But Sturt's "portrait of an unlettered pagan English peasant," with its "picture of rural England during the latter half of the nineteenth century, by one born in the earlier half,"[18] attracts Thomas, it seems, not so much for the content of Bettesworth's knowledge as for the cadence, the "subtle appeal of his talk," and all the sensuous solidity it implies. Fascinated by the turf-laying episodes in both *The Bettesworth Book* (1901) and *Memoirs of a Surrey Labourer* (1907), Thomas quotes Sturt from the latter:

> Half unawares it came home to me, like the contact of the garden mould, and the smell of the earth, and the silent saturation of the cold air. You could hardly call it thought—the quality in this simple prattling. Our hands touching the turfs had no thought either . . . . It seemed as if some-

thing very real, as if the true sound of the life of the village had at last reached my dull senses.[19]

This, then, is not so far from the "sound of sense" principle in Frost's verse—the recovery of physical intonation from beneath the surface meaning of speech, as when the wind blots out the individual words of an overheard conversation and the listener catches only its acoustic rhythm. But Thomas, whose "sound of sense" defines the bounds of his mental understanding rather than blurs conscious thought (Frost's tendency), gained from the American something equally fundamental. What was needed (as with Gurney, when war and exile sent him away from, yet sharpened his relation with England) was the right kind of detachment, in Thomas's case, an acceptance of his apartness as the condition by which he might be more stringently renaturalized inside the limits of the immediate. Frost, the émigré from New Hampshire in England (1912–15), offered him at the right moment the poetic example of American nativeness and alienation, a model that could help Thomas find his own direction without having to carry over the ambivalence that such a position entails in *North of Boston*.

Frost's persona there, as farmer-poet at ease with work, land, and practicality, is in some ways a contradiction (if the biographical record is believed[20]) of his distinctly uneasy and often antagonistic career as an actual New England farmer. Indeed, those difficulties emerge and find expression alongside the seemingly comfortable Frostian voices of the poetry, allowing him to represent the speech of a particular American region in a way that he could never do when he adopted the more commonplace pose of unhappy aesthetic outsider in his first book of verse, *A Boy's Will* (1913). There, as the shades of Rossetti and Swinburne mingle with those of Keats and Shelley, one hears the voice of *Ghost House* ("I dwell with a strangely aching heart / In that vanished abode there far apart"), the recluse of *A Dream Pang* and *The Vantage Point,* the "specter-like" dreamer of *Waiting* who avoids encounter with farm-laborers, and whose only companion in *A Tuft of Flowers* is a butterfly or (as in *My November Guest*) a figure of Sorrow to whose service his language is archaically bound: "She talks and I am fain to list." As Thomas observed in a 1914 review, the Frost of *A Boy's Will* "was still a comparatively isolated, egotistic poet, eagerly considering his own sensations more than what produced them."[21]

The egotism of the first book, however, was countered in *North of Boston* by Frost's giving his conventional alienation a new body and psychology. His standard romantic reclusiveness or achingly sweet sadness now takes on a "female" identity to become part of a dialogue and conflict. It is the sensitive identity that challenges what was flinched from in *A Boy's Will* and that itself takes recognizable shape as the tough-minded sureness, the blunt pragmatism, the terse unsentimentality of actual working Americans. So an interplay is set going between that and the distraught women of the poems, or the laborer in *The Code* who is resentful of a farmer's rough talk, or the timid doctor in *A Hundred Collars* who is frightened by a shirt salesman ("A man? A brute. Naked above the waist"). Indeed the comedy of the last example shows how far Frost has transformed the quailing self-pity of *A Boy's Will* not merely into something jokeable but also into a consciousness that lights up a world of daily solidities and work. To that extent, he has begun to draw upon the tradition of American factuality whose cadences are ultimately so important for Thomas.

Yet Frost is not entirely pledged to the objective and nonegotistic in *North of Boston*. For a poignancy lingers on to blur, in some degree, the concreteness it has begun to reveal. "The fact is the sweetest dream that labor knows," says the poet in *Mowing* (*A Boy's Will*), and though the next book seems to have abandoned such reverie for the hard clarity of fact and work, the temptation to dissolve solidity in dream is still there. It is the abandoning of effort that he denotes by the title of *After Apple-Picking*, where one is offered a film of ice and reverie with which to see a weighty harvest of apples that the poet has *ceased* picking. "My instep arch," he says, "not only keeps the ache, / It keeps the pressure of a ladder-round": an instance of the way the poem accurately registers the thrust and imprint of hard substance (the lineal sticking-out of a "long two-pointed ladder" and "a barrel that I didn't fill / Beside it") only to bed such definiteness in a drowse—just as the word "didn't" impinges sharp actuality while negating its fullness.

It is the implicit emptying of solid ground, of place as a shared and inhabited firmness, that is more seriously visible, or audible, in the dialogue-poem, *The Death of the Hired Man*. A farmhouse has been momentarily taken over by a sleeper, the dying laborer Silas, whose idleness as a worker in the past and whose permission to stay now are debated by Warren the farmer and his wife Mary—not as inhabitants of the house but outside, on the wooden steps of the porch. So, as Silas lingers within, and they hover without, the meaning of "home" remains questionable. To Warren,

> "Home is the place where, when you have to go there,
> They have to take you in."

The American farmer doggedly feels his way towards aphoristic sureness (his "when" pitted against "where," as "there" rhymes a balance), but Mary's defense of Silas's right to die here subtly undermines him. Frost gives her an orchestral pathos ("She put out her hand / Among the harplike morning-glory strings") but it is her restatement of Warren's words—

> "I should have called it
> Something you somehow haven't to deserve."

—that gets inside his attempted straight dealing, his anti-idleness, and occupies it with a coy, nebulous poignancy ("Something . . . somehow . . .").

Another dialogue, *Home Burial,* with its remembrance of a death and with its hysterical wife, undercuts plain talk—and shared, matrimonial ground—even more completely. Wife and husband are inside their house, yet are almost outside when she, looking from the stairs at her son's grave, then getting ready to flee this "home" with her fingers on the latch, flings back at him his commonsensical words on the day their child was buried:

> "I can repeat the very words you were saying:
> 'Three foggy mornings and one rainy day
> Will rot the best birch fence a man can build.'
> Think of it, talk like that at such a time!
> What had how long it takes a birch to rot
> To do with what was in the darkened parlor?

In her mouth, his language is not quite as callous as she, in her mad sensitivity, would make it. Yet her restatement of his New Hampshire pragmatism (by Frost's deliberate clash of "how" against "had" and "To do" against "to rot," so that one may hear the unsmoothed shock of nonliterary cadence) is gradually destroying the stoic sureness by which he lives. One thinks of another poem, *Mending Wall,* where a farmer's solid construction is stealthily crumbled ("Something there is that doesn't love a wall"), or of a husband's resolute view of work parrotted and unwittingly devalued by his crazed drudging wife in *A Servant to Servants*: "Len says one steady pull more ought to do it. / He says the best way out is always through." Amy in *Home Burial* is seen as impossibly demanding, yet her challenge to her husband's would-be normality effectively denies him—and herself—any confident standpoint. At the end, he is uncomprehending and exasperated as he tries to pacify her from his limited perception:

> "There, you have said it all and you feel better.
> You won't go now. You're crying. Close the door.

> The heart's gone out of it: why keep it up?
> Amy! There's someone coming down the road!"
>
> "*You*—oh, you think the talk is all. I must go—
> Somewhere out of this house. How can I make you——"
>
> "If—you—do!" She was opening the door wider.
> "Where do you mean to go? First tell me that.
> I'll follow and bring you back by force. I *will!*—"

With the opening of the door, she has prised from him a cry of naked being, the physical "sound of sense" beneath ordinary talk. Yet his "'I will'", as it meets her own syntax severing force ("*You* . . . How can I make you——"), leaves him poised between bluff and sincerity, just as the poem leaves both people in a void where, homeless yet at home, they neither go nor stay.

Such forceful unrest in poetry taught Thomas a different possibility: how the outsider may reinhabit place and moment. In one of his earliest poems, *Up in the Wind* (1914), the attentive listening to speech that Frost encouraged, brings him (the South Londoner and self-confessed "Clapham Junction man" of *In Pursuit of Spring*[22]) close to a land through the voice of another Londoner—the strange, wild girl whom he finds in an isolated part of Hampshire, looking after a public house:

> "I could wring the old thing's neck that put it there!
> A public-house! it may be public for birds,
> Squirrels and suchlike, ghosts of charcoal-burners
> And highwaymen." The wild girl laughed. "But I
> Hate it since I came back from Kennington.
> I gave up a good place." Her cockney accent
> Made her and the house seem wilder by calling up—
> Only to be subdued at once by wildness—
> The idea of London there in that forest parlour,
> Low and small among those towering beeches
> And the one bulging butt that's like a font.
>
> Her eyes flashed up; she shook her hair away
> From eyes and mouth, as if to shriek again;
> Then sighed back to her scrubbing.

It is as if the *deraciné*'s complaint must be noisily made in order that Thomas can reach back, through her antiromantic cries, to the strange appropriateness of her living here. Just as the plain object has its existence vocally obtruded ("the one bulging butt that's like a font"), so, through potential shrieks, one comes at a quieter working actuality, an accepted concreteness, as she "sighed back to her scrubbing." Through her noise, we arrive at the pulse of the solid world to which she belongs: "The clock ticked, and the big saucepan lid / Heaved as the cabbage bubbled, and the girl / Questioned the fire and spoke." Her discontent and shrieking account of her genealogy (how the smithy became an inn, together with what might have been) energetically bring one back to what must be, in the audible, inevitable present, "When the wind blows, as if a train was running / The other side . . . And the linen crackles on the line / Like a woodfire rising." There is none of the poignancy with which Frost invests the woman crushed by work in *A Servant to Servants*. The wild girl of Thomas's poem, despite her protests against the wind, shares a vocal kinship with it:

> I'd have it blowing that I might go with it
> Somewhere far off, where there are trees no more
> And I could wake and not know where I was
> Nor even wonder if they would roar again.
> Look at those calves."
>
>   Between the open door
> And the trees two calves were wading in the pond,
> Grazing the water here and there and thinking,
> Sipping and thinking, both happily, neither long.
> The water wrinkled, but they sipped and thought,
> As careless of the wind as it of us.
> "Look at those calves. Hark at the trees again."

The poem halts on the verge of animal unconsciousness. A step further and the roar of the objective world ("Hark at the trees again") would become a lulling tune, as mind and speech are dissolved. Yet the noise of active nature need not drown out the perceiving mind, as Tomlinson shows much later when he depicts the waters of an old millrace that "clamour across" a pool—"clamour and clamber / Blindly till again they find their leat / And level" (*The Race*, 1978). So also in *The Mill-Water* (1915), Thomas holds back from the mentally blind state, for "sound comes surging in upon the sense" without destroying consciousness:

> Sometimes a thought is drowned
> By it, sometimes
> Out of it climbs;
> All thoughts begin or end upon this sound

As "climbs" is delicately tugged from "Sometimes," one hears the wakeful adroitness in Thomas's poetry that can speak of the instinctive or indefinite without becoming verbally drowsy. The use of "Sometimes," indeed, makes one realise how much Thomas learnt from Frost without taking over the doughy pathos of "Something you somehow haven't to deserve." Similarly, Frost's inverted word order to create the effect of lounging rumination ("Something there is that doesn't love a wall") points the way for Thomas's inversion (*July, 1915*) where it now becomes alert and definite statement: "Nothing there was worth thinking of so long." In another poem he may celebrate a "pure thrush word" or (in *Sedge-Warblers*, 1915) a bird's wordless song, "Wisely reiterating endlessly / What no man learnt yet, in or out of school." But "Wisely" and "endlessly" have the adverbial wit of a poet looking beyond human speech without forsaking language's lithe, discriminatory power, hence the deft turn of possibility ("in *or* out"), with its counterpart in "All thoughts begin *or* end."

Here again Tomlinson provides a measure of the instinctive yet reasoning mind that Thomas retains as the terms of his human covenant with the nonhuman and animal. In *Poetry and Metamorphosis*, Tomlinson observes how many speakers in Eliot's poems—degraded, violated, or neurotically evasive—are caught inside animal noise or semiutterance—as with the young man in *Portrait of A Lady* who must "Cry like a parrot, chatter like an ape," or the scuttling Prufrock of "ragged claws" who never sings his lovesong, or Philomela metamorphosed to a bird. Yet Tomlinson also sees Eliot striving for a way out of the inchoate, attempting to "reconstitute noise as meaning":[23] that which, in Tomlinson's own poetry, is part of humanity's perpetual coming to conscious speech as it utters or names the world's plurality—a keeping faith with all that we are not. Hence in *Adam* (1969), the "beasts" of all such otherness "Crowd forward to be named ... We bring / To a kind of birth all we can name / And, named, it echoes in us our being." One can go further and say that across centuries (with Adam exiled from Paradise into history, yet retaining a sense of pastoral perfection) cultivators who can win a kinship with local soil have revered it by means of all its nameable variety. Even Thomas in *Digging* (I, 1915), who would "think / Only with scents," cannot help distinguishing the many plants of a savored English earth: bracken, wild carrot's seed, mustard, rose, currant, raspberry, goutweed, rhubarb, and celery. The enduring English countryman of *Lob* carries on his back a multitude of names and localized associations: "Lob-lie-by-the-fire, Jack Cade, / Jack Smith, Jack Moon, poor Jack of every trade, / Young Jack, or old Jack, or Jack What-d'ye-call."

Yet Thomas's Lob, under "hazel and thorn tangled with old-man's beard," escapes from view behind all these names, and remains as elusive as Jack Noman in *May 23* (1915) who goes off, abandoning "his cresses from Oakshott rill / And his cowslips from Wheatham hill." For, although Thomas faithfully records the sense of place shown by previous English generations in their namings, his own poetry recreates no marriage of sensibility and ground. There is a mismatch, an unease, that contrasts, for example, with Tomlinson's ability in *Old Man's Beard* and its companion poem... *Or Traveller's Joy* (1978) to hold together plants' names and their origin in human experiences—seeing man in the plant, and plant in the man, without losing sight of their separateness. Yet there is a vigilance here that still connects with Thomas's unsettled kind of meditation in *Old Man* (1914). For where Tomlinson keeps alert to the ever-changing relation between self and world, Thomas, with his very different sense of disparities, similarly stops the ego blotting out the external scene. His restlessness—the noise of his mind's fidelity to substance—escapes self-absorption when he observes how the names "Lad's-love" and "Old Man" do not entirely fit the herb they describe; how they

> Half decorate, half perplex, the thing it is:
> At least, what that is clings not to the names
> In spite of time. And yet I like the names.
>
> The herb itself I like not, but for certain
> I love it

The sequence of surprises, by which he does not (after all) prefer nameless being to names, then demotes "like" in favor of "love," continues to jolt attention when one passes from the "I" who loves to the child who "will love" in a sudden enlarging of scene round the poet, as she "plucks a feather from the door-side bush / Whenever she goes in or out of the house." This has a located, present solidity made vivid by the to-and-fro, the unease, the apprehension about the child who in the future "will love" and will possibly forget. "Lad's-love" and "Old Man" go together. Yet for all the "old" vision of "ancient" trees and "bent" path, this small, defined ground offers the poet his distinct footing. The herb's bitter scent leads to the sharp fact

> Of garden rows, and ancient damson-trees
> Topping a hedge, a bent path to a door,
> A low thick bush beside the door, and me
> Forbidding her to pick.

Beyond such particularity and beyond his senses, lies a great unnameable void—

> No garden appears, no path, no hoar-green bush
> Of Lad's-love, or Old Man, no child beside,
> Neither father nor mother, nor any playmate;
> Only an avenue, dark, nameless, without end.

Thus the dread vista in the closing lines. Yet Thomas presents it more as his own special fatedness than as a terror that undercuts the reality of all others and all things. Even as a void of forgetting opens up, it does so from the basis of his grip, moment by moment, piece by piece, on the tangibility of the present. It is all, literally, that he holds: "I . . . shrivel the grey shreds / Sniff them and think and sniff again and try / Once more to think what it is I am remembering." He is attuned, "listening, lying in wait," not just for what he cannot remember but to speak for what he can restrictedly possess.

His unease has agitated a ground into view. But never more clearly does one see the difference between that restless quickening and Frost's equivocating presentation of place, home, and substance. For in *The Wood-Pile* (*North of Boston*), one is given from the very start a location that is also a dislocation. "Out walking in the frozen swamp one gray day," he sees lines of trees

> Too much alike to mark or name a place by
> So as to say for certain I was here
> Or somewhere else: I was just far from home.

This cold, nameless place begets no Thomas-like sense of fate (or, more importantly, no keen, attentive consciousness). Instead, Frost offers the confident ego, the unworried nonchalance (almost homely when he says, "I was just far from home") with which he can be superior to a nervous bird he sees keeping its distance. The creature is careful to put a tree between them

> And say no word to tell me who he was
> Who was so foolish as to think what *he* thought.
> He thought that I was after him for a feather—

The bird ("like one who takes / Everything said as personal to himself") comes to resemble the unduly fearful or touchy people in other poems. There, one remembers, Frost's sympathy for the fraught and anxious leaked with poignancy. Now, in his tougher, unbothered guise, he slackens differently, mingling "who's" with the bird, and

4: Between Paradise and History

thus leaving sharp "thought" to such foolish worriers. Consciousness is loosened enough in this prelude to absorb, or begin to blur the edges of, the object now encountered:

> And then there was a pile of wood for which
> I forgot him and let his little fear
> Carry him off the way I might have gone,
> Without so much as wishing him good-night.
> He went behind it to make his last stand.
> It was a cord of maple, cut and split
> And piled—and measured, four by four by eight.
> And not another like it could I see.
> No runner tracks in this year's snow looped near it.
> And it was older sure than this year's cutting,
> Or even last year's or the year's before.
> The wood was gray and the bark warping off it
> And the pile somewhat sunken. Clematis
> Had wound strings round and round it like a bundle.
> What held it, though, on one side was a tree
> Still growing, and on one a stake and prop,
> These latter about to fall. I thought that only
> Someone who lived in turning to fresh tasks
> Could so forget his handiwork on which
> He spent himself, the labor of his ax,
> And leave it there far from a useful fireplace
> To warm the frozen swamp as best it could
> With the slow smokeless burning of decay.

Such an object, burning in the wild rather than a household, could almost suggest Whittier's warmth-in-cold sense of habitation, just as its chanced-on quality might remind one of Williams's *trouvés*. Again, in that respect, Frost shows his closeness to the lineage of American factuality, but he has not sufficiently awakened, or escaped his own inertia, to engage with new relation the concreteness he documents so cleanly and accurately. So he brings to the cut, split, measured wood, with its bark and binding clematis, not an alerted rigor but an idleness of attitude—that which earlier devalued "thought" when he says he "forgot" the bird, and now diffuses "thought" even more with forgetfullness: "I thought that only / Someone who lived in turning to fresh tasks / Could so forget his handiwork on which he spent himself." In the light of such softened "thought," eager effort becomes work abandoned, while zest for the new seems like "spent" vigor. This woodpile, left "far from a useful fireplace," never provides an image with which the mind can grip and reinhabit the world, as when, for example, in Tomlinson's poem, *Night-Piece: The Near and the Far*

(1960), a cloud is lit up suddenly by the moon, and "Over the houseless space, a hearth spills down." Frost's woodpile centers no realization and earns back no homing point. "Far from a useful fireplace," it warms only a lazy, unconcentrated idea of homeliness—a dream that aptly mingles with the wood's slow dissolution.

Thomas, by contrast, who was more obviously cut off from his England, could more genuinely inhabit boundaries. When he reviewed *North of Boston,* he said that *The Wood-Pile* belonged with Frost's "masterpieces of deep and mysterious tenderness."[24] But he allowed himself no easy softening in *Fifty Faggots* (1915). He is modified by what is objectively *there:*

> There they stand, on their ends, the fifty faggots
> That once were underwood of hazel and ash
> In Jenny Pinks's Copse. Now, by the hedge
> Close packed, they make a thicket fancy alone
> Can creep through with the mouse and wren. Next Spring
> A blackbird or a robin will nest there,
> Accustomed to them, thinking they will remain
> Whatever is for ever to a bird:
> This Spring it is too late; the swift has come.
> 'Twas a hot day for carrying them up:
> Better they will never warm me, though they must
> Light several Winters' fires. Before they are done
> The war will have ended, many other things
> Have ended, maybe, that I can no more
> Foresee or more control than robin and wren.

There are no large time perspectives, as in Gurney's *Felling a Tree.* But this chopped wood—a sanctuary of present fact against transience, fate, and the uncertain future—shows how much closer Thomas is to the hard work and tangibility of Gurney's poem than to Frost's *Wood-Pile* laxness. "Close packed" (like the *p*'s and *s*'s of "Jenny Pinks's Copse" in its English particularity), the faggots are an obstruction to reverie and assumptions about the future. So tight is the "thicket" that "fancy," squeezed into it by Thomas's consonantal humour, can only just "creep through"—not rushing ahead, but keeping to the smaller scope of mouse or wren. "Next Spring" (as we peer further), "A blackbird or a robin will nest there," though, since their *nest* resides too comfortably on time's *Next* unsettling, fancy lies in thinking "they will remain / Whatever is for ever to a bird." Such optimism, however, is not patronized in any Frostian way, but is given Thomas's wry, melodious tolerance ("Whatever . . . ever") before he reins back sharply: "This Spring it is too late; the swift has come."

Abruptly returned to the present by "too late," one feels the threat of incessant change that turns trees to faggots, faggots to later fires.

Yet within that unsteadying reality lies Thomas's sensuous grip on savored time, on all that has been sufficiently kindled between man and solid substance to make him say, "Twas a hot day for carrying them up: / Better they will never warm me." The impact of "Better" (shifted from its predictable place at the end of the line to a freshly forceful position at its beginning) contains both an ironic grimness about the fires that won't warm him and an unapologetic relish for what he *has* known. There is pain here, but Thomas's understatement with regard to the "many other things" ending ("maybe") before the war's end seeks no pity from us. Rather, his personal intimations of fate bring him back more definitely into that modest homeground— those fifty faggots—shared unforeseeably with robin and wren. At the end, Thomas's achievement in the poem is inseparable from its cost—the necessity of not looking impossibly far, either forward or back, but touching, hearing, solidity's tremor.

III

Gurney, however, reminds one of continuities. Thomas's poem *Roads* (1916) has its solitudes, its companies of the dead, and its inevitable direction: "Now all roads lead to France." But Gurney's *Roads—Those Roads* (1919–22) brings him back along English highways with their poplar and hawthorn, to a more reachable past—to "the different people / That ruled and had shaping of this land at their periods." Such are the Severnside Danes he pictures kneading clay for bricks in *Kilns* or the Norman builder of another postwar poem, *Tewkesbury*. It is with a Tomlinson-like feeling for the tutelary responsibility of a past people ("how the makers gathered and guarded," as Gurney says in one poem) that he meets with his own sense of guardianship in *Up There* (1919–22), where a modern farmer is imagined unearthing a Roman coin and by the grasp of the hand almost touching the past's close-yet-far cultivated soil. One is as near to the worked contours of the Roman farm as "the single kite hovering still / By the coppice there, level with the flat of the hill." It is like the "touch of sight" in *The Dearness of Common Things* (1919–22), with "finger-traced curves . . . When concrete objects grow." But Gurney's touch is keenest when a land's mettle (or Roman "metal") calls up his soldierly alertness in *The Bare Line of the Hill* (1919–22):

> The bare line of the hill
> Shows Roman and

> A sense of Rome hangs still
> Over the land.
>
> So that one looks to see
> Steel gleam, to hear
> Voice outflung suddenly
> Of the challenger.
>
> Yet boom of the may-fly
> The loudest thing
> Is of all under the sky
> Of the wide evening.
>
> And the thing metal most
> The pond's last sheen
> Willow shadow crossed
> But still keen

Once he can "see" such "Steel gleam" and sense that challenging edge within the land, he too is on guard—not celebrating old romance, but a firm voice heard in the mayfly's "boom," or in the "metal" that protrudes on us the very look of a water's lit surface. Caesar, Carausius, and Maximus have gone, but

> The regal and austere
> Mantle of Rome is thrown
>
> As of old—about the walls
> Of hills and the farm—the fields.
> Scabious guards the steeps,
> Trefoil the slopes yield.

"Trefoil"—more like the subject of the sentence than its object—partners the watchful tutelary, "Scabious." Indeed, Gurney tautens what might seem casual in Rome's thrown mantle when his words become equal to the guarded reality found in walls, in "fields," and, most strongly of all, where "slopes *yield*."

It is the pressure of felt fact on language and the outer voicing of a land's inwardness that make the first lines of *The Valley Farm* (1919–22) seem to resemble Tomlinson's divining of buried currents:

> Ages ago the waters covered here
> And took delight of dayspring as a mirror;
> Hundreds of tiny spikes and threads of light.
> But now the spikes are hawthorn, and the hedges

> Are foamed like ocean's crests, and peace waits here
> Deeper than middle South Sea, or the Fortunate
> Or Fabled Islands.

Water's spiky twinklings glimpsed anew in today's hawthorn—the observation might almost be Tomlinson's except that on this occasion Gurney loses sharpness when hedges become "foamed" and semilegendary "peace" waits inertly. Even the efforts of the woodchopper with his "noble weapon" a few lines later ("peace works an act through him") lack enough vitality to suggest how man in nature and Eden's replenishments are close to each other. Tomlinson, however, must freshly reearn such kinship, often through the very grain of language. *The Metamorphosis* (1978) shows him rediscovering a way along the track of a lost watercourse in a valley wood:

> Bluebells come crowding a fellside
>   A stream once veined. It rises
> Like water again where, bell on bell,
>   They flow through its bed, each rope
> And rivulet, each tributary thread
>   Found-out by flowers.

Sinuously fluent yet earth-solid (with "bell on bell" chiming upon the hardness of *"bed"*), a whole new pathway rises into view and hearing—a channel where one's mind can dance with instinct, sight with speech. "Each tributary thr*ead*" of the old path not only rhymes reminder of its former *"bed,"* but also takes one, in mind, senses, and tongue (the latter unthickening the "thread" with dexterous *f*'s) into a newly rippling wide-vowelled space, "Found-out by flowers." At the poem's end, where the sight of wind across bluebells lets one rightly believe that "Water itself might move like a flowing of flowers," Tomlinson, in the fullness of eyes, ears, tongue, and thought, has opened out a "flow" inside nature and the versatile vowels that speak it.

It is the energy caught to view between image and reality, the current that elsewhere in Tomlinson's verse starts to move between Adam and Eden, but only because opposites are not dreamily or willfully merged—for the separateness of contrary things vitalizes the joint relation perpetually being remade. Again, then, one comes back, with a sense of added relevance, to Tomlinson's poem on Gurney. The latter could "regain the gate" to Eden by death, but the living man found his time-and-space way of rhyming with, dancing alongside, eternal intimations. With similar care, Tomlinson's pastoral poem *In Arden* (1978) parallels vision and locality. Here there is no egotizing of place (although Macadam threatens). Nor can one drift into paradisal innocence. For "Eden lies guarded" with a wakeful wariness that is learnt by readers as well as poet:

> Pardonable Adam, denied its gate,
>   Walks the grass in a less-than-Eden light
> And whiteness that shines from a stone burns with his fate:
>   Sun is tautening the field's edge shadowline
> Along the wood beyond: but the contraries
>   Of this place are contrarily unclear:
> A haze beats back the summer sheen
>   Into a chiaroscuro of the heat:

That a "haze" should beat back "the summer sheen," and not the other way round, makes one realize, in new sharpness, how "contrarily" resistant and unpredictable is Tomlinson's presentation of contraries. They are opposite, yet with every moment that passes they seem to become more interlocked and interdefining. The sun "tautening the field's edge shadowline / Along the wood beyond" burns within an increasingly specific time and place—a point of negotiation and encounter where heat eventually touches another contrary, water:

> The down on the seeded grass that beards
>   Each rise where it meets with sky,
> Ripples a gentle fume: a fine
>   Incense, smelling of hay smokes by:
> Adam in Arden tastes its replenishings:
>   Through its dense heats the depths of Arden's springs
> Convey echoic waters—voices
>   Of the place that rises through this place
> Overflowing, as it brims its surfaces
>   In runes and hidden rhymes, in chords and keys
> Where Adam, Eden, Arden run together
>   And time itself must beat to the cadence of this river.

Powers stir also in the Tuscan landscape of Pound's *Canto I*: "all the leaves are full of voices...." But Tomlinson who quotes that early version in *Poetry and Metamorphosis* has here evoked the collective, vibrant speech of a distinctively English scene—a tradition's marvelous potency and the individualized realization through which it rises. The writing's splendor owes everything to the agility with which Tomlinson maintains the verbal differences between things in order to enact a quickening likeness—as when (like "*c*hords and *k*eys") "Adam," "Eden," "Arden" bound off each other, in hard-edged singularity, yet move together in one flow, one river, one beating rhyme of history with paradise. So, contraries beget relation, and, by the working of that principle, Tomlinson's poetic kinships again take on importance. There is Blake, of course, with his special relevance to the early poetry of the 1940s. But, in a less obvious way, it is Lawrence—the one contemporary of Gurney equally able to make English possibilities out of Whitmanian idiom—who in the end is to prove closer to Tomlinson's art.[25]

5
Contraries and Relations

I

By its title, *Relations and Contraries*, Tomlinson's first book of verse (1951) shows the theme that had engaged him from his beginnings as a poet. For contraries—if not always relations between contraries—were at work on his imagination when, as a student at Cambridge just after the war, he found himself admiring Cézanne's paintings in the Fitzwilliam Museum and at the same time avidly reading Whitman. But opposites first coexist on the page, even if unconsciously, in the extract from his long prose poem, *Nightbook*, that was published in a 1949 issue of the magazine *Nine*. In the fragment called "Art and Chaos," he is championing flux while actually presenting a textual stability—reasoned, balanced, aphoristic:

> All living art is temporal, even fragmentary.
>
> Art which pretends ultimacy or permanency should be suspect, for the reign of ultimates is tyranny. Greek art pretends to an ultimacy of Proportions, all things Roman to an ultimacy of power, and Gothic things to an ultimacy of Spirit.
>
> Gothic cathedrals, along with the skyscraper, should be consigned to the graveyard of giants. The cities of the West are full of monstrous tombstones.
>
> Let us beware of imposing Forms: of the pyramids at Gizeh, of Corinthian temples, of the arch and the basilica. Beware of petrified Forms. *For all life flowers on the edge of chaos.*[1]

Despite the italicized drama of the last sentence, it is there, at the fine "edge" between fixity and fluidity, that one hears Tomlinson's later voice. Although, according to a footnote, the whole work's intended effect is that of "a Blake prophetic book", the future art that is intimated here has less in common with Blake the large-scale visionary than with the man who wrote the proverbs in *The Marriage of Heaven and Hell*. The small, stony instancing in "Art and Chaos" is particularly noticeable:

> Hence the effectiveness of unfinished statuary, as in certain carvings of Michelangelo and Rodin. *For all life flowers on the edge of chaos.*
>
> Hence the enlivening union of art and primal things, as when the bushman paints on rock or on rock or shells.
>
> Hence the beauty of weathered stone and lichen stains. Hence the nostalgia of old walls and decaying houses.

"Nostalgia" is not to survive in Tomlinson's vocabulary as a poet. Yet this excerpt from the never published *Nightbook* points forward thirty-five years to the time when, in his preface to *Eden*, Tomlinson is speaking about his graphics. Poems and pictures, he says then, comprise "the place where the civilised, discriminating faculties and the sense of the elemental, of origins, reinforce each other." It is this "place"—not somewhere geographical, but the point at which one's intelligence takes grip on the nonhuman world and its representation by art—that Tomlinson finds so lacking in visionary Blake. His 1959 review of a new edition of *Vala, or The Four Zoas* notes "shadowy transitions" and "endless cycles of gargantuan turmoil" where there "occurs so little in the actual turns of the story for the mind to take hold on or to draw sustenance from."[2] Yet his distrust of such art (Whitman included, one feels), which is colossally unaccountable to the mind and to groundlevel concreteness, also suggests what he could find valuable inside such work: the factual, particularized confine within the gigantic. It would take several years before he discovered in Williams's art, and drew upon, the qualities that he had instinctively relished in Whitman's.

But with Blake, it seems, he could sooner gain a foothold upon the solid particularities of the world—luminous not with "fourfold vision," but with a manifold nature separated out into opposites: "Without contraries is no progression. Attraction and repulsion, reason and energy, love and hate, are necessary to human existence."

These are principles of distinctness in Blake's *Proverbs of Hell*. The being of a mouse is not to be confused with that of a tiger. The eagle's knowledge is quite separate from the crow's. So also, more subtly, in the *Innocence and Experience* poems, Blake's adopted voice in *The Lamb* (where he impersonates a child's way of uttering a Christ-given relationship between creatures) is to be set apart from the aghast tones he ironically assumes in *The Tyger:* the voice of the adult who is horrified by the distant, mechanical God of nonrelatedness whom he has constructed out of his Promethean-Frankenstein mind. There is to be no confusion either in *The Divine Image* where Blake, through the unsentimental logic of his quatrains, keeps separate yet parallel the virtues of God and the virtues of man:

> To Mercy, Pity, Peace and Love
> All pray in their distress;
> And to these virtues of delight
> Return their thankfulness.
>
> For Mercy, Pity, Peace and Love
> Is God, our Father dear,
> And Mercy, Pity, Peace and Love
> Is Man, his child and care.

The clear discipline of such a form, rather than its Christianity, is almost certainly the reason why quatrains appear so frequently in *Relations and Contraries*. Yet Tomlinson's need for confines in verse—the boundary and limit that, by being acknowledged, release a dynamism—quickly finds such Blakean structures less flexible than those he presents in his second book, *The Necklace* (1955). After that time, developing a variable verse-line through the example of Williams, he was to leave Blake's forms behind, although still sharing his perception of the lit, myriad world. By the 1960s, Tomlinson is able to command in verse what he could only attempt in *Relations and Contraries*—the halting of the reader in front of the text as a still, fixed entity that itself parallels the fact and experience before which the poet has been arrested. With that stillness granted, that otherness acknowledged, one can move forward again—through surface and closure into depth and openings, through the past into a presentness. *A Sense of Distance* (1969) shows it clearly, for a surface "sense of distance" (the poet in England remembering a moment far away in the American Southwest) leads to one more deeply native:

> The door is shut.
> The red rider
> no longer crosses the canyon floor
> under a thousand feet of air.
>
> The glance that fell
> on him, is shafting

> a deeper well:
> the boughs of the oak are roaring
> inside the acorn shell.

Vast American scale, "under a thousand feet of air," is gradually being transformed into "acorn shell" grasp, an English realization of an inward, potent space. A few lines later, the unheard animal of the past becomes audible in a new way: "The hoofbeats—silent, then— / are sounding now." "Sounding" suggests not external noise, but the process by which a land is plumbed as one touches the interior roar of nature's growth and the pulse of time. Moment by moment, through the confine of the mind, one draws closer to—and more sensuously understands—the energies of the "animal" universe that the red horseman originally rode:

> And it seems as if a wind
> had flung wide a door
> above an abyss, where all
> the kingdoms of possibilities shone
> like sandgrains crystalline in the mind's own sun.

No Blake-like quatrain would have ever allowed Tomlinson to elongate the last line so extraordinarily, or to open up, in its separate parts, the bold verbal weight heard in "kingdoms of poss-ib-il-it-ies," which themselves take on glittering refinement in "sandgrains cryst-all-ine." It is, indeed, the crystallizing out of word and syllable that lets "sun" emerge in bright acoustic from the comparatively blurred "shone." But if Tomlinson uses no Blakean form, he nevertheless seems to remember the spread of gleaming terrain in *Mock On, Mock On, Voltaire, Rousseau!* For Blake, each fragment is part of God's immense energy, confounding sceptics, rationalists, and would-be reducers of the universe:

> And every sand becomes a gem
> Reflected in the beams divine;
> Blown back they blind the mocking eye,
> But still in Israel's paths they shine.
>
> The atoms of Democritus
> And Newton's particles of light
> Are sands upon the Red Sea shore,
> Where Israel's tents do shine so bright.

Yet Blake's poem only emphasizes Tomlinson's differences. The wind flinging the door open in *A Sense of Distance* is, undivinely and unsymbolically, a force of nature. The threshold upon "kingdoms of possibilities" is not the same, for all its shared sense of a radiantly enterable world, as the shore where the Israelites wait to cross. Tomlinson reaches that starting point at the end of his poem not by spiritual transcendence, but by enclosure within nature. His oak boughs inside the acorn could not be more different from the "precious odours" of the infinite that Blake perceives in every flower: "within that centre Eternity expands / Its ever-during doors" (*Milton,* book 2). What expands for Tomlinson are the vitalities of time and space brought to view by boundaries. Hence the pulse of relation *between* nature's many singularities that make up solid ground in the poem *Stone Speech* (1972), a terrain that is visionary not through any sublimity, but because of the neighborship it implies. The pebbles on this beach are no stepping-stones towards a Red Sea miracle; instead, concreteness has its own wonder—of myriad separate things moving towards the communal. Thus

> flints
> edged out of flinthood
> into smoothness chafe
> against grainy ovals,
> pitted pieces, nosestones

The idiosyncratic hardness of "nosestones" (verbally unsoftened, kept strange, by the hyphen's absence) forbids any overhuman projection on nature; nevertheless, one finds valuable images and resemblances. Reading this poem, as the poet "reads" the beach, one notes kinships and recognitions—

> chalk-swaddled babyshapes,
> tiny fists, facestones
> and facestone's brother
> skullstone

—as well as the stones' quirky impersonality, set apart from us and mimicked by hyphenless compound words. Without pathetic fallacy, therefore, the hard stones, chafed against each other to make an interfitting whole, offer an image for human community: of abrasive energies that have been tempered but not tamed in a world of coexisting parts,

> all
> rubbing shoulders:
> a mob of grindings,

5: Contraries and Relations 151

> groundlings, scatterings
> from a million necklaces
> mined under sea-hills, the pebbles
> are as various as the people.

As with the kingdoms spread out at the end of *A Sense of Distance,* the Blakean example has taken on an extraordinary power in regard to *this* world. It only suggests the more why Tomlinson's instinct for relations, despite his early use of quatrains that probably derive in the main from the *Innocence and Experience* poems, could never be satisfied with Blake's tying of kinship to Christian love:

> Can I see another's woe,
> And not be in sorrow too?
> Can I see another's grief,
> And not seek for kind relief?

Relations and Contraries, on the other hand, seeks a more dynamically charged expression of the bond between creatures. In *Poem of the Neighbours,* from that collection, the verb may be immaturely labored in the pairings that Tomlinson presents:

> Bird neighbours the rising tree,
> Leaf neighbours the waiting soil

Yet the potentiality of action, downward or upward, lies beneath the still surface of a word; and the connective force in "neighbours" begins to take on more interesting, dangerous implication at the end of the poem, when the form's neat boundary contains animal energy waiting to strike:

> Cat neighbours the bird in death,
> Lion neighbours the doe in death,
>
> Snake neighbours the hidden toad,
> Hidden toad neighbours the fly:
>
> That life shall know increase.

The last line is very explicitly Tomlinson's version of Blake's "Without contraries is no progression." But in a less overt and more deeply far-reaching way, it is another influence—Lawrence's—that the poem reveals, as do several others in *Relations and Contraries.* For it is Lawrence, as novelist and essayist rather than pre-1920 poet, who has the greater effect in showing Tomlinson how opposites quicken and renew truths between them. It is Lawrence, after all, whose affirmation of duality and rejection of fixed oneness lies behind Tomlinson's attack on absolutes (the "ultimacy" of "Proportions", "Power," and "Spirit") in "Art and Chaos." Moreover, for a poet like Tomlinson, working so often at the border between human and nonhuman, mind and senses, there is special affinity with a novelist who, in *The Rainbow* and *Women in Love*, dramatizes the creative fight between man and woman—that which neither side may win separately in order that both may win jointly. Two opposing energies thus hold between them, in time and in nature, a bond, a relation, that has the timelessly infinite within it—whether it is called the rainbow, the angel, or the crown that hovers above the lion and unicorn in the arms of England.

For Lawrence, contraries prevent the collapse of relation into the docile or stale. In a 1917 essay he characteristically finds a state of "peace" not through the conciliation of lion and lamb, but in that poise where the doe is "balanced against the bright beam of the leopard like a shadow against him. The two exist by virtue of juxtaposition in pure polarity."[3] It is such polarity, indeed, that is celebrated by *Etruscan Shades*, the first poem in *Relations and Contraries*, where not only the title seems Lawrentian (*Etruscan Places, The Shades of Spring*) but also the imagery that depicts marriage:

> Between the lion and the doe
> We moved as calm and passion flow

Setting these lines inside a tight quatrain, Tomlinson has little in common with the Lawrence of 1914 who likens poetic meter to "a bird with broad wings flying and lapsing through the air."[4] Yet Lawrence's feeling for the dynamic and fluid still remains important. After all, when Tomlinson spoke in "Art and Chaos" about "unfinished statuary, as in carvings of Michelangelo and Rodin," he was echoing *Women in Love* where Birkin derides the imprisoning quality of possessions: "You have to be like Rodin, Michael Angelo, and leave a piece of raw rock unfinished to your figure. You must leave your surroundings sketchy, unfinished, so that you are never contained, never confined, never dominated from the outside."[5] Yet the fact that Lawrence is only indirectly acknowledged in *Relations and Contraries*, with his influence usually hidden inside a Blake-like quatrain, suggests a slight uneasiness in Tomlinson—a reluctance, despite his Lawrentian blow against rigidities, to accept the rootless dispossession, without bounds or community, which could lead from such an attitude. Tomlinson's concern, as one has seen, is to speak for the elemental, rippling potency that enters the housed, the bounded, and the civilized. For him, it is not a case of the wild destroying the fold, but of providing the terms, in rock, sky, and water, for a vitalization.

When Lawrence also sees the communal as a bond to be invigorated rather than a prison to be escaped from, he is then remarkably close to the civic kind of Englishness at work in Tomlinson's poetry. Such is the Lawrence, for example, who compares Siena with amorphous Nottingham in the late essay, "Nottingham and the Mining Countryside" (1929) and says "we have frustrated that instinct of community which would make us unite in pride and dignity in the bigger gesture of the citizen, not the cottager."[6] For the "pride and dignity" of the communal instinct, not the cosily meek, would bring to the sense of place the renewing power it needs—the very same imaginative resource, it can be said, that Tomlinson more fully opens out as the energy to make or remake cities in poems like *Geneva Restored, More Foreign Cities* (1960), and *Eden* (1969), where nature's wind unfancifully "stirs in the thicket of the lines / In Eden's wood, the radial avenues / Of light there, copious enough / To draft a city from."

The question, however, for Tomlinson as a young poet was how to unearth such sources and verbally draw upon them. It is no accident, then, that his discovery of potencies is crucially linked to his rearticulation of Lawrence. Thus the poem, *Peace Between Us, William Blake (Relations and Contraries)*, may seem, by its title and contents, as if it has an obvious literary forebear:

> The brindled tiger burns by night
> Before the deer;
> The blameless lamb in fields of light
> Crops flower on flower.

But here one sees a Lawrentian rather than a Blakean vision of opposites balanced against each other and inter-defining: "Both singly celebrate / The thing they are." There is also the perception, derived from Lawrence, that when separate creatures lose their singleness—and tigers become sweet lambs—there is a collapse of polarity and a world brought to confusion:

> Lamb beholds its brindled prey:
> Tiger cropping blameless flowers.
> Then, among the fields of day
> Lamb-grown tiger lamb devours.

Tomlinson's comedy of uncertainty in the last line (who devours whom?) is not, after all, so far removed from Lawrence's satire on those who deaden the flame in his essay "The Novel" (1925). There he sees Tolstoy attempting to deny his own sensuous being when he tries to cram his passionate "lion" inside his "lambkin" self of spirituality and would-be universal brotherhood. It is the kind of confusion that Tomlinson's later poetry presents (*Through Binoculars, Farewell to Van Gogh*) in different terms, not as Christian love inflated at the expense of the body, but as a romantic egotizing of the physical world that must be quarreled with so that one may reach beyond it to a cleansed sense of the objective and solid. Even here, though, in *Peace Between Us, William Blake,* Tomlinson implicitly reveals Lawrence offering him a direction as the poem moves through a perceived tiger-and-lamb muddle towards a final clarifying:

> Between the tiger and the lamb,
> Between the other and the self,
> Each in perfect counterpart
> What third, then, knits the single heart?
>
> Between the eagle and the dove,
> Between the Father and the Son,
> Power by night and by day love—
> The paradox: God is one.

The only "one" that Lawrence conceives is that which springs from the fusionless meeting of opposites: when "the two are related, by the intervention of the Third"—the Holy Ghost—"into a Oneness."[7] Ultimately more important, however, than adherence to Lawrentian vocabulary is Tomlinson's inherited sense of the "third" thing—the flash struck between two contraries—as the basis on which he develops his own artistic consciousness. The final poem of *Relations and Contraries, The Light and Dark,* offers a hint of this:

> Life is the spark
> Thrown off by grinding opposites, whose power
> Relates the world of fearful symmetry with blood and flower.

Blake's "symmetry" now refers to the deadlocked, urban rigidities ("The verticals of waste, the lost street-ends") that the Stoke man knows well. But "blood and flower"—like the antitragic "blood consciousness" of Lawrence pitting potencies against fated ugliness—suggests again how much Tomlinson shares with his fellow Midlander. For although the novelist's great theme is the man-woman relation,

Tomlinson's subject is an allied one: the fresh remarryings of the physicalized mind, or "enlightened carnality" (*Apples Painted*, 1989), with the phenomenal universe.

Reengagement with such pulsing fact, beyond stale cerebrality, is Lawrence's concern, significantly, in his 1921 story, "The Ladybird." Here he depicts the exhausted "white" consciousness of wartime England: the mental surface that the Austrian soldier, Dionys Psanek, describes to Lady Daphne when he tells her that we fail to see the sun straight:

> Well then, the yellowness of sunshine—light itself—that is only the glancing aside of the real original fire. . . . There would be no light if there was no refraction, no bits of dust and stuff to turn the dark fire into visibility. You know that's a fact. And that being so, even the sun is dark. It is only his jacket of dust that makes him visible . . . and the yellow beams are only the turning away of the sun's directness that was coming to us.[8]

The physics of refraction shaped Lawrence's portrayal of Gerald Crich and his external whiteness in *Women in Love*. But it is "The Ladybird" that most clearly offers suggestions to Tomlinson, particularly in the *Relations and Contraries* poem *Swan*. The bird's pure white surface is there distrusted as a symbol, and its ferocity is remembered. Moreover,

> The sun we see is light thrown back,
> The outside of the sun—no more;
> The sun we do not see is black,
> And blackly molten to its core.
>
> For as it blackly burns away
> Its darkness propagates no light;
> Only to hide its inner ray,
> Permits this change from black to white.

Of all Lawrence's contraries, it is this one—inner substance/outer image—that is the most essential in Tomlinson's development, though it is ultimately given an emphasis that might seem un-Lawrentian. For Lawrence usually regards the illusions offered by art as an intervening form, a false consciousness, that one must escape in order to arrive at the naked universe. Thus, as theorist, he ignores what his artistry actually presents—the means by which the mind takes grip on word, image, and textual surface as a way of proceeding into a world of animate energy. Tomlinson, then, in making so conspicuous the process of movement from illusory surface to tangible solidity, restores what is lost to view in Lawrence's practice, as well as finding his own route forward. The sun's refraction in "The Ladybird" can, therefore suggest to Tomlinson, together with Constable's art, the truth that counterfeit illusion reveals—as when sunlight, distorted by a window in *Glass Grain* (1960), throws an image of "combed-down hair" upon a wall, so that through it one touches the rippling texture of sun-in-earth.

Yet the Lawrentian inheritance in *Swan* also suggests the animal means by which human beings are taught entrance into a world of cleansed revelation. The swans lead the way later in *Canal*, as do the Fiesole oxen. In *A Sense of Distance*, the poet inwardly follows the American horse as it sounds out new space; and the reader of *Far Point* (1989) gazes with the Canadian deer through the window of a bayside bar and through waste at a nature unveiling itself to those who will genuinely look. But, in *Relations and Contraries*, it is specifically Lawrence's feeling for the way that animal singularity challenges the human to a new attentive awareness that has notable results. For Lawrence, in the early poem *End of Another Home Holiday* (1913), the animal signifies a need in the self, as consciousness fights its way out of pathos towards some nontragic articulation. So, even though a "yearning-eyed, / Inexorable love" drags at his feelings, he can respond—briefly—to a different emotional impulse:

> The moon-mist is over the village, out of the mist speaks the bell,
> And all the little roofs of the village bow low, pitiful, beseeching, resigned.
> —Speak, you my home! What is it I don't do well?
>
> Ah home, suddenly I love you
> As I hear the sharp clean trot of a pony down the road,
> Succeeding sharp little sounds dropping into silence
> Clear upon the long-drawn hoarseness of a train across the valley.

The love that "suddenly" comes with the pony's "sharp clean trot" has, for a moment, the verve and distinctness that lifts it out of old, resigned emotion. Another animal, later in the poem, offers a further hint:

> The wild young heifer, glancing distraught,
> With a strange new knocking of life at her side
> Runs seeking a loneliness.

But the "loneliness," or "sharp clean" singularity, separated out from blurring sentiment, never finds its full speech in the poem, which concludes in fatalism with the valley corncrake's "plaintive, unalterable voice." *End of Another Home Holiday* lets Tomlinson imagine a comparable situation in *Relations and Contraries* with his *Beginning of Another Home Holiday* ("Returning to familiar rounds again / Our limbs fall foul of love's mired hawser-ropes"). But Lawrence also offers a way into the most interesting continuity that Tomlinson begins to explore in *Poem*. What Lawrence has broached, with the pony's "sharp clean trot" can be developed, but in Tomlinson's own way—for, in *Poem,* he is a listener roused by animal hoof beats that signify a larger speech, the articulation of a communal ground:

> Wakening with the window over fields
> To the coin-clear harness-jingle as a float
> Clips by, and each succeeding hoof fall, now remote,
> Breaks clean and frost-sharp on the unstopped ear.
>
> The hooves describe an arabesque on space,
> A dotted line in sound that falls and rises
> As the cart goes by, recedes, turns to retrace
> Its way back through the unawakened village.
>
> And space vibrates, enlarges with the sound;
> Though space is soundless, yet creates
> From very soundlessness a ground
> To counterstress the lilting hoof fall as it breaks.

"Each *succeeding* hoof fall" opens out a space of neighborhood, and, as Tomlinson's adjective takes on special significance, the sense of time expands from the "Succeeding sharp little sounds" in Lawrence's poem. Yet, even if Tomlinson is partly remembering that (and explicitly quoting "unstopped ear" from Pound's *Hugh Selwyn Mauberley*), he is finding his own particular direction in verse by his representation of the experience as a *read* event. One must consciously separate out the verbal parts ("coin-clear harness-jingle") and hear the pieces that make up a "dotted line" of textual stillness as prelude to further movement. It is the acoustic discovered by tongue and ear ("From very *sound*lessness a ground / To *counter*stress") that, by contraries, takes one from pieces to whole. It is the sensuous apprehension made reachable by acknowledging the syntax as a surface that the mind takes purchase on in its own right. Thus, in not treating it as a form to be escaped from, or a transparent window through which the eye simply glides, one is accepting reason as an essential part of the human state—that which negotiates a way back, in felt thought, to contours and textures.

Poem is Tomlinson's best, earliest instance of such textual fastening.

5: Contraries and Relations

But *How Still the Hawk* in *Seeing is Believing* shows what could be achieved by a tauter verse-form in which a previous Lawrentian duality ("Lion neighbours the doe in death") takes on an extra dimension—for predator and prey are joined by a human witness, the "reader" who is poised at a distance from an equally hovering hawk. There is space yet parity between human and bird. The hawk is suspended over ground containing unrevealed prey, while one scrutinizes a textual surface whose static words hide mobile implications:

> How still the hawk
> Hangs innocent above
> Its native wood:
> Distance, that purifies the act
> Of all intent, has graced
> Intent with beauty.
> Beauty must lie
> As innocence must harm
> Whose end (sited,
> Held) is naked
> Like the map it cowers on.
> And the doom drops:
> Plummet of peace
> To him who does not share
> The nearness and the need,
> The shrivelled circle
> Of magnetic fear.

The poem begins with a sense of discrepancy between the bird's "innocent" image and murderous purpose, yet Tomlinson's demeanor, as human perception and winged stillness hover together, avoids downfall into irony. Instead, as the reader waits to strike down and through to meaning, not flesh—a felt body of realization at groundlevel beneath the words—there is an increasing sense of the link across space between opposites. Human consciousness stays separate from the hawk, as the hawk does from the prey (for the moment); yet hardly has one read the word "intent" in the fifth line before the "graced / Intent" of the next line has given the noun a new keenness that connects beauty to dangerous, physical implication, without losing its airy suspense. The word "beauty" (supposedly still, poised, hovering in line 6) has itself been barely read before it too is on the move in "Beauty must lie / As innocence must harm": a further linkage of contraries, even as Tomlinson preserves one's human awareness of a less deterministic vision.

For although, in that "must," one accepts the inexorability ("the doom drops") of killer against killed in the animal world, the "doom" is not ours, nor is human consciousness hypnotically caught inside that "end (sited, / Held)." There is flexibility still in one's perceptions: a sense of space that does not merge creature into creature, human into animal, but that, on one's reading of an unidentified prey and "the map it cowers on," begins to single out a live body. The victim is more than a mere target on a hawk's "map." Similarly, the "magnetic" clinching of bird and victim, "The nearness and the need," where "need" to kill and be killed fuses both, is a close-up view that, at the same moment, allows one's discriminating mind to set things apart. There is space between image and reality in "Plummet of peace"; but in that gap, the instinct and reason move together, plumbing the sense of vitalistic "peace" in the world. It is the movement in and through a dimension from which Tomlinson draws further strength in his development as a poet, diverging from Lawrence in verse-form and influences, yet essentially sharing a perception of the impersonal and *other*.

II

In order to develop at all, both Englishmen had to escape from art that overpersonalized the world: Lawrence by his attack on the absolutism of possessive, spiritualizing love; Tomlinson by his rejection of a lazy romantic sensuousness that devalues the body of the tangible universe, not just of human flesh, and the spry senses of those who speak it. Indeed, what unites Lawrence and Tomlinson, in their differing emphases, is their reaching for the rigor of a clean impersonality; more dynamically alert in feeling than Eliot's idea of a tradition beyond the self, yet all the same offering a resource and standard that puts the self inside the greater framework of the past or of the universe.

In this respect, Cézanne provides a guide to shared attitudes. Lawrence's essay, "Introduction to These Paintings" (1928), praises Cézanne's achievement in setting the object free of the self's projection. The painted apple, which is allowed to "exist in its own separate entity,"[9] emerges from a great artistic effort that breaks out of "the enclosed ego in its sky-blue heaven self-painted."[10] Tomlinson, quoting these words in the preface to his book of graphics and poems, *Eden* (1985), writes as one who, with *Paring the Apple (Seeing is Believing),* had already created a poetic parallel to Cézannian movement—the verbal peeling of a fruit in order to reconstitute it. The apple, seen objectively, will not be a victim of the ego's luscious fantasizing: neither a Dylan Thomas kind of verbal debauchery nor the pictorial subjectivism of another artist that Lawrence mentions. "Van Gogh's earth," says Lawrence in his essay, "was still subjective earth, himself projected into the earth."[11] Tomlinson's *Farewell to Van Gogh (Seeing is Believing)* offers a language of continuity and concreteness—of things allowed to exist in their otherness—as he says goodbye to such insistent romanticism: "Stone by stone / Your rhetoric is dispersed until the earth / Becomes once more the earth." Much later, in *Van Gogh* (1984), he changes his mind about an artist whose madness (it is now seen) impeded his sane desire for objective earth: "It was not seeming, but solidities / That took your glance." But the principles are the same as when earlier, in *Seeing is Believing*, he spoke of the evening as a solidity the ego cannot adulterate: "A tangible block, it will be no accessory / To that which does not concern it" (*Tramontana in Lerici*).

Lerici on the Ligurian coast is an apt place for clear vision, for it was here that Tomlinson first developed a way of seeing and speaking in verse that brought about his earliest mature poems. Most of the work that eventually comprised *The Necklace* arises from the period of late 1950 and just after when he was briefly employed as secretary to Percy Lubbock in the villa, Gli Scafari, between Lerici and Fiascherino on the Gulf of Spezia. It is a period of artistic development comparable with Lawrence's when he came to the same area thirty-seven years before, in autumn 1913, lived in a cottage near Fiascherino, and wrote the first drafts of *The Rainbow*. Struggling to articulate a new art of "carbon" reality—deeper than the "diamond" or "coal" levels of the personal self[12]—he speaks in his letters of "the eternal stillness that lies under all movement, under all life, like a source . . . the great impersonal which never changes and out of which all change comes."[13] Significantly his words arise from his sight of the "great, level, massive blue sea" and his sensation of "slow, sure stooping into the spaces"[14] when he crossed the Gulf to La Spezia in autumn 1913. For the steadiness of the same sea, in its formings and reformings, was the basis for Tomlinson's recuperation after dismissal and breakdown. It was here that he found a constancy greater than the self's turmoil and, therefore, a power that taught the individual talent how to build back, piece by piece, to wiry resilience.

Six years after Tomlinson first came to Liguria, he evoked in *Gli Scafari* (written in December 1956 and collected in *Seeing is Believing*) the rocky headland that gave Lubbock's house a name and the poet a way of inhabiting the elemental:

5: Contraries and Relations 161

>   Rock reproduces rock
>   In miniature
>   On rock; and where
>   The sheerness fails
>   Particularity resumes:
>   Layers, in flakes;
>   Piled shale; or
>   Minutest slates
>   Not slatted—packed and pitted
>   Against each
>   Barbarous element,
>   For all four
>   Climb with this sea
>   Save fire (and fire
>   Galls from above)
>   To will a corrosion
>   In so much silent decision among
>   Toy fortresses
>   Which can resist.

The reader climbs dexterously. As Tomlinson's short verse-line scales a surface where "Rock reproduces rock / In miniature" and is verbally duplicated "On rock," there is grip yet wakeful surprise at each turn of line. No grandiose reach of mind, no predictable vistas, can exist "where / The sheerness fails" but where, nimbly modest, "Particularity resumes." On such a basis, the consciousness can inch its way forward through "Layers" in "flakes," "shale," and "slates," none of which, one soon realises, is loose or inert. For as the long *a*'s become short—and as "slates / Not slatted" take on density in "packed and pitted"—a taut, compact energy is emergent in the stone. What was gouged and "pitted" is active: "pitted"—in the line-turn's agile shift—"Against each / Barbarous element." Indeed, as one textually grips a rockface that repels its enemies, there is a human moral equivalence to be found: a vigorous civil poise, deft in its footing, antibarbaric yet not arrogantly assertive. Thus one can challenge "corrosion," the disintegrative will in human affairs, with a countering exactness—like the rock's "silent decision" unexcessively decisive against insidious attack. So, at the end, voiceless stone remains itself yet possessed of an inner dynamic that one shares and can utter, as when the last two syllables of "fortresses" speak of a power that (with a new shift of emphasis) "can *resist*."

The poem's flexible toughness, however, draws not only on Ligurian rock, but also on an Italian verse-form that uses hard, syllabic particles.

When Tomlinson first came to Italy (and long before he adapted Williams's brevity of line for his own purposes), he translated a number of poems from Giuseppe Ungaretti's early collection, *L'Allegria*, which had been written in 1914–19 and influenced by Apollinaire's prewar cubist verse. Most importantly, Ungaretti's line-breaks expose the working sinews of speech. One hears a voice that, as in the opening of *Girovagi* (*Wanderer* in Tomlinson's *Translations*, 1984) goes beyond the overpersonalized:

> With each
> new
> region
> that I reach
> I find myself
> wearied
> at having been
> bored before
> by the very
> scene's familiarity
>
> And I break out of it always
> an alien

Significantly, it was Ungaretti's contemporary and fellow-Italian, Filippo Marinetti, who provided Lawrence's art with a similar example of particles that cluster into an impersonal strength. While writing *The Rainbow* (June 1914), he found in Marinetti's futuristic physics, or "physiology of matter," an image of resistance ("the binding of the molecules of steel or their action in heat") that spoke partly for his own sense of human individuality aligned upon rhythms and forces beyond the personal.[15] It is an inviolable separateness of being that he articulates in *The Rainbow* itself, through characters such as Tom Brangwen, Lydia, and Ursula, and then later, with further discrimination—an awareness of the dehumanized fatalism in the "impersonal," as distinct from its religious singularity—when he portrays Gerald Crich in *Women in Love*. Marinetti's materialism, which Lawrence had earlier quarreled with, even as he took from it an image, is now seen through American literature (especially via Lawrence's reading of Poe's *Tales* and *Moby Dick*) in all its deadly implication. So at the end of *Women in Love*, Crich in the Tyrolean heights moves ever faster towards his fate, like an essentialized figure of futuristic mechanics, outsoaring all "in an intensity of speed and white light that surpassed life itself . . . whirling along one perfect line of force."[16]

Ursula Brangwen in the novel turns away from such mountaintop cold and speed—back to a ground and growth implied in the "patient wintry vegetation"[17] of Italy. But if she descends, as it were, from the icy boundary between self and nonhuman where extreme impersonality has met its end, Lawrence does not abandon his interest in that frontier of invigoration. The Dana of *Two Years Before the Mast,* as described by Lawrence in *Studies in Classic American Literature* (1923), has been purged of his sentimental idealism by the rigors of a voyage through "sleet and black ice-rain, a sea of ice and iron-like water."[18] He is almost like Melville, "a futurist long before futurism found paint";[19] and, although Lawrence no more applauds American "iron" materialism than he does Marinetti's (so that Melville is judged almost dead in his "human-emotional" self, but "spell-bound by the strange slidings and collidings of Matter"[20]), he finds an honesty in Dana's "dispassionate statement of plain material facts."[21] It is the chastening objectivity through a voyage, with its antiromantic discipline, that Tomlinson, one remembers, found in Stevens's *The Comedian as the Letter* C and—with reservations akin to those of Lawrence about Dana's emotional numbness—in *The Snow Man*. For both Englishmen, indeed, a journey to the frontier where self meets elemental fact does not imply a necessary deadening of responses, but rather a cleansed alertness of feeling. In Lawrence's story, "The Captain's Doll" (written 1921), it is significantly a man of the Borders, Captain Hepburn, the Scottish soldier, who climbs to a glacier in the Tyrol and a new borderline of realization—leaving behind his wife's smothering domination of him by love and walking upon the "naked translucent ice" in a kind of purgative struggle: "The wonder, the terror, and the bitterness of it."[22] But that, for him, is a vital ascent and clarification—the winning of a resistant yet unbrutalized self—from which he returns to groundlevel.

It is a long way down from the ice field to the captain's new relation with Hannele and the contest of opposites that, Lawrence suggests, will be the conditions of any peace that they hold between them. The contest will also go on with the world outside the self: not a glacier but the farmland in Africa that Hepburn will struggle to cultivate. Yet such descent to earth after cold heights and "marriage" with a ground through contraries is, in his individual way, very much Tomlinson's predilection as a poet. So, in *The Glacier* (1984), he walks a cold, upper world of slate : "blackened razors" where feet and mind are carefully tutored for descent. One comes back from edges and monochrome to color, flow, and tillable earth more sharply seen, as "moraines staining the torrents brown" lead back to "soil which fructifies / In the plains a wide and level shore." There has been an implicit moral tempering in the walking of an upland, the way by which the self is taught to pace out a lower terrain, balancing between a sense of the life and death, growth and detritus that shape it. But in *The Snow Fences* (1966) such ground is the result of a hard-won and perpetually endangered balance, for northern English farmers must struggle to maintain a definable earth against the force of the elements. Since Saxon times in "these airy and woodless spaces" of the hill country, they "froze here before they fed / the unsuperseded burial ground." But what will *not* be buried in them or us—the muscular resilience coming awake at the border of human with nonhuman—is the poem's discovery:

> They are fencing the upland against
> the drifts this wind, those clouds
> would bury it under: brow and bone
> know already that levelling zero
> as you go, an aching skeleton,
> in the breathtaking rareness of winter air.
>
> Walking here, what do you see?
> Little more, through wind-teased eyes,
> than a black, iron tree
> and, there, another, a struggle
> of low and broken wall between, grass
> sapped of its greenness, day going.

We ("you"), as walkers of the cold upland, as readers of a visually bleakened text, have a pared-down yet irreducible presence that partners the anonymous "They"—those who, minus self-assertion (yet tenaciously "*They*" versus "this," "those," or "that") match the impersonality of "this wind, those clouds . . . that levelling zero." Such tightly massing forces (word crushing on word: "the drifts this wind, those clouds") would level the human to the merely fleshless and skeletal, would flatten us to frozen sameness where "brow and bone / know already that levelling zero / as you go." But, in the movement of the poem towards a church and burial ground, "you" can discover the blood and flesh—the animal in the human—which has not been erased. It is a clue to a regainable physical identity, that which, in sinewy stride, brings "you" down from winter heights and "aching skeleton," to walk, with newly flexed "joint and tendon," a ground of burials and resurgence. Here "you" of the quickened present belong, in understanding, to "they" who resist across centuries:

> Between the graves, you find
> a beheaded pigeon, the blood and grain

> trailed from its bitten crop, as alien to all
> the day's pallor as the raw
> wounds of the earth, turned above
> a fresh solitary burial.
>
> A plaque of staining metal
> distinguishes this grave among
> an anonymity whose stones
> the frosts have scaled, thrusting under
> as if they grudged the ground
> its ill-kept memorials.
>
> The bitter darkness drives you
> back valleywards, and again you bend
> joint and tendon to encounter
> the wind's force and leave behind
> the nameless stones, the snow-shrouds
> of a waste season: they are fencing
> the upland against those years, those clouds.

One thinks of another coming to earth after ascent in Tomlinson's *For Miriam* (1981). There also "mind and muscle / Learned to dance their balancings" as the poet climbs through snow to the "high village" of the dead woman preacher. Consciousness physically rises through a ground without transcending it, for here a "pagan" poet's yearning for resurrection in nature's secular sense meets Miriam's unorthodox Christianity and its promise of everlasting life. Moreover, the ground of realization descended into at the poem's end (where summer's heat is poised against wintry memory; where destruction and renewal quiver together) is grasped with an animal keenness not shown so extensively in poems like *The Snow Fences* or *How Still the Hawk*. The hawks who hover as predators throughout *For Miriam* now move from the periphery of human consciousness to the center, as "My body measures the ground beneath me / Warm in this beech-foot shade." It is here, as the poet remembers Miriam's "eagerness and anger," that

> The hawks come circling unappeasably. Their clangor
> Seems like the energy of loss. It is hunger.
>   It pierces and pieces together, a single note,
> The territories they come floating over now:
>   The escarpment, the foreshore and the sea;
> The year that has been, the year to be;
>   Leaf on leaf, a century's increment
> That has quickened and weathered, withered on the tree
>   Down into this brown circle where the shadows thicken.

Human "anger," rhyming with animal "clangor," then piercing further in animal-human realization—"It is hunger"—breaks open, yet brings into a whole, one's sense of nature's destructions and renewals: the zest for a fullness that comes out of the empty, the "single note" that speaks for a plurality of terrain in escarpment, foreshore, and sea. More lies inside this "brown circle" of weathered-withered pulsing than in the "circle / Of magnetic fear" that tightens in Tomlinson's previous hawk poem. Yet an agile poetic decorum continues. Human awareness neighbors the animal: a close pairing that deftly avoids a mingling.

It also suggests a standard by which one comes back to Lawrence with particular appreciation. For in the best of his *Birds, Beasts, and Flowers* collection (mainly the European poems written in Italy or Germany from 1920 to 1921 and a few of the poems written in America, 1922–23), he creates a decorum of alacrity—a verse-line and tone that have been modified by, made conspicuously adaptive to, the animal otherness he celebrates. It is a fitting of form to strange fact that recalls Williams, the admirer of both Lawrence and Tomlinson. But ultimately it is Tomlinson's verse—balancing against, not overwhelmed by the world's sensuous density—that is the clearest guide to Lawrence's progress as a poet.

III

The 1914 poem, *Song of a Man Who has Come Through,* is an instance of what Lawrence developed *from*:

> Not I, not I, but the wind that blows through me!
> A fine wind is blowing the new direction of Time.
> If only I let it bear me, carry me, if only it carry me!
> If only I am sensitive, subtle, oh, delicate, a winged gift!
> If only, most lovely of all, I yield myself and am borrowed
> By the fine, fine wind that takes its course through the chaos of the
>   world
> Like a fine, an exquisite chisel, a wedge-blade inserted;
> If only I am keen and hard like the sheer tip of a wedge
> Driven by invisible blows,
> The rock will split, we shall come at the wonder, we shall find the
>   Hesperides.

Instinctively he is right. He does need a hard, keen "wedge-blade"— not to find the Hesperides, but to cut through redundancies of word and style. He needs a toughness to set against the poem's elastic linger-ings and joyous eternality. Then it might more genuinely be set, in moment-by-moment unfolding, upon a "new direction of Time"; and all the energy now diffused by the soaring and lapsing verse-line could find its voice and proper ground. But one is only on the threshold of possibility at the poem's end when "three strange angels" knock for admittance.

When, however, Lawrence began to write poems again in 1920 after a gap of two years, it is the "wedge-blade" sharpness of his subjects that significantly engage him. *The Mosquito* and *Humming-Bird* (written May and June 1920 respectively, according to Keith Sagar[23]) mark the start of his new kind of verse. *Humming-Bird* especially (if one follows Sagar and does not place it in the later New Mexican period where other editors implicitly locate it[24]) is the initial key poem of *Birds, Beasts, and Flowers*. In it Lawrence shows his ability to use Whitman's verse-line with an alertness to its factuality not shown earlier when he employed Whitmanian rhetoric—to challenge its egotism—in a 1917 poem, *New Heaven and Earth*:

When I gathered flowers, I knew it was myself plucking my own flowering.
When I went in a train, I knew it was myself travelling by my own invention.
When I heard the cannon of the war, I listened with my own ears to my own destruction.

But *Humming-Bird* reveals the change of attitude that has come about since Lawrence began to write the several versions of his American Studies. Whitman there is now the poet who, for all his bombast, can allow the separate being of others to exist—notably at the borderline of self with elemental world that Lawrence sees in *Out of the Cradle Endlessly Rocking* ("on the edge of the great sea, in the night"[25]) and to which he more generally pays tribute when he acknowledges Whitman's "wide, strange camp . . . on the edge of a great precipice."[26]

It is the frontier sense of beings that are separate yet in relation that he notes in the account by Hector St. John Crèvecoeur (*Letters from an American Farmer*) of feeding quails in the snow: "over the mysterious, dark gulf reaches his tenderness and the wild confidence of the quails, leaving their two natures uncommingled, yet strangely in contact."[27] Yet it is the "uncommingled" distinctness of the humming-bird (with eyes "like diamonds,"[28] as Crèvecoeur describes it) that specifically attracts Lawrence—both in his revised Crèvecoeur essay of 1920 (when he remarks on "a curiously sharp, hard bit of realisation . . . a jewel-sharpness . . . inherent in the little soul of the creature"[29]) and his poem of the same year. Four years later, in *An Octopus,* Moore was to write of the goat as a "scintillating fragment" broken off American rock where bears live in caves of gems, crystal, and quartz. But for Lawrence the breaking-off is from a past—into the present's "curiously sharp, hard bit of realisation":

> I can imagine, in some otherworld
> Primeval-dumb, far back
> In that most awful stillness, that only gasped and hummed,
> Humming-birds raced down the avenues.
>
> Before anything had a soul,
> While life was a heave of Matter, half inanimate,
> This little bit chipped off in brilliance
> And went whizzing through the slow, vast, succulent stems.
>
> I believe there were no flowers then,
> In the world where the humming-bird flashed ahead of creation.
> I believe he pierced the slow vegetable veins with his long beak.
>
> Probably he was big
> As mosses, and little lizards, they say, were once big.
> Probably he was a jabbing, terrifying monster.
>
> We look at him through the wrong end of the long telescope of Time,
> Luckily for us.

Clear focus—"Luckily for us"—comes sharp, poised, and wryly teasing, out of the penultimate line's "telescope" distance. So also, in the first stanza, Lawrence extracts from the inarticulate, prehistoric blur that he mimics with his distancing *that*'s ("that most awful stillness, that only gasped and hummed") a sudden close-up speech—the vividness that comes out of murmured hum and audibly lets fly "*Humming*-birds." Without soaring, they wing "down the avenues" of a rooted world—both the bird as a separate utterance out of the mass and language itself broken into finite, singular pieces. It is fragmentation that not only looks toward a similar poetic practice by Williams and Tomlinson, but seems here to enact a splitting away from the "heave of Matter, half inanimate." Thus the dull *i*'s of that last word yield in the next line to the audibly bright distinctness of their counterparts, as "This little bit chipped off in brilliance / And went whizzing." Yet, for all the speed, there is time and space for a cooler tempo, a meditation, as the reader moves through sensuous thickness and as Lawrence muses, "I believe he pierced the slow vegetable veins with his long beak." Penetrative instinct goes with reasoned detachment to make a flexible voice—semi-amused, semiserious—that can imagine a "jabbing, terrifying monster" yet hold the bird in one's mind, here, now, as a creature of sharp-billed presentness. For the humming-bird is not to be limited by a retrospective view or "telescope" diminutions, just as in bygone ages it "flashed ahead of creation."

"Invincible fore-runner," one might say, using Lawrence's praise of the baby tortoise in the poem of that name (September 1920), for here also, but with more tender humor, Lawrence addresses a small thing that can take the weight of physical immensity—a "tiny shell-bird" keeping balance and undauntedly moving forward under a "huge vast inanimate" universe; "pitching through immemorial ages / Your little round house in the midst of chaos." The continuity and equilibrium are important: a perception by Lawrence of how one might make "house" in and not be submerged by the nature of which one is part. Tomlinson takes the principle further when contemplating a "profusion of possibilities" in sun, cloud, and water (*Northern Spring*, 1960). Against "variegated excess," he conceives placing a counterpoise: "a square house / Washed in the coolness of lime." Later (*Poem*, 1981), he enacts the regaining of the balance he has nearly lost in the interchange between self and world. Nature's pourings overflow the consciousness. But, at a crucial moment,

> a bird's veering
> into sudden sun
> finds me for a pen
>
> a feather on grass,
> a blade tempered newly

"Tempered", indeed—human awareness is both moderated and freshly steeled, enough at least to hold back the overflow, and with new, fine-tipped clarity write out nature's unconscious "script." Balancing against such a textuality is hardly, one might think, Lawrence's interest. Yet the movement of the verse-line in *Snake* (July 1920) indicates otherwise, for here the watcher of the snake, and the reader, must suffer the unrelieved burdening of mind by a nonmental heaviness—the creature drinking at the water trough, making man wait out time's process, and gradually storing up the force of human reaction:

> And looked around like a god, unseeing, into the air,
> And slowly turned his head,
> And slowly, very slowly, as if thrice adream,

> Proceeded to draw his slow length curving round
> And climb again the broken bank of my wall-face.

The trancelike compulsion of the *And*'s is part of a seamless, unhurried ceremony: line joined to line in a wondrous, terrible serpentine continuity, and all provoking the break-up ("A sort of horror, a sort of protest") when, in revulsion at the snake's "withdrawing into that horrid black hole," human consciousness splits off. Lawrence's verseline must also enact the holding back from hypnotic immersion. There has to be an awkward, if remorseful, balancing out again—a grasping at a world of separate concrete things:

> I looked round, I put down my pitcher,
> I picked up a clumsy log
> And threw it at the water-trough with a clatter.
>
> I think it did not hit him

What he must expiate, after immediate regret and final cherishing of the kingly snake, is

> A pettiness

—its paltry nature isolated by the line. For the moment, the gulf between man and snake is not to be crossed. Yet the space opened up, when syntactic smallness counterweights sensuous length, is to remain important for Lawrence's verse.

It shows how remarkably he adapted for his own purposes the kind of balance that Whitman could offer—not as the bard of democratic love who must inflate himself in *A Song for Occupations* so that he may encompass multitudinous facts ("House-building, measuring, sawing the boards, / Blacksmithing, glass-blowing, nail-making, coopering, tin-roofing . . . "), but as the poet who matches to the varying world with a steadiness—with that figuring of a calm Gurney admired. *Song of the Open Road,* one remembers ("To see nothing anywhere, but what you may reach it and pass it, / To conceive no time . . . but what you may reach it and pass it") need not encourage a grandiose poetry in others but Gurney's infinitive-relished moments: "to sit still and sip with all–appreciative lip." But Lawrence, admiring the unexaggerated Whitman of *Sea Drift* as he stands alone on the great edge of existence, is encouraged by the American's phrasing not to celebrate distinct moments, but rather the isolate thing or animal. So, in *Fish* (August 1921), he may use Whitmanian length to suggest the creature's apparently merged and drowsing life:

5: Contraries and Relations   171

> To sink, and rise, and go to sleep with the waters;
> To speak endless inaudible wavelets into the wave;

But the "To" form, like the fish itself, is also innately wakeful inside that sleep. As with *Humming-Bird,* a spry brevity waits to dart out:

> To have the element under one, like a lover;
> And to spring away with a curvetting click in the air,
> Provocative.

Set in space, poised with danger, "Provocative" suggests how much Lawrence has taught himself as a poet by making the single word or syllable the springy basis of his line. Tomlinson, of course, is to find his way there with the help of a different American example. Yet, whatever the stimulus—Williams or Whitman—each Englishman discovers the means by which the singled-out verbal fragment can be alone on the page's blankness yet also part of a collective whole:

> To be a fish!
>
> So utterly without misgiving
> To be a fish
> In the waters.
>
> Loveless, and so lively!
> Born before God was love,
> Or life knew loving.
> Beautifully beforehand with it all.
>
> Admitted, they swarm in companies,
> Fishes.
> They drive in shoals.
> But soundless, and out of contact.
> They exchange no word, no spasm, not even anger.
> Not one touch.
> Many suspended together, forever apart,
> Each one alone with the waters, upon one wave with the rest.

So also swarm the one and the many in Tomlinson's *Sea Poem,* with its Williams-like flotation:

>   each
>   shift
>   with its separate whisper, each whisper
>   a breath of that singleness

> that "moves together
> if it moves at all"

Chaste, cool statement in Lawrence's verse-line—"Not one touch"—demonstrates the stylistic sureness with which the isolated fish and shoal hover in relation. One line, sociable and conceding ("Admitted, they swarm in companies") is followed by the next where "Fishes" linger in detachment—the communal and solitary "suspended together" in apposition. They are also, by a precise delight, "Beautifully beforehand"; the adverb measuring to its adjective, as word to wordless creature who, like the humming-bird, was ahead of creation in the past, is beyond one now, yet remains utterable.

American objectivity brings Lawrence here, but not his quarrel with a mechanistic America—"the iron click of your human contact" that he fears, for example, in *The Evening Land* (May 1921). In *Turkey-Cock*, the bird at Fiesole is said to have the hard metal of a "raw American will," its wattles "the colour of steel-slag which has been red hot." Yet in the same month as *Turkey-Cock* (September 1920), and in the same Italian town, Lawrence writes *Cypresses* with an implicitly different sense of American fact and surface. Then a more cautious attentiveness comes into play:

> Tuscan cypresses,
> What is it?

Arrested, as it were, by something unsaid just before the poem begins (and by a culture that has lost its voice long before that), Lawrence's speech is disciplined from the start by tact and surmise:

> Tuscan cypresses,
> What is it?
>
> Folded in like a dark thought
> For which the language is lost,
> Tuscan cypresses,
> Is there a great secret?
> Are our words no good?
>
> The undeliverable secret,
> Dead with a dead race and a dead speech, and yet
> Darkly monumental in you,
> Etruscan cypresses.

"Tuscan" widens to "Etruscan," but Lawrence has found the anchoring centre of gravity in "Etruscan cypresses," which ensures that the long verse-line risking overextension, excess verbalizing of silence ("Dead with a dead race and a dead speech, and . . .") can aurally be brought back within bounds. Treelike, the poem's branching out—the "wavering" play of speculative idea—defines the quiet axis on which all turns. Without a verbal overstretch, "Darkly monumental" is held by such a centering. It is also why "Dark" in the next two lines—

> Ah, how I admire your fidelity,
> Dark cypresses!

—avoids loose glamor and fits its noun with flickering exactness. The slim, flame-shaped trees, swaying on a pivot, and as reticent as a people's lost speech, have their own Lawrentian fidelity of style in representation: one that will not be seen again in English verse until Tomlinson's *Cézanne at Aix* and other *Seeing is Believing* poems. Recovery of a verbal discretion in front of wordless nature, after neoromantic excess, is to be Tomlinson's concern; but as Lawrence's adjectivally full lines wheel about their rooted center in *Cypresses,* he is discreet in his own way:

> Is it the secret of the long-nosed Etruscans?
> The long-nosed, sensitive-footed, subtly-smiling Etruscans,
> Who made so little noise outside the cypress groves?
>
> Among the sinuous, flame-tall cypresses
> That swayed their length of darkness all around
> Etruscan-dusky, wavering men of old Etruria:
>
> Naked except for fanciful long shoes,
> Going with insidious, half-smiling quietness
> And some of Africa's imperturbable sang-froid
> About a forgotten business.

The wit that confines the long-shoed, "long-nosed" Etruscans—of the tomb paintings and pottery—inside the "sinuous" cypress shapes, also controls the daring length of line that imagines an "insidious, half-smiling quietness / And some of Africa's imperturbable sang-froid." What risks being a garrulous mouthful is actually a precise verbal measure that keeps poise with the Etruscans' lean, unnoisy sureness of movement, going their own idiosyncratic way, just as the sentence, with its own "sang-froid" oddness and adjectival surprise, takes its confidently nonchalant course. "Insidious" is a reminder of the "vicious" and "evil" charges against the Etruscans by their Roman conquerors, which Lawrence rebuts at the poem's end. Here, materialist America has a share of the blame: "There is only one evil, to deny life / As Rome denied Etruria / And mechanical America Montezuma still." But this is an aberrant conclusion for a poem that, by staying within the confines of the cypress groves, has allowed a range of voice to become audible—a propriety of modern speech for one that has been lost.

Cypresses is one of Lawrence's first works to show admiration for the people he was to celebrate at greater length in *Etruscan Places* (written 1927). Tarquinia's painted tombs show him, for example, the "wonderfully suggestive *edge* of the figures":[30] all belonging to a world where "each thing had a clear outline, visually, but in its very clarity was related emotionally or vitally to strange other things, one thing springing from another."[31] Again one sees his interest in the related yet "uncommingled." This time, however, the Mediterranean, animistic setting is shared with Pound who speaks, in his essay on Cavalcanti (1934) of "the radiant world where one thought cuts through another with clean edge, a world of moving energies ... magnetisms that take form."[32]

Tomlinson's affinity is also evident, since he has used Pound's words on several occasions to articulate his own delight in the rediscovery of such energies. The poems show the same intentness: as in *Tarquinia* (1972), where Tomlinson observes how "The eyes of the winged horses / That rode on the citadel are still keen / With the intelligence of a lost art." With *Swimming Chenango Lake* (1969), far from Etruscan places but close to an aboriginal America near Cooperstown, there is a "lost language" that the swimmer "begins to construe." Yet it is Lawrence's sense of a "wonderfully suggestive *edge*" to things—the hard distinctness yet interrelation—that, more than Pound's vision, is awake in such a poem. Here, however, the interrelation takes the form of a metamorphic shimmer, the "angles and elongations" that, by watery illusion, spread out from objects' reflections on the surface of a lake. Things on land retain their finiteness. Yet in the autumnal water of Chenango

>   every tree
> Appears a cypress as it stretches there
>   And every bush that shows the season,
> A shaft of fire. It is a geometry and not
>   A fantasia of distorting forms, but each
> Liquid variation answerable to the theme
>   It makes away from, plays before:
> It is a consistency, the grain of the pulsating flow.

5: Contraries and Relations 175

The observer visually, like the swimmer physically, enters that changeful flux, but still retains an unsubmerged awareness: what Lawrence calls the human soul's "wide-eyed responsibility / In life" (*Man and Bat*, September 1921). As with the climbers of other Tomlinson poems, one remains an alert reader of text and texture: seeing the difference between thing and image, swimmer and cold element, as the basis for moral distinctions on the move. Thus the swimmer takes "hold / On water's meaning . . . to be, between grasp and grasping, free." The last word, indeed, has a swimmer's grip—neither drowningly possessed, nor an egotistic possession. The self is not anarchically doing what it likes and has kinship with Lawrence's idea of freedom in the American *Studies*, when one is bound by place and obedient to the "IT," the "deepest self."[33] To reach it, says Lawrence, "takes some diving." But Tomlinson's swimmer locates that special freedom upon the surface:

> He reaches in-and-through to that space
> The body is heir to, making a where
>   In water, a possession to be relinquished
> Willingly at each stroke. The image he has torn
>   Flows-to behind him, healing itself,
> Lifting and lengthening, splayed like the feathers
>   Down an immense wing whose darkening spread
> Shadows his solitariness: alone, he is unnamed
>   By this baptism, where only Chenango bears a name
> In a lost language he begins to construe—

Like "free" earlier, "Willingly" rides the line with special balance: neither willful in suggestion or timidly willing, but with an exact bold verve. Just as each tree radiates out a "cypress" image on the water, so also this self, free because of its defined bounds, is both solitary and, in a feathered, winged extension, part of the universe's wider animal being. Such nature has no voice but seeks it; thus the swimmer is also a kind of answerer to the element in which he moves, like the boy who hears the bird in Whitman's *Sea Drift* or the poet who must ask, "Tuscan cypresses, / What is it?" Therefore the swimmer "begins to construe" the water's

>   speech of densities and derisions, of half-
> Replies to the questions his body must frame
>   Frogwise across the all but penetrable element.
> Human, he fronts it and, human, he draws back
>   From the interior cold, the mercilessness
> That yet shows a kind of mercy sustaining him.

In this space of meaning defined by contraries, human awareness has swimmer's sinews: the working muscularity by which, at the poem's end, the self moves between constancy and flow in a nature where breakage becomes recreation and conclusion continuity:

> The last sun of the year is drying his skin
> Above a surface a mere mosaic of tiny shatterings,
>   Where a wind is unscaping all images in the flowing obsidian,
> The going-elsewhere of ripples incessantly shaping.

IV

In *The Poem as Initiation* (1967) Tomlinson speaks of *Swimming Chenango Lake* in terms that link it with the Hopi initiation ceremony. In this rite an Indian child's coming of age is ritually celebrated by clansmen wearing masks and impersonating tribal spirits. Just as the Hopi adults remove their disguise at the end of the ceremony and show the child a kinship he rejoins on fresh terms, so for Tomlinson the poem is a guise, a surface, that, having engaged the consciousness in its own ceremony, can then be set aside to reveal the actual world one is heir to. As Tomlinson says of *Swimming Chenango Lake*, "the naked reality, the spreading, pulsating water takes over from the swimmer, the mask of the poem (so to speak) is being put by, and the elusive reality of the lake, or of life, is admitted back into its own."[34]

Tomlinson also speaks of the Pawnee ceremony for crossing water: the moment-by-moment pausing over the separate stages of an action that shows an aboriginal reverence for time and space. It leads to other Tomlinson poems in which ceremony unmasks a reality, and also to Lawrence again. By this one does not mean the willed artistry of *The Plumed Serpent*—not the insistent drums and Huizipochtli ceremonies of Lawrence's devizing, but his description of an actual event, the Navajo Dance of the Sprouting Corn, in *Mornings in Mexico* (1927). This particular narrative (written in April 1924) is preceded in the book by his account of Indian animism. In such instinctive sense of existence, he says, no god of spirit looks down on a world of separate matter, for god is in everything, with all creatures sharing the same pulse of creation, though in different ways; the yell of the mountain lion is distinct from the breeze in the aspen trees. In Lawrence's Corn Dance chapter, the awareness of distinctions, through the ceremony's disciplining of his narrative, takes the overt form of a piece-by-piece realization. Indian artifice is a means to an artless entirety; in shadowing it closely with his prose, Lawrence touches again (as with the stook-gathering scene between Will and Anna in *The Rainbow*) the process by which man and woman reconstruct, in acknowledged separate phases, a sense of whole relation. Therefore pieces of perception build gradually into something larger across several pages in the Corn Dance chapter. First, as the car moves from the desert towards the pueblo, "You realize that you had heard the drum from the distance." Then, coming nearer, "You realize" the line of dancers, the singers, and the jester-figures called the Koshare. After that, as the eye takes in the women dancers, and then the men ("down, down, down, down, in the downward plunge of the dance") the agile Koshare are seen—catching a word from the singers that refers to a thing of the sky and miming its connection with the earth. So also when "they catch a word that means earth . . . the hands flutter softly down, and draw up the water, draw up the earth-quickening, earth to sky, sky to earth . . . to meet in the germ-quick of corn, where life is."[35]

Moment by moment also, in a similar narrative enactment, Tomlinson presents the Indian dancers of his New Mexican poem, *Cochiti* (1981) as they bring earth to sky and sky to earth. Here, by ceremony, they extend what has been shared increasingly between man and bird in *How Still the Hawk* and *For Miriam,* and by the winged swimmer of the Chenango poem. Now, though, by Tomlinson's deliberate syntactic ambiguity, the dancers seem almost to be entering the bird's element—only to reveal, through their cries of the air (and the poem's aeration of mass into separate parts) a world breathed open:

> The cries
> of the eagle
> dancers at Cochiti
> rise to such a
> complete complicity
> with the way it is
> when eagles
> speak what they have to say
> that the sky
> brings down
> over thinning snow
> unfurling the black
> line of wings
> slackening then
> tautening them back
> to take the thrust
> of the wind and mount it
> to wander away

> above the pocked snow-whitenesses
> of plain hills mesas
> an eagle

Tomlinson long ago saw in Rosenberg's *Moses* the poetic possibilities of "syntactic entanglement," where human consciousness can appear possessed by the energy of an animal, yet not forsake its meditative reason: "Startlingly, / As a mountain side / Wakes aware of its other side, / When from a cave a leopard comes . . . Sprang an intelligence." Now one has the nimbler entanglement of human with nonhuman: the syllabic close match of rhyme, by men of Cóchiti in "complete complicity," with nature's being ("it is")—then the apparent fusion, by extended sentence, adjectives, and participles ("thinning . . . unfurling . . . slackening . . . tautening"), which seems to make eagle and men indistinguishable. It is an ambiguity, "unfurling the black / line of wings," in a bird-human suspense, which Tomlinson prolongs—not to lose human identity in the eagle, but to maintain the sense of animistic energy shared by dancers with bird—even when, in the last lines, the creature more obviously flies separate:

> to wander away
> above the pocked snow-whitenesses
> of plain hills mesas
> an eagle

After the absence of formal punctuation and the mingling participles, the use of "to" ("to take the thrust . . . to wander away") separates out the "pocked," contoured plurality of a land. The commaless "plain hills mesas" that might have seemed an undifferentiated block, now require (after the syllabic breakage of "snow-white-ness-es") punctuation of their differences. One must pause over a world's manifold parts that have been made distinct by a single bird, and that is, like the dancers, articulated: "an eagle."

In the ceremony of such a poem, the sky and land pulse together with the hovering energy seen in Tomlinson's *High Summer* (1984). There a pair of buzzards who are teaching their young one "The fields of prey" that lie below it, are "two / High Aztec messengers of the sun / Telling over and over the sources of blood." Their "telling over" in cries is not just a reckoning up of victims, but also a birdlike narration of the forces that connect flesh and blood to air, ground to sky. The buzzards are part of an interplay that Lawrence's poem, *Eagle in New Mexico* (October 1922) presents only in narrow terms. Writing on American ground and battling against the deathly presences that he feels there, Lawrence challenges the unappeased cruelty of the eagle who picks the heart from a rabbit or bird: "Do you lift it to the sun, as the Aztec priests used to lift red hearts of men?" But, less defensively, there is elsewhere the voice of another Lawrence: the patient observer of the dances in *Mornings in Mexico* who can say of the moments before the Hopi Antelope Dance, "We stand and wait on a house-roof . . . We wait without event."³⁶ On similar stillness Tomlinson bases an entire poem, *Before the Dance* (1969):

> the waiting
> for the Indian
> is half the dance,
> and so they wait
> giving a quality
> to the moment
> by their refusal
> to measure it.

Here, at Zuni, human confines open out into the world's vast currents, yet a sense of limit and locality remains clear. As before in both Lawrence's and Tomlinson's perception, the impersonal energies of the infinite are entered only by respect for an earthbound finiteness, here and now:

> the moment
> is expansible
> it burns
> unconsumed
> under the raw bulbs
> of the dancing chamber:
> the Navajo faces
> wear
> the aridity of the landscape
> and 'the movement
> with the wind
> of the Orient and
> the movement against
> the wind
> of the Occident'
> meet
> in their wrinkles:
> they wait, sitting
> (the moment)
> on the earth floor
> (is expansible)
> saying very little

> or sleep
> like the woman
> slipping along the wall
> sideways
> to wake
> in the clangour of the pulse of time
> at the beginning
> drum....

The final surprise, after so much restraint, is also an inevitability. For the predance wait is a slow tuning in to origins, beginnings, and powers. It is the gradual matching-up of consciousness to outer universe that one experiences as a reader of the poem by adjusting to the "mask" it wears. For in fitting oneself to the text's disciplining surface and variable line length (now suggesting the "expansible," now holding imagination inside the bounds of the dancing chamber), one is also observing a fidelity to the wrinkled Navajo faces—weathered against overexcitement, yet supple enough to countenance a larger, dynamic world. Thus the "mask" of the text can also bend without losing firmness:

> they wait, sitting
> (the moment)
> on the earth floor
> (is expansible)

Still Indian figures in space, poised upon "expansible" time: it is a crisscross suspense in a poem where Tomlinson quotes from John Cage's lecture *On Something* (1959), itself drawing on Buckminster Fuller's idea that "men leaving Asia to go to Europe went against the wind and developed machines, ideas, and Occidental philosophies in accord with a struggle against nature," while, "on the other hand, men leaving Asia to go to America went with the wind, put up a sail and developed ideas and Oriental philosophies in accord with the acceptance of nature. These two tendencies met in America, producing a movement into the air, not bound to the past, traditions, or whatever."[37] When Cage adapts the notion for his lecture, it is space, Zen, and transcendence that come to the fore:

> the movement   with the   wind of the Orient   and the movement
> against   the wind of the Occident   meet   in America and
> produce   a movement   upwards   into the air—the
> space, the silence, the nothing that supports us   .[38]

5: Contraries and Relations 181

One might equally remember Whitman's address to an America defined between east and west in *A Broadway Pageant*: "You shall sit in the middle well-poised thousands of years." But for Tomlinson, contrary impulses locate more tightly a sense of place between them. The wind of human struggle with a land and the wind of men's movement with it

>   meet
>   in their wrinkles:

Earthbound, the Navajo poise is no traditionless vacuity or airy nothing.

Seated on their "earth floor," these inhabitants of New Mexico are not so far, in geography or grounded reality, from those of an older Mexico whom Tomlinson first depicted in verse in the 1960s. He observed a people whose civility is untranscendental. One can exist in a land without religiously or politically trying to domineer and soar. A character in Lawrence's *The Plumed Serpent* also understands the need to be grounded: "Mexico pulls you down, the people pull you down like a great weight! But it may be they pull you down as the earth's pull of gravitation does, that you can balance on your feet . . . . It may be you need to be drawn down, down, till you send roots into the deep places again. Then you can send up the sap and the leaves back to the sky, later."[39]

Listening down the shaft of water in *The Well* (1966), Tomlinson finds that center of gravity on which depends the peace of a people—like the couples of Oaxaca who stroll a barrack square, or like the varied walkers of another square in the same town, with its "democracy / of the tierra templada" (*The Plaza*, 1989). Against such comity, the vehemence of the past looks stranded and isolated, both in the revolutionary slogan at the end of *The Well* and in the boast of the busdriver, Lukenbac, written up in Gothic script and to be translated as "I flew for the Fuehrer" (*On the Tlacolula Bus*, 1966). Like his political creed, the words of the German exile now seem as fixed and abandonable as the goat on a string that the bus leaves behind when it swings out of the market square. For that willful past is outgone (along with Lukenbac's subservience) now that "today" the bus is not driven by the German but, in cheery mastery, by "a Mexican with the brown / face of a Mayan." The onward life he embodies has the kind of Mexican presentness that, in a different poem, *At Trotsky's House* (1984), makes the fortified home of another ideological European seem equally caught in its past. Hardened against life's flow, the Trotsky vision—before the murder and after—seems now as static as the dried ink in the dead man's study and the ashes waiting their return to a long-gone Russia, "kremlined forever in historic snow."

Yet if Mexico in Tomlinson's poetry is a land that civilly outlasts foreign dogmas, invasions, and violence, he is also presenting an account that differs from Lawrence's only in its emphasis on community, not in its sense of anomaly. Lawrence sees historical incongruity: the mismatch of European Catholicism or "white" spiritual consciousness imposed on Mexico at the conquest. In the postrevolutionary Mexico of the 1920s, he also regards socialism as failing to meet the inner needs of the people. Tomlinson similarly portrays discrepancy between the religio-political dimension of the country and its living actuality; but he is closest to Lawrence in his understanding of the consequences suffered by the body after the spirit's utopian or resurrection flight. Thus in *Constitution Day* (1966), there is high political exaltation—a group of well-dressed Mexicans on a platform, "perched there beyond the doom / of the ragged rest," while, "Ablaze / in his laundered white," an adolescent recites a poem on Mexico's political saints: "*Juarez, Madero, Cárdenas* / the names go by / like faces in a fresco / just as Diego / would have painted them." Yet the higher the "white" flight, the worse the physical ruin—the "doom" endured in time's consequences, as the poem remembers "God's desolate mother, Eisenstein / dead of a weakened heart / and Stalin rifled from his tomb."

The contrast is harsher, however, between painted spiritual flight and the temporal body's suffering of the cost, in another 1966 poem, *Weeper in Jalisco*. Here, contemplating a frieze of saints, "hacked, mauled, bound" and bleeding, in a Tlacolula chapel "under the gloom of the central / dome of gold," Tomlinson observes not just the body martyred so that the spirit can fly, but also, in the Christian era that follows, the degradation of earthly time, with "a blood- / bought early resurrection / leaving us this / tableau of wounds." The woman in the chapel, wailing to the saints, is therefore like the perpetually wounded aftermath, or constant epilogue of weakness, to which the temporal and the carnal have been reduced:

> she is the voice
> those wounds cry through
> unappeasably bleeding where
> her prone back shoulders
> the price and weight
> of forfeited paradise.

By contrast, the stoic beggars of *Los Pobrecitos* (1984), "a courteous race . . . gentle and cunning," outgo such finality and Fall. "Dogging the porches" of churches—sitting there as one goes in and as one goes out—"they are both prologue and epilogue / to each gold interior." However, for the full strength of Mexican continuity, alive in spirit *and* body, with no devaluing of secular existence, one must go to *The Tax Inspector* (1987). Written after Tomlinson's return to the chapel of hacked saints at the Tlacolula church, it counters the "forfeited paradise" of *Weeper in Jalisco* with celebration of a regainable whole in this world—the dance of companionable resurrection as a people bear up in communal onwardness the burden that the weeping woman once shouldered alone. At the church where the chapel is shut and the tax inspector's funeral service is officially over ("the event / was closed"), there is life after such endings:

> The organ
> whose punctuations
> had accompanied the rite
> broke into a waltz
> and the women
> rose and the *compañeros*
> *de trabajo* of the dead man
> shouldered the coffin forth
> to daylight. The waltz
> seemed right as did
> the deathmarch, the woe
> of the inconsolable brass
> preceding to the *campo santo*
> the corpse, the women
> and the *compañeros*
> who sweated from street to street
> under the bier,
> swaying it like a boat.
> And this was the way—
> a banner declaring
> what work he and his *compañeros*
> had once shared—
> the tax inspector,
> ferried across on human flesh,
> was borne to burial.

Death's "inconsolable" finality is not danced away. Rather, its closing-down is syllabically opened up by the poem's long o's—enacting the physical labor of those workmates, the *compañeros de trabajo*, who, after the organ "broke into a waltz" and the women "rose," "shouldered the coffin forth." Even "the woe / of the inconsolable brass" has its sturdy aeration as all enter the space (actual and syllabic) outside the church, the "*campo santo.*" So the dance goes on, with waltz balancing deathmarch and life's airy-vowelled breath playing against closure, as the bier sways like a "boat"—the long *o* coffined by the final consonant, but sailing onward in a Charon-like ferrying.

Nevertheless, Tomlinson celebrates here and elsewhere a mythless Mexico, freed from the weight of Aztec Gods, flesh-torturing Christianity, or the creation of new myth. There is no giving of wings, as Lawrence does symbolically in *The Plumed Serpent*, to the deathly snake that sensuous existence has become. Instead, with a sense of related contraries that he shares more profoundly with Lawrence, he touches again the terms of community he began to articulate long ago in *Poem of the Neighbours*. Moreover, death in Mexico—and life—lead him back from the Americas to Europe: to a clearer perception of the way that poetry, with its feeling for fluid possibility, can engage with the fixities of history.

6
Ends and Beginnings

> Every phrase and every sentence is an end and a beginning,
> Every poem an epitaph.
> T. S. Eliot

> Every poem is an attempt to reconcile history and poetry for the benefit of poetry.
> Octavio Paz

I

In the late 1960s and the following decade, Tomlinson wrote four major politico-historical poems. All of them—*Assassin* (1969), *Machiavelli in Exile* (1972), *Charlotte Corday* (1978), *For Danton* (1978)—draw from widely differing sources in Europe and the Americas, and in philosophy, poetry, and film; but all share a view of history that goes back to Tomlinson's literary relationship with Eliot—one that is combative in regard to the author of *Four Quartets,* yet more fruitful as regards the author of *The Waste Land* and "Tradition and the Individual Talent." It is this earlier Eliot who shows the presentness of the past. Furthermore, as Tomlinson makes clear in *Poetry and Metamorphosis* and his 1989 recorded reading of *The Waste Land,*[1] this Eliot is a poet of constant rearticulation, striving to deliver the human voice back to a larger music out of submersion in babel or silence, stone or desert, thunder or bird's cry. Whatever the aridities into which Eliot does fall in *The Waste Land,* he is not, one sees, the poet of *Four Quartets* who has lost belief in the efficacy of words and the value of the temporal. There the future is a "faded song," and "beginnings," as they emerge from "ends," must be perpetually swallowed by them and perpetually reemerge in the form of unstable paradox. So there are "endless" timeless moments, but no time and space continuity nor concreteness worth celebrating when

6: *Ends and Beginnings*

>   any action
> Is a step to the block, to the fire, down the sea's throat
> Or to an illegible stone:

For Tomlinson, however, a stone's potential *legibility* is a commanding interest, particularly when "stone" signifies the dense, varied substance of things in the world—the singular, opaque being that, grappled with, unclenches a way into the lit pluralities of time and space. So his view of the figures in his politico-historical poems who must suffer the fateful consequences of their actions or go to their executioner's "block," also involves his countersense of "beginnings": the fluid possibilities that still play against fate's congealments.

In this he is encouraged even further by his admiration for the poetry of Octavio Paz, which he first read on his initial visit to Paz's native Mexico in 1963. One sees in the older poet (born 1914) the kind of internationalist range that also attracted Tomlinson to the best of Eliot—that which in Paz draws on the art of India, on the poetry of medieval and baroque Spain, as well as from the French symbolists and surrealists and the English romantics. Paz's poetry and his view of poetry as a challenge to historical determinism (especially in the essay "Poetry and History," which Tomlinson included in his 1979 edition of Paz's *Selected Poems*) directs the Englishman even more vigorously towards an antifatalistic flexibility. Eliotic "endings" or the degradation of time into meaningless exercise can be seen as implicitly contested by Paz's essay where the poem is celebrated as "a Fiesta, a precipitate of pure time." "Every poem," he says, "is an attempt to reconcile history and poetry for the benefit of poetry." So a renovatory power is claimed for poetry, "a secret fertility" that is "ever returning to inaugurate a new period."[2]

Tomlinson does not necessarily endorse the Pazian flight into extravagance, where time's processes are overleaped too readily. But, more importantly, he does share Paz's affirmation of time's "beginnings" in a poem such as *Himno entre ruinas* (1948). Indeed, there Paz is joined by Williams in a qualifying of Eliot's surface aridity, because the poem, translated by Williams as *Hymn among the Ruins*, sets against a *Waste Land* of "unreal city" and temporal enervation ("New York, London, Moscow ... Now and then an anaemic sun shivers") a delight in time's firm fruits: "Day, round day, / shining orange with four-and-twenty bars." There is also the pleasure in being able "To see, to touch each day's lovely forms.... Midday, ear of wheat heavy with minutes, / eternity's brimming cup." The wheat image may brim more fully of Blakean vision and eternity than Tomlinson wants in his own poetry, yet he is already very close to

6: Ends and Beginnings

Paz's sense of growth in a *Seeing is Believing* poem, *Farewell to Van Gogh*, where he plants artistic sensibility back on the earth after the painter's apocalyptic flight:

> The world does not end tonight
> And the fruit that we shall pick tomorrow
> Await us, weighing the unstripped bough.

A poet who can turn meditative patience ("A*wait*) into a slowed-down concreteness ("*weigh*ing") is less close to Paz when the latter speaks too easily in a language of weightless lubricity. But Tomlinson has no demurral when he appreciates, as reader and translator, the Mexican's creation of a rippling space in poetry—the means by which the mind can dance out of, yet back to, solidity. In *Lo idéntico* (translated by Tomlinson as *One and the Same* from a 1962–68 collection), Paz portrays Webern's music in terms of surrealistic metamorphosis; yet Mexico's native rock crystal exists as mineral fact amidst change:

> Hanging
> From night's sheerness
> Black gardens of rock crystal
> Flowering along a bough of smoke
> White gardens that explode in air
> Spaces

"Spaces"; but for Tomlinson they seem like openings, inlets upon density, as with the actual gardens—not music's kind—which are remembered in Paz's poem, *Cuento de dos jardines* (or *A Tale of Two Gardens* from *Hacia el Comienzo* [or *Toward the Beginning*] of 1964–68). Indeed, these are grounds of beginning and relation: both the garden in Mexico that Paz knew as a child and the garden in India where he was married. As Tomlinson says in the introduction to the dialogue he recorded with Paz, one moves in his finest work "through a garden of words that flicker with the weather of the world, yet stay in place."[3]

When Paz's words do not stay in place, however, and he insists on seeking paradisal beginnings uprooted from circumstance, the vision loosens:

> we must dream backwards, toward the source, we must row back up the centuries,
> beyond infancy, beyond the beginning, beyond the waters of baptism,
> we must break down the walls between man and man, reunite what has been sundered,

> life and death are not opposite worlds, we are one stem with twin
>   flowers,
> we must find the lost word, dream inwardly and also outwardly

This is Paz in *El cántaro roto* (1955), translated by Lysander Kemp as *The Broken Waterjar*. But although Tomlinson, with his sense of contraries, is sceptical about a dream of oneness, it is the act of dreaming itself—the power to unclench the mind—that crucially affects his response in verse to these particular lines. Paz's yearning need not be a groundless fantasy if it touches a clean vitality of beginnings and brings the mind forward again to a fresh, onward present. In extravagance lies a dynamic for precision, which is why, very literally, the Spanish of *El cántaro roto* ("Hay que . . . soñar hacia dentro y también hacia afuera" [we must . . . dream inwardly and also outwardly]) is a "beginning" for Tomlinson when it forms the epigraph of the brief *Variation on Paz* (1972):

> We must dream inwards, and we must dream
>   Outwards too, until—the dream's ground
> Bound no longer by the dream—we feel
>   Behind us the sea's force, and the blind
> Keel strikes gravel, grinding
>   Towards a beach where, eye by eye,
> The incorruptible stones are our witnesses
>   And we wake to what is dream and what is real
> Judged by the sun and the impartial sky.

Out of a dream sea rises the clear, discriminating mind. But as it locks on grit-sharp concreteness ("gravel, grinding") and escapes from subjectivity into judgement (its own as well as nature's), one has a particularly solid instance of the way that Paz offers valuable provocation to Tomlinson in the writing of politico-historical poetry.

There had, of course, been earlier poems by Tomlinson that point in this direction. *Antecedents,* a suite of poems from *Seeing is Believing,* depicts nineteenth- and twentieth-century egos in their solitudes, yet signalling a more communal, verdurous ground. *Up at La Serra,* one remembers, shows the lone self of Paolo Bertolani opening out into a larger realization. But it is not until *Assassin* that the movement from isolation to a wider perception takes a distinct historical incident as its starting point. Based on Trotsky's murder in Mexico in 1940 and provoked in part by Che Guevara's assertion that revolutionaries must turn themselves into "killing machines,"[4] the poem is also indebted to Paz's antimechanical suppleness of mind—the metamorphic consciousness that combats would-be political transfiguration

6: Ends and Beginnings

by the will. Significantly, Paz's long poem, *Sunstone* (*Piedra de Sol*, 1957) supplies Tomlinson with an epigraph for *Assassin* and a world of suggestion, for here are the figures of history, including Trotsky, caught by a deadening kind of time: Socrates chained, Moctezuma sleepless, Robespierre counting the minutes on his way to execution, Lincoln with his steps numbered as he goes to the theater and his own murder. Where their death is "a statue of their life" ("la estatua de su vida"), the Pazian escape from petrifaction is either through the spirit, as the world peels away its masks to reveal "at its heart, a transparent shimmer / that we call God" ("en su centro, vibrante transparencia, / lo que llamamos Dios") or through the flesh—Man reaching towards paradisal oneness with Woman, in her archetypal guise as Mary, Persephone or Heloïse.

The physicality that Tomlinson makes central in his choice of epigraph for *Assassin*, however, is not sexual but animal: "The rattle in Trotsky's throat and his wild boar's moans" ("el estertor de Trotski y sus quejidos / de jabalí"). Here, characteristically, he dramatizes the struggle back to ground and body—the "animal" self from which human utterance and realization must ultimately come. If the killer, however, triumphed in his precalculation, none of that would occur:

> Blood I foresaw. I had put by
>   The distractions of the retina, the eye
> That like a child must be fed and comforted
>   With patterns, recognitions. The room
> Had shrunk to a paperweight of glass and he
>   To the centre and prisoner of its transparency.
>
> He rasped pages. I knew too well
>   The details of that head. I wiped
> Clean the glance and saw
>   Only his vulnerableness. Under my quivering
> There was an ease, save for that starched insistence
>   While paper snapped and crackled as in October air.
>
> Sound drove out sight. We inhabited together
>   One placeless cell. I must put down
> This rage of the ear for discrimination, its absurd
>   Dwelling on ripples, liquidities, fact
> Fastening on the nerve gigantic paper burs.
>   The gate of history is straiter than eye's or ear's.
>
> In imagination, I had driven the spike
>   Down and through. The skull had sagged in its blood.
> The grip, the glance—stained but firm—

    Held all at its proper distance and now hold
This autumnal hallucination of white leaves
    From burying purpose in a storm of sibilance.

I strike. I am the future and my blow
    Will have it now. If lightning froze
It would hover as here, the room
    Riding in the crest of the moment's wave,
In the deed's time, the deed's transfiguration
    And as if that wave would never again recede.

The blood wells. Prepared for this
    This I can bear. But papers
Snow to the ground with a whispered roar:
    The voice, cleaving their crescendo, is his
Voice, and his the animal cry
    That has me then by the roots of the hair.

Fleshed in that sound, objects betray me,
    Objects are my judge: the table and its shadow,
Desk and chair, the ground a pressure
    Telling me where it is that I stand
Before wall and window-light:
    Mesh of the curtain, wood, metal, flesh:

A dying body that refuses death,
    He lurches against me in his warmth and weight,
As if my arm's length blow
    Had transmitted and spent its strength
Through blood and bone; and I, spectred,
    The body that rose against me were my own.

Woven from the hair of that bent head,
    The thread that I had grasped unlabyrinthed all—
Tightrope of history and necessity—
    But the weight of a world unsteadies my feet
And I fall into the lime and contaminations
    Of contingency; into hands, looks, time.

    In such extraordinary inversion, where to "fall" is to stand upright again, surrealistic dreaming is the force that lands the self back inside clear fact. But where distortion occurs (with Trotsky's papers magnified to "gigantic . . . burs" in a room that a killer's mind fails to shrink and clamp down beneath "a paperweight of glass"), the surreal also makes possible a retributive moral effect—the daring that has to go beyond conventional moral viewpoint if it is to be a match for a

6: Ends and Beginnings

murderous ego's attempt to nullify place and relation. Historically, the place was Trotsky's fortified house at Coyoacán, Mexico City, to which the assassin, a Stalinist agent called Jacson, had gained access by posing as a follower. In a 1963 biography read by Tomlinson, *The Prophet Outcast: Trotsky: 1929–1940*, Isaac Deutscher tells how the killer devised a "dress-rehearsal" three days before the actual crime in August 1940. "He had enticed Trotsky into the study for a *tête-à-tête*, made him read a manuscript, and placed himself above his head. He had come to the dress-rehearsal with ice-axe, dagger, and pistol concealed in the coat he clutched in his arms. In his pocket he may already have had the letter purporting to explain his motives—the text had been typed out well ahead of time."[5] Too well ahead of time, the poet seems to observe, when he entitles his first version of the poem in September 1967, *The Rehearsal*,[6] for Tomlinson's perception of a Macbeth-like murderer who would escape from his coexistence with his victim in the present, shows him leaping beyond the moment in political predeterminism: "Blood I foresaw . . . In imagination, I had driven the spike / Down and through . . . I am the future and my blow / Will have it now." Like the claim of the Marxists to be carried by the force of irresistible history, this has the willful belief in clairvoyant authority expressed by the writers and makers of nineteenth-century history whom Edmund Wilson takes as his subject in *To the Finland Station* (1940).[7]

Not only a source for *Assassin*, Wilson's narrative on the complex impetus that finally brought Lenin back to Russia via the Petrograd terminus from Finland to start a revolution, also gave Tomlinson an image for a companion poem, *Prometheus* (1969). Shelley and Beethoven celebrated Prometheus, but the thief of fire and maker of man, says Wilson, had special mythic importance for Marx, the major spokesman for his century's secularizing of divine providence. Through such a vision, Promethean man not God was the self-creator, the ordainer of history. In Tomlinson's poem, as he listens to Scriabin's *Prometheus* symphony, it is a myth acted out across time by murder—that which "arrived by train at the Finland Station, / To bury its hatchet after thirty years in the brain / Of Trotsky." Such violence takes one back to Trotsky's own brutality when he suppressed all opposition to the early Soviet state:

> Trotsky, was it not then you brought yourself
> To judgement and to execution, when you forgot
> Where terror rules, justice turns arbitrary?

Yet in *Assassin*, Tomlinson offers no severity of judgement on Trotsky. What matters instead is the need to rearticulate a justness of relation between man and man, or between self and the bodied world, which the Promethean murderer would crush into silence. He would nullify all shared meanings; any civil, social literacy—the means by which one "reads" the other as a separate, coexisting individual—would be reduced to the speechlessly unread. Voice, sound, body, space—all would shrink like the room

> to a paperweight of glass and he
> To the centre and prisoner of its transparency.

The image of such threat may well derive from Mexico and the verse of Paz. In Paz's poem *The Prisoner* (1948), he addresses the Marquis de Sade, narcissistic captive of so many gaols and of himself, as "Prisoner in your castle of rock crystal" ("Prisionero en tu castillo de cristal de roca"); and Mexican "cristal de roca" (still, it seems, imaginatively present for Paz in *Sunstone* and its "transparent shimmer," divine "centre") provides Tomlinson's own poem *Mictlantecuhtli* (1984) with a reminder of the land's more ancient cult of murder—when "the accurate Aztecs / carved the skull god's device / out of rock crystal / as transparent as ice."

Tomlinson's concern in *Assassin* is to break out from such crystal finality and its mythic congealment of life, whether Aztec or Marxist. It is as if he needs to let time breathe again, to let the voice of fuller meaning, suppressed in victim and his writings, begin to split open the killer's glassy perfection "While paper snapped and crackled as in October air." Yet Tomlinson, with his unrushed sense of time's process, avoids the rapid Pazian efflorescence he translates in *One and the Same* with "black gardens of rock crystal / flowering along a bough of smoke." For now he carefully draws upon a different kind of surrealist art—not just literary but cinematic. As he says in an interview, he was a student of films by Buñuel, Dulac, Man Ray, and Welles, while at the same time—during his Cambridge days and just after—he himself wrote film scripts (unproduced). He tells of disliking the fatalism into which the metamorphic flow of many films tended to collapse, and he describes one of his own scripts, *The Lepidopterist,* ending with a death's head moth that changes on screen into a massive skull. One comes nearer the anti-egotistic art of *Assassin,* however, in his description of his "*Kane*-influenced script," rewritten as a novel, *Project 95,* about a "technocratic giant . . . obsessed with harnessing the wind,"[8] who is eventually blown off a mountain together with his contraption. In such an account, one has a clear suggestion of Tomlinson's acknowledged debt to Welles's *Citizen Kane,* the film made in the summer of 1940 that Trotsky was killed.

6: Ends and Beginnings

Significantly it is an American sense of possibility that breaks open a "rock crystal" hardening of time, as with the visually fluid movement at the beginning of Welles's film. The camera passes through the barred gates of Kane's Xanadu, across desolation, and up to the window of his encastled Gothic chamber where (another barrier dissolving) the viewer is inside the room and sees the dying man in monumental silhouette upon a bed. Kane's hand, unclenching, lets fall a glass globe—a child's toy with an enclosed winter scene that, dreamlike, is already spilling its snowflakes before the glass breaks on the floor. Looking through that glass, one sees a room strangely warped—the door and walls bent askew. But although, as Tomlinson acknowledges, this particular visual effect influences *Assassin* and the killer's distortion of Trotsky's room, the voice heard on film a moment before is even more important. For, in a huge close-up and with an amplified echo on the soundtrack, the lips of Kane open to say the one word—"Rosebud." In Welles's film, it is the word that starts the search for its meaning and the uncovery of a man's life by the reporter from the newsreel, *Time on the March*. In Tomlinson's poem, it suggests the potency of speech, the living time shared by killer and victim, that will not be silently glassed inside an eternal "October" or 1917 apocalypse. Such time, suppressed by the murderer's foreseeings, now has its revenge on him—firstly by an "autumnal hallucination of white leaves," then with the fall of a bizarre winter. It is as if the seasons are beginning to speak again from Trotsky's uncensorable papers that

> Snow to the ground with a whispered roar:
>   The voice, cleaving their crescendo, is his
> Voice, and his the animal cry
>   That has me then by the roots of the hair.

The voice that makes hair stand up in fear, and thus roots the killer back to the shared physicality he would deny, speaks for the difficult balance between contraries—the perilous standing between rise and fall, life and death—that is the human state. Yet Tomlinson's recreation of such voice and "whispered roar" from an American source is no accident. The magnifying of a word in Welles's film (and the search to recover a life's momentum, buried like Kane's youth under a looted Europe at Xanadu, with its objets d'art and statuary) brings one again to Lawrence's view of a native America hidden by layers of European consciousness and needing its own special utterance. Lawrence's review of *In the American Grain* speaks of the "sensitive awareness" wanted by the great continent, "the still-unravished bride of silences[9]"; and Williams, whose book had clearly taken encouragement from Lawrence's early American *Studies*, was to attempt a literary, mythic marriage in *Paterson*.

Yet Lawrence's "myth of America"[10] in the *Studies*, inspired by the back-yet-forward chronology of the *Leatherstocking Tales* ("She starts old, old, wrinkled and writhing in an old skin. And there is a gradual sloughing of the old skin, towards a new youth"[11]) takes its most extraordinary form in *Citizen Kane*. Here is a film that moves back through time—back through the rigidities and self-importance of old men stiffening inside their monuments—to a young, irreverent America whose onward vitality may founder yet be refound. Indeed, the nativeness of *Kane* (originally called *American*[12]) was only arrived at by Welles's abandonment because of cost of his 1939 plan to film *Heart of Darkness* and give it a contemporary European significance. Thus Conrad's Kurtz would have been a fascist ruler with a temple of skulls, and the "whispered roar" would, if heard, have been the cry of the European liberal-turned-exterminator—"A voice! a voice!"— that haunts Marlow: "He cried in a whisper at some image, at some vision—he cried out twice, a cry that was no more than a breath— 'The horror! The horror!'"[13]

Kane's vast whisper, like the film's movement between past and present, denotes a potency alive inside static tragedy. "Rosebud" speaks in a particularly American way for a vitality buried under nostalgia and pomp, for the trajectory of a childhood sled halted in the past (covered by snow while young Kane is borne away by train to a millionaire's life and then destroyed in a furnace at the film's end) whose sharp momentum, cutting against finality, is continually being rediscovered in the course of the film itself. Cinema's fluidity will not let *this* life be written off by dead words and signatures on paper. The *Time on the March* investigation, as it records the fall of Kane's newspaper empire (signed away by a bald, bankrupt Kane "in the winter of 1929," according to the memoir of his former guardian, Walter Thatcher), still touches the eruptive spirit it has uncovered in the snows long before, of a different winter. In fact, the newsreel reporter who sits to read the delimited pages of the memoir in the Thatcher Memorial Library under the gaze of its founder's statue, is the eye of a cinematic medium that, as in the film's opening moments, flows through surface barriers to a snowy zest and a voice.

In Tomlinson's poem, "papers / Snow to the ground", while in Welles's film the camera eye, traveling across Thatcher's copperplate script ("I first encountered Mr. Kane in 1871 . . ."), dissolves its way through paper pomposity to the defiant energy inside its pages—to young Kane, with his delighted cries, playing outside his mother's boardinghouse in the West. The snowball he flings at the written sign of the house, while within she is signing the child away to a fortune and Thatcher's legal care, is like his butting of his new guardian with his sled soon after: a playful vitality that, in the helter-skelter of years swiftly traveled by the film, becomes defiantly perverse. Not only does Kane, "the emperor of newsprint," strike against America's trusts and financial exploiters, he also hits at his own moneyed power. Now, literally caught within papers (his sensationalist press by which he ruins others and is politically ruined in turn), his energy becomes self-contradictory. Grand magnate yet baiter of capitalists, denounced both as communist and fascist, he is at the film's end (when his childhood delight in play exists as hideous pastiche with the opera house and jigsaw puzzle for his second wife) a figure cut into many pieces, like the infinitely repeated image of himself in the mirrors of the Xanadu mansion.

There still remains, in the remembrance of possibility, the glass globe, the child's toy, that breaks open at his death. Here is the flow, the spilling forth, which only cinema would seem able to depict. Yet for Tomlinson, observing the clash of vitality and deadness in Eliot's art, especially the filmlike quick cutting he sees in *The Waste Land*,[14] poetry can also present the juxtapositions—the release versus containment—of an unsettled psychology. In *The Waste Land*, one sees, it is that of a Europeanized American. Yet such a Europe yields for Eliot, as in *Kane*, the memory of young zest—of a pre-1914 voice at "the arch-duke's, / My cousin's" where another sled is in motion: "He said, Marie, / Marie, hold on tight. And down we went." At this point Eliot filmically "cuts" from past daring to the aged fear of the present: "I read, much of the night, and go south in the winter."

For Tomlinson, as an interpreter of Eliot and in his own poetry, such change does not have to suggest only a collapse into irony and defeat. Contraries mean consciousness perpetually rewon, where a sense of balance and stability is worth nothing unless earned out of the subverting and disintegrative. Danger defines the poise of the dancer, just as the distorting "glass" in Welles's film and the rock crystal of Paz's poetry center one again on the unfantastically exact. It is what Tomlinson imagined long before in one of his earliest poems, *Through Binoculars* (1955). There "normality" becomes desirable through its opposite—the "congealed light" of binocular vision, the "last phase in a romanticism" that shrinks space, makes everything "clear-cut, but bodiless," and, like Trotsky's killer, forbids individual recognition: "what we had taken for a face / Has neither eyes nor mouth, / But only the impersonality of anatomy." Movement is also silenced. To dispense with binoculars, however,

> Is to make audible the steady roar of evening,
> Withdrawing in slow ripples of orange,
> Like the retreat of water from sea-caves.

That "steady roar" heralds the "whispered roar" of the later poem: of a world speaking its way back to body, relation, and continuity. In *Assassin,* surreal distortion also makes possible the accuracy not complacency of sharpened moral judgement. For this, regained in startling clarity ("Objects are my judge"), has the unforeseen freshness that could only be arrived at through—and in challenge to—the killer's attempted foresight. His would-be prediction of everything gives energy to one's sense of an undetermined time and place, with its incalculable changes and constancy. It is the killer's perverse horror at being enclosed by "Mesh of the curtain, wood, metal, flesh" that energizes a normality of perception—one's *unhorrified* sense of the individual placed back in his surroundings. So also the murderous thrust at Trotsky, with its "arm's length" distancing and attempted disembodying, curiously invigorates a muscular sense of the near and reconnected: "As if my arm's length blow / Had transmitted and spent its strength / Through blood and bone." Like Theseus in a later Tomlinson poem, *Ariadne and the Minotaur* (1972), the killer would "unlabyrinth" the world's complex fullness, although here with ideology's narrow thread. Yet the "animal" reality that he cannot kill (the "warmth and weight" of existence's contraries: "A dying body that refuses death," in a reversal of *Macbeth's* ghost rising on body and in remembrance also of the actual, wounded Trotsky amazingly fighting back) has the unpredicted strength that his more destructive energy brings into view. By his own desperation, the "weight of a world" rises against his "paperweight" vision—against the last attempt by his mind to thin away corporeal solidity that now has to be so strenuous that he must clutch not at straws but at a hair: that "Tightrope of history and necessity," that he surrealistically wills it to become, and that he would step across before, brought down from this mental travesty of time, he stands again, with new balance, inside the broad, perilous world of contraries. For where "lime" and "time" rhyme together with corrosive *and* creative implication, the unsteadying can also steady, just as "contingency" dances alongside "contamination." It is a ground where nimble judgement is perpetually on its toes; a space of nonironic consciousness opened out by *Assassin* from its Mexican and American sources. Now one sees the further gain, as poetry tutors history in a European setting with *Charlotte Corday* where Tomlinson keeps in balance his presentation of a very different murderer.

II

The young girl from Normandy who killed Jean-Paul Marat in his Paris house on 13 July 1793, in the belief that this would halt further bloodshed in the French Revolution, has been called by Tomlinson "the 'good' assassin."[15] Corday, he says, "actually misread history somewhat—Marat being no longer in the political forefront and not really the right man to kill. The irony was that her action, in some degree, only served to stiffen events in the direction of the reign of terror."[16] Corday, indeed, might seem to invite posterity's indictment:

> How should she know
> The Terror still to come, as she was led
> Red-smocked from gaol out into evening's red?
> It was to have brought peace, that faultless blow.

Yet Tomlinson's poem, drawing here especially on Carlyle's *The French Revolution* for its description of the "serene" girl "sheeted in red smock of murderess,"[17] is notable for a poise in style and word that refuses history its ironic subversions. Thus the adjective in "faultless blow" may suggest the dangerously pure idealism that, like the perfect accuracy of Corday's knife thrust, prepared the way for the Terror's guillotine. But "faultless" also speaks for that unguarded, unknowing quality in Corday that has a defensible innocence: "How *should* she know . . . ?" For all her naïveté, she has the belief in a civil peace and a time outlasting revolution, which posterity can share with her. Her dagger therefore opens up an unwounded (and unwounding) consciousness, even though one is aware at the poem's end how, in a more deadly way, "the blade / Inherited the future now." Then, on the scaffold, she

> Entered a darkness where no irony
> Seeps through to move the pity of her shade.

Impervious to irony, Corday is also unshaken by a sense of pity developing too late. But poetry's careful words can suggest, without undercutting or overstating, the human possibilities in her—all that André Chénier ignored when he glorified Corday before the eyes of history: "Toi qui crus par ta mort ressusciter la France . . . O Vertu, le poignard, seul espoir de la terre, /Est ton arme sacrée".[18] Quoting from Chénier's ode in his epigraph to *Charlotte Corday,* Tomlinson both translates part of it in the poem itself and remembers another contemporary eulogizer of Corday (Adam Lux, who demanded the tribute *Greater than Brutus* on her statue) when he speaks of "daggered Virtue ... Action unsinewed into statuary!" For such high, rigid monumentality is merely Tomlinson's point of departure as he steadily moves towards a sinewy, breathing life in Corday. Indeed, his opening stanza is like a challenge to the finality of his own last lines where "she / Entered a darkness"—and to the bombast of the Chénier epigraph. For "Courteously" she enters, alive in the poise of murderous *and* civilized aims:

> Courteously self-assured, although alone,
> With voice and features that could do no hurt,
> Why should she not enter? They let in
> A girl whose reading made a heroine—
> Her book was Plutarch, her republic Rome:
> Home was where she sought her tyrant out.
>
> The towelled head next, the huge batrachian mouth:
> There was a mildness in him, even. He
> Had never been a woman's enemy,
> And time and sickness turned his stomach now
> From random execution. All the same,
> He moved aside to write her victims down,
> And when she approached, it was to kill she came.
>
> She struck him from above. One thrust. Her whole
> Intent and innocence directing it
> To breach through flesh and enter where it must,
> It seemed a blow that rose up from within:
> Tinville reduced it all to expertise:
> —What, would you make of me a hired assassin?
>
> —What did you find to hate in him?—His crimes.
> Every reply was temperate save one
> And that was human when all's said and done:
> The deposition, read to those who sit
> In judgement on her, 'What has she to say?'
> 'Nothing, except that I succeeded in it.'
>
> —You think that you have killed all Marats off?
> —I think perhaps such men are now afraid.
> The blade hung in its grooves. How should she know

6: Ends and Beginnings

The Terror still to come, as she was led
Red-smocked from gaol out into evening's red?
It was to have brought peace, that faultless blow.

Uncowed by the unimaginable result,
She loomed by in the cart beneath the eye
Of Danton, Desmoulins and Robespierre,
Heads in a rabble fecund in insult:
She had remade her calendar, called this
The Fourth Day of the Preparation of Peace.

Greater than Brutus was what Adam Lux
Demanded for her statue's sole inscription:
His pamphlet was heroic and absurd
And asked the privilege of dying too:
Through the republic raised to her no statue,
The brisk tribunal took him at his word.

What haunted that composure none could fault?
For she, when shown the knife, had dropped her glance—
She 'who believed her death would raise up France'
As Chénier wrote who joined the later dead:
Her judge had asked: 'If you had gone uncaught,
Would you have then escaped?' 'I would,' she said.

A daggered Virtue, Clio's roll of stone,
Action unsinewed into statuary!
Beneath that gaze what tremor was willed down?
And, where the scaffold's shadow stretched its length,
What unlived life would struggle up against
Death died in the possession of such strength?

Perhaps it was the memory of that cry
That cost her most as Catherine Marat
Broke off her testimony . . . But the blade
Inherited the future now and she
Entered a darkness where no irony
Seeps through to move the pity of her shade.

The poem's composure and questions match those of its subject, implying her tone, yet never overbearing or losing balance. "Why should she not enter?" There speaks the insistent girl at Marat's door, her murderous purpose in "should" hidden behind the "could" or "could do no hurt." Yet equally one hears the tone of a balancing innocence, rightfully protested, like Tomlinson's wondering, "How should she know / The Terror still to come . . ?" As with the hovering bird of *How Still the Hawk*—"innocence must harm"—deadly motive and outward calm go together in that "Courteously self-assured" voice that Tomlinson derives from the "voix assurée"[19] and "assurance extraordinaire"[20] attributed by Jules Michelet to Corday in his *Histoire de la Revolution Française* (1853).

Moving in step with her poise also means the poet must keep in proportion her own potential extravagance as an idealistic republican. She is not here, for instance, playing the part of a descendant from Corneille, as Michelet records her: a woman who wants to reenact her ancestor's *Cinna* by striking down a tyrant on the Champ-de-Mars. Instead, with Tomlinsonian tact, she is one "whose reading made a heroine": both a misreader of sick Marat's actual state and herself read amiss, "made a heroine" in the wrong sense by later glorifiers. In modesty, therefore, Tomlinson rhymes Corday's "Rome" of the mind with "Home"—her naïveté scaled down, yet treated without ironic condescension, inside the domestic confines where the man she would envisage as her monstrous objective ("The towelled head *next*, the huge batrachian mouth") is seen as a human being with his mildness and qualms. In fact, Michelet's description of Marat, with his "grande bouche batriacienne,"[21] sounds, when translated, like Corday's own bookish, "batrachian" misreading of her victim, as a monster—and one that seems incongruous with the "towelled head." That domestic intimacy is still a reminder of human limits and proportions as she brings him names of anti-Jacobins in Normandy—an occasion that shows the murderous intent in both of them: "He moved aside to write her victims down, / And when she approached, it was to kill she came." Yet even as she aims the blow and downfall awaits, her innocence does not lose its poise and become morally fallen. For Tomlinson takes note of Michelet's description of the thrust she delivers "d'en haut . . . frappé avec une assurance extraordinaire"[22]—an assuredness in the poem that holds together the double-sided quality of her action, as she proceeds, murderously yet untaintedly, to make a further confident entrance ("Why should she not enter?"):

> She struck him from above. One thrust. Her whole
> Intent and innocence directing it
> To breach through flesh and enter where it must,
> It seemed a blow that rose up from within:

An entirety of feeling, "Intent and innocence," exists still in "One thrust." Where the blow she has struck "from above" also seems to have risen "up from within," there is an indignant passion that lifts her action higher than the low crime her enemies would make it—

"faultless" in a mere technical sense. The public prosecutor Tinville "reduced it all to expertise," but her reply, "What, would you make of me a hired assassin?" (the words recounted by Michelet from the trial report in Le Moniteur[23]), shows courage against belittlement—a rising also, in her innocence, against posterity's knowledge of a doom about to drop:

> —You think that you have killed all Marats off?
> —I think perhaps such men are now afraid.
> The blade hung in its grooves....

Mass terror—we know—is the real consequence of her attempt to frighten a few. But though "blade" waits to follow close upon "afraid," she does not fall beneath one's indicting irony. Her idealism and her modesty ("I think perhaps...") still affirm a moral height. But its scale must be suggested with verbal care by Tomlinson, for she is neither the great statue imagined by her admirers nor, as she rides to execution, a person to be safely looked down upon by "heads" (soon to fall) in an abusive crowd ("un peuple abject, servile et fécond en outrage," as Chénier says). Amid error lies proportion:

> She loomed by in the cart beneath the eye
> Of Danton, Desmoulins and Robespierre,
> Heads in a rabble fecund in insult:
> She had remade her calendar, called this
> The Fourth Day of the Preparation of Peace.

It is the calm tone of Corday's mind, not just her voice, which Tomlinson suggests—the "Uncowed" thoughts that can remake the calendar in *her* revolutionary way; the idealistic yet civil style which sets her against the mob's insults.

Yet Tomlinson, in defining that equitability, earns the right to ponder its emotional cost. There have been previous questions in the poem: "Why should she not enter?"; "How should she know / The Terror still to come...?"; "What, would you make of me a hired assassin?" Now he adds another—giving no ground to her detractors or glorifiers, but enquiring about her "faultless" state at its more felt, human level:

> What haunted that composure none could fault?

The occasion is her glance, "dropped" when shown the knife and modestly lowering Chénier's claim that when she killed Marat she wanted nothing more than a martyr's end—"She 'who believed her death would raise up France.'" For it is her desire for life that she reveals when asked about her actions if she had gone uncaught:

> Would you have then escaped?

"I would," she says, with a "would" of possibilities, of humble yearning as distinct from the stern, marmoreal will that has brought her to seem as high as the guillotine over France. Another question—

> Beneath that gaze what tremor was willed down?

—touches that "would" yet again: the tremor of potencies that are there, seeking embodiment, without excessive height, as the poem goes on to ask,

> What unlived life would struggle up against
> Death died in the possession of such strength?

The "would" of the "unlived" life in herself and thousands more is weakened, but not so weak that it is to be read as a feeble "could." It still trembles into view as Corday's poise is affected by Marat's sister at the trial. But here such upsurging life is only a might-have-been—or the modest *might be* of "Perhaps" in sympathetic feeling—before her will shuts down and the guillotine blade falls:

> Perhaps it was the memory of that cry
> That cost her most as Catherine Marat
> Broke off her testimony . . . .

But Corday "lives" in unexaggerated possibility, against history's distortions and waste. Hers is the precise, daring "innocence" that not only makes reply to a Chénier but also to the painter David in Tomlinson's companion poem, *Marat Dead* (1978), who left her out of his glamorized version of the murder scene. In that painting she is only present through the "truthless scrawl" of paper by which she gained entry. But in *Charlotte Corday* she is given her own "truth": the sustaining of a difficult, calm equilibrium, an inner temperate space she carries unshaken through all the turmoil of murder, tribunal, gaol, rabble, and scaffold. Danton, however, in Tomlinson's other poem of the revolution, must seek it in an actual place of fruits, health, and renewal. Before it is too late, his instincts drive him back to the ground and continuity he would almost seem to have forfeited as founder of the revolutionary tribunal, regicide, and instigator of massacres. He too, so near the conclusion of his life, enters a space of beginnings.

III

But Danton stands there, at first, with less realization of the downfall that awaits. To be locally exact, *For Danton* imagines the unknowing man paused by the river at his birthplace, Arcis-sur-Aube, in the autumn of 1793, just before his return to Paris in November and his condemnation the year following. Danton's confidence, though, is like Corday's: not just blindness, but a valuable corrective to the reader's knowledge of imminent doom. As with the girl who did not know the Terror to come, the unaware Danton provokes questions—seemingly ironic at his expense, yet preparing the way for the alert, speculative consciousness that holds him back from merely being history's victim:

> Who is the man that stands against this bridge
> And thinks that he and not the river advances?
> Can he not hear the links of consequence
> Chiming his life away? Water is time.
> Not yet, not yet. He fronts the parapet
> Drinking the present with unguarded sense:
>
> The stream comes on. Its music deafens him
> To other sounds, to past and future wrong.
> The beat is regular beneath that song.
> He hears in it a pulse that is his own;
> He hears the year autumnal and complete.
> November waits for him who has not done
>
> With seeings, savourings.

"Not yet, not yet," goes the refrain, by contrast with the more deadly tune that is also heard—the fate that, in the poem's last line, "Will spring the trap whose teeth must have a man." But what of "*the* man" at the start? Poetry still has time and space to inquire about the individuality of the man who has not yet been blindly swallowed up by the depersonalizing processes of brutal revolution. As with Corday, one still has latitude to see the double-sided nature of a human being, except that with Danton it is not a temperateness simultaneously murderous and innocent, but two kinds of audacity in one. Thus there is the ego of the revolutionary, believing "that he and not the river advances," while coexistent with that is the different daring of a man who submits to a restorative nature beyond self-delusion. The latter Danton is not Robespierre's dupe, vainly "unguarded" in the belief that he controls events, but one who "fronts the parapet" and "stands against this bridge" with an "unguarded," healthy openness to all that stands over against him. That is a nonironic sense of order, with its own music—though mistaken by the more egotistic (and ironically subvertible) Danton for the rhythms of another order, his imagined power over history. Since he hears in the river's regular beat "a pulse that is his own," it is inevitable that the mind's self-assertion *(is his)* continues to be enacted by Tomlinson in the rhyming insistence of "hears" itself: "He *hears* the *year* autumnal and complete." The illusory completeness of grasp means that the time to come seems almost deferential: "November waits for him . . . ."

Yet, as the sentence carries on from the second to third stanza, poetry's syntax momentarily suggests a Danton who is led out of history's grip. The man of fated finality and wrong foresight becomes more fully the man brought alive in the senses, open to the uncalculated, unfinished and continuous:

> November waits for him who has not done
>
> With seeings, savourings.

Now it is Danton who waits on time, in hungry savoring not complacent relish. But fate also bides its moment ("Can he not hear the links of consequence . . . ?") with an imagery in the poem that has its American and English resonance. Tomlinson does not forget George Oppen's *Of Being Numerous* (1969) where "motes / In the air" can be

> an iron mesh, links
>
> Of consequence
>
> Still, at the mind's end
> Relevant

Closer to Danton's time, however, is Wordsworth in book 10 of *The Prelude*, "Dragged by a chain of harsh necessity"[24] from revolutionary France to England. Yet before that ("To soothe regret, though deepening what it soothed"), Wordsworth speaks of a refreshment against determinism:

> When by the gliding Loire I paused, and cast
> Upon his rich domains, vineyard and tilth,

6: Ends and Beginnings 205

> Green meadow-ground, and many-coloured woods,
> Again, and yet again, a farewell look;
> Then from the quiet of that scene passed on,
> Bound to the fierce Metropolis.

The last line becomes the epigraph of *For Danton*, while the river scene appears to suggest the place of Danton's pause—fate and its assuagement, with a Wordsworthian basis for both. Yet Danton is "Bound to the fierce Metropolis" by his past as well as by his future: a commitment, as well as a striving from it, which Hilaire Belloc's *Danton: A Study* (1899) reinforces in Tomlinson's poem. The biography tells how Danton, leader of a revolution, briefly escaped it; how, after leaving the convention and imagining he saw the Seine run with blood, he was exhausted. "He had at this moment a hunger for his native place, for the Champagne after the harvest, and for the autumn mists upon the Aube ... needing the country as a parched man needs water."[25] Belloc speaks of Danton's six weeks of sleep and recuperation at Arcis, but also of decisive events long before:

> He ran off in his last year [of school] to Rheims, seventy odd miles away, that he might see the crowning of Louis XVI. Going and returning on foot, he satisfied the desire which he had expressed to his school-fellows of "seeing how they made a king." So as a boy he went to look at the making of a king, and afterwards, when he grew older, Danton himself unmade him.[26]

In this account the poet sees Danton's ego at work: remembering the past as it leads to personal, future success, yet lacking all sense of a presentness shared with his victim or with others. It is a past-to-future symmetry of retribution, without space for a present discriminative consciousness, that brings the king's unmaking and Danton's undoing more and more tightly together. However, in the drama of mind—and poet's word—Danton has not yet finished here, now,

> With seeings, savourings. Grape-harvest brings
> The south into the north. This parapet
> Carries him forward still, a ship from Rheims,
> From where, in boyhood and on foot, he'd gone
> 'To see,' he said, 'the way a king is made',
> The king that he himself was to uncrown—

> Destroyed and superseded, then secure
> In the possession of a perfect power
> Returned to this: to river, town and plain,
> Walked in the fields and knew what power he'd lost,
> The cost to him of that metropolis where
> He must come back to rule and Robespierre.
>
> Not yet. This contrary perfection he
> Must taste into a life he has no time
> To live, a lingered, snatched maturity
> Before he catches in the waterchime
> The measure and the chain a death began,
> And fate that loves the symmetry of rhyme
> Will spring the trap whose teeth must have a man.

A man who "Must taste" present fruits is doomed by a different *must*—the inescapable momentum (Arcis to Rheims, Rheims to Paris) that comes from the Louis-Danton entanglement ("'To see,' he said ... the king that he himself was to uncrown") where the revolutionary's ego, confused by pronouns with the king, leads to a fate ("Destroyed and superseded") in which the participles cannot distinguish one man from the other. Depersonalization is such that "secure" cannot be attributed to Danton as an individual with any political or grammatical confidence. Yet, out of "Destroyed and superseded," with its blind mechanics, a different, more perceptive sense of the impersonal comes to Danton. Syntactically, consciously, he is a man "Returned." The word's suggestion of passive conveyance turns active as one reads—an aware "return" that strides anew in "Walked" where the verb does without a pronoun or ego and admits him to understanding of a "perfect power" that is no political delusion. Eden-like, there is another sense of the perfect, even as he

> Walked in the fields and knew what power he'd lost,
> The cost to him of that metropolis where
> He must come back to rule and Robespierre.

One notes the use of "he." But this nonegotistic pronoun sees what the old "he" could not—the tightening entanglement of self with Paris and ambition, where all space of present awareness will be squeezed out, as the words press upon each other: "lost" on "cost" with the willful insistence that self-destructively for Danton brings "he'd" and "to him" within the swallowing grasp of "*metropolis.*" There lies for him a placeless place: a "where" subverted by "Robespierre." Yet in a poetry that reprieves a consciousness from history's extinction, words like thoughts can attempt a different rhyme and a larger ground. In an Arcis of "river, town and plain," Danton must strive to keep measure with a "life" he has no time to "live," but which can be "lingered" before his snatching by fate and a different music of consequences. It is a lingering, however, that has urgency rather than autumn melancholy—the need felt by a man who unmade a king for the sovereign value of the lived moment.

IV

The Italian who "may perfect / A prince" in *Machiavelli in Exile* establishes the conditions for such sovereignty; and now the poetic art that shows Machiavelli's imagination surviving downfall is one more than ever at variance with that of Eliot in *Four Quartets*, particularly the purgative form of Christianity demonstrated by *Little Gidding*. There, one remembers, a "secluded chapel" and "broken king" give particularity to a place—but only as the spiritual means by which time lets through the timeless. The individuality of a ground matters only so far as it is part of a sameness of purpose, for "There are other places / Which also are the world's end. . . ." Above all, the "beginnings" that are possible from such "ends" are taught with Eliotic rigor:

> If you came this way,
> Taking any route, starting from anywhere,
> At any time or at any season,
> It would always be the same: you would have to put off
> Sense and notion. You are not here to verify,
> Instruct yourself, or inform curiosity
> Or carry report. You are here to kneel
> Where prayer has been valid.

It is the "parsonorial"[27] tone and the depletion of the senses ("while the light fails / On a winter afternoon") that have already been challenged by Tomlinson's *Something: A Direction* from the group of poems, *Antecedents*, for in *Something*, he imagines the ego moving beyond sunset tragedy and romantic solitude into a greater community of the living, objective world. The "shriven self" is also greeted in a manner and phrasing that implicitly contest the prohibitive Eliot style ("You are not here to verify . . . You are here to kneel")—

> You are downing
> Back from that autumn music of the light . . .

>. . . . .   You accept
> An evening, washed of its overtones
>   By strict seclusion, yet are not secluded
> Withheld at your proper bounds. From there
>   Your returns may enter, welcome strangers
> Into a civil country (you were not the first
>   To see it), but a country, natural and profuse

There is discipline but also welcome. Grounded in such new territory, language, and relation, "You" may read things afresh: "Sun is, because it is not you . . . It downs / Recovered, coverless, in a shriven light."

With the first line of *Machiavelli in Exile*, that "country, natural and profuse" finds both place and time: "A man is watching down the sun." For here, at a specific historical moment—1513, in the countryside south of Florence where the disgraced Machiavelli lives on his farm and writes *The Prince*—the fallen self is coming to ground with a deeper sense of time than he has known in his frustrated political career. Corday knew "Four Days of the Preparation of Peace," while Danton lingers in "a life he has no time / To live" ("Who is the man that stands against this bridge?"). But "A man" like Machiavelli, "watching down the sun," not only has a larger timespan in his humbled state; he also implicitly shows how the questions provoked by Corday and Danton in their poems belong to the wider, more flexible, inquiring consciousness that poetry plays against history. By attempting to answer questions (and go beyond his own failed political opportunism), Machiavelli enters the largest space of developing realization that Tomlinson conceives in the history poems:

> A man is watching down the sun. All day,
> Exploring the stone sinew of the hills,
> For his every predilection it has asked
> A Roman reason of him. And he has tried
> To give one, tied to a dwindling patrimony
> And the pain of exile. His guileless guile,
> Trusted by nobody, he is self-betrayed.
>
> And yet, for all that, Borgia shall be praised
> Who moved and, moving, saved by sudden action:
> The Florentines, despite their words, will have
> Faction and the blood that comes of faction:
> The work of France and Spain others begin—
> Let him who says so exercise his powers
> With dice and backgammon at a country inn;
>
> Where, for his day's companions, he must choose
> Such men as endure history and not those

6: Ends and Beginnings

Who make it: with their shadows, magnified
And spread behind them, butcher, publican,
Miller, and baker quarrel at their cards,
And heights and hill-roads all around are filled
With voices of gods who do not know they're gods.

Nor are they, save for a trick of light and sound:
Their fate is bound by their own sleeping wills.
Though lateness shadows all that's left to do,
Tarde non furon mai grazie divine:
The sun that lit his mind now lights the page
At which he reads and words, hard-won, assuage
What chance and character have brought him to.

He enters that courtly ancient company
Of men whose reasons may be asked, and he,
Released from tedium, poverty, and threat,
Lives in the light of possibility:
Their words are warm with it, yet tempered by
The memory of its opposite, else too soon
Hopes are a mob that wrangle for the moon.

Adversity puts his own pen in hand,
First torture, then neglect bringing to bear
The style and vigilance which may perfect
A prince, that he whom history forsook
Should for no random principle forsake
Its truth's contingency, his last defeat
And victory, no battle, but a book.

Tomlinson says in a footnote that the poem is based in part on Machiavelli's letter to a friend in Rome, Francesco Vettori. Yet it also recalls Pound's quotations from Malatesta's letters in the *Cantos*, together with the voice of the prisoner outside Pisa in *Canto LXXIV*: "a man on whom the sun has gone down." Although, in Tomlinson's poem, "A man *is* watching down the sun" with the active attentiveness that comes from Machiavelli's letter and his dawn to evening account of his day ("I rise with the sun . . .": "Io mi levo col sole"[28]), this individual is beginning to share in an identity beyond the ego that for Pound was Odyssean, the state of being "noman" or "Oŭtis." In Machiavelli's case, Tomlinson imagines the movement into the impersonal and communal as similar to the responsibility asking to be taken up in his poem *Appearance* (1972). There "the cold / Hills drawing us to a reciprocation, / Ask words of us, answering images." Indeed, the tutelary spirit of his poetry—letting nature's fact be given voice and reenter as humanity's guest—now assumes an historical form.

But the "Roman reason" asked of Machiavelli in his moral trial under the sun, deepens in meaning as the poem continues. At first such "reason" seems the quality of mind—the *virtù*—that Machiavelli admires in the ancient republican Romans and he celebrates in his *History of Florence* (1521-25). For him, it has the civic, unifying reasonableness that distinguishes Rome from Florence with its factional strife. In chapter 17 of *The Prince,* it is the power for unity shown by Cesare Borgia in his pacification of the Romagna—harsh yet better than the behaviour of the Florentines who, in order to avoid seeming cruel, thereby let Pistoia be destroyed. Machiavelli also seems to be invoking the spirit of "Roman reason" against fragmentation when he speaks (*The Prince,* chapter 3) of the ambitious Venetians who invited the French into Italy, allowing them to conquer most of it and to divide the kingdom of Naples with Spain. So, rising high above the petty and mingling with the powerful—at least mentally—Machiavelli, in Tomlinson's first stanza, seems possessed of *that* "reason" at least. A man who has been tortured, imprisoned and exiled by the Medici and who now seeks to win back favor by his book, has at that level a kind of reasoning, vigorous impersonality—set beyond his own particular troubles, even though Tomlinson, summarizing the robust, dispassionate tone, also shows its willful manner:

> And yet, for all that, Borgia shall be praised
> Who moved and, moving, saved by sudden action:
> The Florentines, despite their words, will have
> Faction and the blood that comes of faction:
> The work of France and Spain others begin—

Indeed there are "others", for the next line's fiat ("Let him who says so . . .") immediately reminds one that it is not Machiavelli who decides the fate of nations. He "who says so" only exercises "his powers" in a game of chance at a country inn—with the shouts of his gambling associates now more obviously to be heard in his own noisy insistences as historian. Lacking godlike transcendence, he watches the power politics of his day as things of chance and anarchy rather than order. His attempt at a grand impersonal view is but "guileless guile." Yet inside the nonpersonal there *is* an unpretentious vitality and sense of order: an unegotistic perception of the real masteries possible in history when "reason" is not loftily Roman, but is grounded in daily consciousness. Then it can extend across the ages in a chastened way—humbled, but not humiliated as his rural companions and shared energy lead him towards a different sense of the communal.

6: Ends and Beginnings 211

In "A Note on Machiavelli" (1949: collected in *Signs*, 1960)—an essay that seems to have suggested the Florentine to Tomlinson as a subject—Maurice Merleau-Ponty remarks: "There will always be two kinds of men, those who live through history and those who make it. There are the miller, the baker, and the innkeeper with whom the exiled Machiavelli spends his day, chatters, and plays backgammon. ('Then,' he says, 'disputes, vexatious words, insults arise; they argue at the drop of a hat and utter cries that carry all the way to San Casciano....')."[29] But these are "sleeping wills" in contrast with Machiavelli's waking, unwillful awareness. As with his earlier clamor ("Borgia shall be praised... The Florentines... will have / Faction"), the shouts of excess fade. "The sun that lit his mind now lights the page." He enters that quieter understanding that Merleau-Ponty describes in another book with importance for Tomlinson, *The Primacy of Perception* (1964). Phenomenology and poetry come together when it is said that "the experience of perception is our presence at the moment when things, truths, values are constituted for us ... that it teaches us, outside all dogmatism, the true conditions of objectivity itself; that it summons us to the tasks of knowledge and action."[30]

The vigilance of Machiavelli from the start ("watching down the sun. All day...") is towards such objectivity and knowledge—or so it becomes clearer when he no longer seems the theorizer who mentally organizes men of power, but one who sees the order and civility that can exist in human affairs if dangers are squarely faced. Again Tomlinson is helped in such definition of Machiavelli by Merleau-Ponty in *Signs*. There the Italian's achievement is seen as his astute humanism, an acceptance of the unreason in men or events that is balanced by his awareness of the intelligence and careful government that are necessary to political life. Left unwatched, the random gains control; but "Chance takes shape only when we give up understanding and willing."[31] So Machiavelli, whose better "reason" knows the cost of the arbitrary gamble—and whose "hard-won" words of understanding in *The Prince*

>   assuage
>   What chance and character have brought him to

—combines, as Merleau-Ponty sees, "a most acute feeling for the contingent and irrational in the world with a taste for the consciousness and freedom in man." This is a Machiavelli who sees human society as capable of self-responsibility, not giving way to despair or seeking for some "transcendent principle" above the "givens of our condition." In Tomlinson's poem, Machiavelli, forsaken by history yet not forsaking "Its truth's contingency" for a "random principle," is even more firmly nontranscendent and secular. The Christian hope in the quotation from Petrarch in the fourth stanza, "*Tarde non furon mai grazie divine*" ("Divine graces were never late"), seems misplaced, even though the words appear at the beginning of the Vettori letter, for the poem suggests that it is nature and tutored human reason that are the assuaging powers. It is the sun, not God, who questions his predilections, and it is the sun, lighting his mind as he goes home from work, who lets his sense of reason expand and find solace in time's grace.

He is no longer simply a figure who is questioned—and politically questionable—but one who can also question, for, as he says in his letter—and the poem recognizes (when he takes off his everyday clothes to put on the robes of court and palace, so that he may resume his studies for *The Prince*)—he comes into the more reciprocal world of dialogue, where he may seek "reasons" from others in history. "I enter the antique courts of the ancients" ("entro nelle antiche corti degli antichi uomini"[32]). There, as one sees in *The Prince*, he can converse with such figures as Alexander, Theseus, and Moses. Not only is he able to "ask the reasons of their actions" ("domandare della ragione delle loro azioni") but also to experience the courtesy of those who, says Merleau-Ponty, "always answer *him*. ('And during four long hours . . . I no longer feel any boredom; I forget all misery; I no longer fear poverty; death no longer terrifies me')":[33]

> He enters that courtly ancient company
> Of men whose reasons may be asked, and he,
> Released from tedium, poverty, and threat,
> Lives in the light of possibility:

Such "light" is a consciousness across time—steadied against the politically impossible and against the arbitrary rule of strong men where chance is mere tyrannous whim that cannot be questioned. In fact, Tomlinson's poem touches the necessary balance between the accountability of government and its potential paralysis. Merleau-Ponty speaks of such balance in terms of a continuous dialogue between rulers and ruled in humanistic, democratic communities—what Machiavelli articulated, he says, as the social need of "holding power in check without annulling it. It was necessary to have leaders capable of explaining the reasons for their politics to those subject to power."[34] There is also, as Tomlinson sees, the value of a "style and vigilance which may perfect / A prince": the watchfullness that is against despair or utopian dream and against the egotism of mob or dictator, but which is *for* a realizable sovereignty of being.

Williams was also struck by Machiavelli's perfecting of a prince. A chapter of *In the American Grain* begins with a remembrance of how Machiavelli, "coming home at evening from the fields dusty and tired out . . . doffs his outdoor clothes, dresses himself for a new part and entering his study becomes a king."[35] Williams's book also reaches out to a larger, historical community. His "ancient company" is not courtly but includes those essentially native "Americans"—De Soto, Rasles, Champlain, Boone, and others—who touched the quick of the new continent. Such local realization stands in implicit contrast to what Williams felt was Eliot's betrayal of America in the Europeanism of *The Waste Land*.

But as one sees from Tomlinson's history poems and their relation to Eliot's work, the Williams viewpoint can now be especially qualified. *The Waste Land* has its own inner American vitality, its striving towards a communal speech or music that is beyond tragedy. So too reach out the fated Europeans in Tomlinson's poems from *Assassin* onwards—and never more so than with the exiled Machiavelli. His individual talent finds itself by means of a tradition, but, in an un-Eliotic way, he witnesses to that sense of beginnings versus ends by which poetry counters yet again the tyrannies—and tyrants—of history.

7

To Marry with a Land

I

Tomlinson's challenge to a culture of "endings" also defines his place among postwar British poets. His affinities are clear in his 1983 lecture, *The Sense of the Past*, where he speaks of Basil Bunting and David Jones (together with Geoffrey Hill in *Mercian Hymns*) as poets who connect us to "a larger . . . spiritually denser England"—to "a sense of scale that English poetry was to stand in danger of forgetting when, after the exhaustions of the war and the end of Empire, it took its stand on narrowed ground."[1] Bunting's and Jones's ways of reaching beyond insularity bring them close to Tomlinson's own voyagings. But the sense of scale in all three poets becomes the more sharply evident if one briefly considers Tomlinson's differences from the poetry of lowered horizons and cultural retreat that emerged in the England of the 1950s.

The verse of Philip Larkin, Kingsley Amis, and others, as exemplified in the anthologies *Poets of the 1950s* (1955) and *New Lines* (1956), presented itself as the "moderate" reaction to the Apocalyptic poets of the preceding decade and the neoromanticism of Dylan Thomas in particular. But, as Tomlinson saw, rejection of excess meant in their case an atrophying of the senses and the imagination: the "provincial laziness of mind,"[2] the adherence to a Little Englandism and "suburban mental ratio" that prevents a "vital awareness of the continuum outside themselves, of the mystery bodied over against them in the created universe."[3] So, when Amis asserted in *Poets of the 1950s* that "Nobody wants any more poems about . . . foreign cities,"[4] Tomlinson's poem, *More Foreign Cities* (*Seeing is Believing*) directly defies "movement" preconceptions. Here the mind dances beyond the stale, as in the Mozartian kind of city,[5] Fiordiligi, where consciousness is both caught and freed by

>   its sun-changes
> Against walls of transparent stone
> Unsettling all preconception—a city
> For architects (they are taught
> By casting their nets
> Into those moving shoals);

It is a meshed yet unpossessive grasp of a constantly shifting universe that brings one again to the humanized landscapes in many Tomlinson poems. "Unsettling" is there the basis for a hard-won settlement of place by people or sensibility—"the wedding of the mind / with . . . the further fields, the seamless / spread of space" (*Four Kantian Lyrics*, 1963). That is one way "to marry with a land." Another is to have the adeptness of Hopi farmers (*Arizona Desert*, 1966), whose villages "mean / marriage, a loving lease / on sand, sun, rock." Even when the desert is the dust of a demolished British city (*The Way In*, 1974), and all that remains is debris to be scavenged by "A race in transit," Tomlinson suggests desire for a permanent purchase on place and relation in the eyes of the salvagers as "their pale / Absorption . . . Gazes the new blocks down." They imply a human persistence towards a bond or marriage with terrain that the industrial workers of *Steel: the night shift* (1963) look toward more commandingly. Here among Tomlinson's own Stoke people, above the furnaces of Shelton Bar-Iron Works, "men / facelessly habituated to the glare / outstare it"—gaze beyond all that would mechanistically seem to degrade them, as *they* control the movement of the girders and the feeding of the slag trucks. In the controlled acoustic—"regular, successive, sea-on-shore / concussive bursts"—space enlarges with the sound, yet at the same moment "time / is all this measured voice would seem / to ask."

In such undefeated reaching out to a temporal ground, Tomlinson's difference as a poet from Philip Larkin could not be more marked. Larkin, even as he contemplates the same England as Tomlinson, travels away from the latter's sense of relation and possibility. There is to be no marriage with a land—or with anyone—by the bachelor poet of *Dockery and Son* (1964), as Larkin travels home by train, after seeing a married friend, and finds himself

>   waking at the fumes
> And furnace-glares of Sheffield, where I changed,
> And ate an awful pie, and walked along
> The platform to its end to see the ranged
> Joining and parting lines reflect a strong
>
> Unhindered moon.

"Joining and parting": this is not an England where, in Tomlinson's words, "all moves / Towards encounter," but one where the irritated ego, enduring fumes, glares, and pie, curtly severs itself from pairings. "Unhindered" gleams alone across the stanza gap with that dismissal of linkage that gradually shows itself on another train journey through England in *The Whitsun Weddings* (1964). The nonchalant fatalism with which the poet sees environmental shoddiness passing by the carriage window (canals with "industrial froth," a "new and nondescript" town, with "acres of dismantled cars") gives way to seaside postcard caricaturing as Saturday wedding parties meet the train— "fathers with broad belts under their suits," "mothers loud and fat," and girls so "unreally" adorned that they seem less like people than a catalogue of gaudy goods: "the perms / The nylon gloves and jewellery-substitutes." The "tenderly nursed sense of defeat"[6] that Tomlinson saw in Larkin's earlier poetry here reveals more obviously its willed dampening when hopes, lives and marriages *must* fail in the regulated bathos to which Larkin consigns them as the train reaches London

> and what it held
> Stood ready to be loosed with all the power
> That being changed can give. We slowed again,
> And as the tightened brakes took hold, there swelled
> A sense of falling, like an arrow-shower
> Sent out of sight, somewhere becoming rain.

The arrow-sharp image seems only to be there in order to make more acute the effect of dissipation, the inexorable falling-apart of lives and energies momentarily wedded or fortuitously clustered together on a train. So vitality is "loosed," not as a seeding fecundity that pinpoints place and gives it fruitful reality, but as an enervated looseness, scattered in a blank, placeless "somewhere"—the keenly visual and present "Sent out of sight, somewhere becoming rain" in a distanced dreariness.

It is a poetic subversion of time and space that "dulls to distance all we are" in Larkin's *Ambulances* (1964). Across time, in *An Arundel Tomb* (1964), a married couple, a medieval earl and countess, memorialized in quaint "stone fidelity," also provide a blurred and distancing image for our "unarmorial age"—their "hardly meant" constancy rigidified into an "Untruth," yet proving "Our almost-instinct almost true: / What will survive of us is love." Since "love" is verbally worn away by Larkin's weakening "almosts" (like the features of the married pair themselves), any continuity is only a posture accidentally frozen by time. What humanly "survives" is a mere equivocal comfort—and even hardly that in a poem such as *Here* (1964) where humanity itself is to be escaped from. For a sense of peopled place does not lie for the poet in the city's "cut-price crowd" and their late 1950s affluence—"Cheap suits, red kitchen-ware, sharp shoes, iced lollies, / Electric mixers." All such catalogue of vulgar desires is patronized and outdistanced by a poetry that does not slow down in its perpetual journeying until one comes to

> Isolate villages, where removed lives
>
> Loneliness clarifies.

Like "Unhindered" in *Dockery and Son*, "Loneliness" must be reached in its solitary insistence across the blank space that separates stanzas. Asserted against normal word order (and thereby becoming more important as an abstraction than the "removed lives" of human beings whom it supposedly clarifies), "Loneliness" has the decontaminating force, rid of human taint, by which Larkin suggests, a few lines later, that the air is more "Luminously-peopled" than a village or land. Thus all place—*here*—to which the reader has traveled from the beginning of the poem is not a habitable ground that has been worked, cultivated, or cherished across time, nor even struggled for against nature's resistance. It is a recluse's void, free of claim upon the untrammeled ego that surveys it:

> Here silence stands
> Like heat. Here leaves unnoticed thicken,
> Hidden weeds flower, neglected waters quicken,
> Luminously-peopled air ascends;
> And past the poppies bluish neutral distance
> Ends the land suddenly beyond a beach
> Of shapes and shingle. Here is unfenced existence:
> Facing the sun, untalkative, out of reach.

Larkin's romanticism (finding grand solace in the distant rather than the near, the "unfenced" rather than defined) looks out "beyond a beach / Of shapes and shingle" in a way that Bunting could not. The human and nonhuman, words and wordless, are to grip close together in *Briggflatts* where "blades" of surf

> fall crisp on rustling grit,
> shaping the shore as a mason
> fondles and shapes his stone.

Similarly, on another English shore, there is no Larkinesque unshaping and dehumanizing in Tomlinson's *Stone Speech* (1972) when the poet finds faces in the pebbles that the elements have sculpted. This is to discover relation, without anthropomorphism on the one hand, and without, on the other, that "immense exercise of will"—with "Self-purification and anti-humanity"—by which Hugh MacDiarmid, in the Shetland setting of *On A Raised Beach* (1934), imagines us becoming "Adamantine and inexorable" like the stones. But the Scotsman's vision, for all its movement towards the depersonalized, takes note of the close particularity of things. There he anticipates Tomlinson's regard for the discipline of stony otherness, if not the way by which the self in *Cézanne at Aix,* made alert rather than hardened by nonhuman fact, finds "Untaught / Unalterable, a stone bridgehead / To that which is tangible." By contrast with the merely null in Larkin's prefixes ("unnoticed," "unfenced," "untalkative"), Tomlinson's *un*'s and *not*'s in *Seeing is Believing* are the verbal barrier that has to be faced and grappled with before the negative yields to the positive and to "tangible" possibility. Indeed, the contrast is not just with Larkin, but with W. H. Auden; in *Tramontana in Lerici,* where the air is "Unfit for politicians and romantics," the cold singularity of an evening—

> A tangible block, it will be no accessory
> To that which does not concern it

—shows Tomlinson echoing Auden's *The Watershed* (1927):

> Stranger, turn back again, frustrate and vexed:
> This land, cut off, will not communicate,
> Be no accessory content to one
> Aimless for faces rather there than here.

The Auden who later became a precursor of Larkin in an English tradition of commonplace feeling and bathos (as with *Musée de Beaux Arts,* 1937) is visible already in the alienated, hortatory manner that allows the stranger to be no more than "frustrate and vexed." Even so, *The Watershed* does reveal how close Auden is to a different tradition of concrete objectivities, where he is responsive to the northern England of his youth and to all that will "not communicate"—a respected mystery rather than source of alienation—in this place of abandoned workings. *Missing* (1929) has a similar regard for the border country he knew well as an amateur geologist and walker. Despite posturing heroics, a poem that begins, "From scars where kestrels hover," can go on to observe

> The slow fastidious line
> That disciplines the fell,
> Hear curlew's creaking call
> From angles unforeseen,

Yet such native ground (as suggested by the "region / Of short distances and definite places" that Auden celebrates in a 1948 poem, *In Praise of Limestone,* written during his years in America), never impinges sufficiently on his sensibility, with its aloofness and evasions, to exert a shaping discipline. Instead, the limestone poem, with its landscape composed from English and Mediterranean scenes, is notable for his pleasure in the escape from solidity into underground secrecy and flux:

> If it form the one landscape that we, the inconstant ones,
>   Are consistently homesick for, this is chiefly
> Because it dissolves in water. Mark these rounded slopes
>   With their surface fragrance of thyme and, beneath,
> A secret system of caves and conduits;

For Adrian Stokes in *The Stones of Rimini* (1934), with a Poundian sense of interplay between water, light, and stone, "Limestone is the humanistic rock."[7] Although Auden, like Tomlinson, would surely agree, his interest, as seen in *New Year Letter* (1941), is not the adjustment of self to surface world, in a humanizing that avoids the impress of the ego, but the dissolution of that world into the subjective and the subterranean. It shows the extent to which Auden, writing from America (that "fully alienated land," he says) remained proof against the examples of poetic objectivity that were offered to him not only by Williams but also by Moore whom he particularly admired. *New Year Letter* has no belief in any community of understanding outside the self: "No longer can we learn our good / From chances of a neighbourhood." Nor is there much human good to be observed in the drama of man's Fall, which Auden imposes on the geology of northern England. "Those limestone moors that stretch from BROUGH / To HEXHAM and the ROMAN WALL" are turned into a *paysage moralisé* that includes the river Eden and the descent of the poet, with more portentous capitalization and verbal clamor, into supposed "knowledge" at a County Durham mine where he enters the embrace of Ur-Mothers:

> In ROOKHOPE I was first aware
> Of Self and Not-self, Death and Dread:
> Adits were entrances which led

> Down to the Outlawed, to the Others,
> The Terrible, the Merciful, the Mothers;

In Tomlinson's poetry, however, "knowledge" is sharper: not the dark balefulness of Auden's *Urmutterfurcht,* but the wakeful realization of time's possibilities before and after the Fall. Eden is lost, but not the Edenic freshness of perception that lies potently at hand. So in Tomlinson's poem, *The Shaft* (1978)—its scene an old mine in the Lake District—there is moral awakening rather than moralizing of place when the adit is entrance to a past, "A vertigo that dropped through centuries." Undizzyingly, though, it is also a way out at last to a regained future and present:

> the adit you entered by
> Filtered a leaf-light, a phosphorescence,
> Doubled by water to a tremulous fire
> And signalling you back to the moist door
> Into whose darkness you had turned aside
> Out of the sun of an unfinished summer.

This is a long way from a poetry of alienation or subjectivized place, particularly when Tomlinson, in a journey through the Carlsbad Caves[8] of a Texas mountain (*The Cavern,* 1966), finds features in stone and crystal that offer recognitions yet forbid over-familiarity: "mosses not of moss . . . prints / of feet where no feet ever were." Without submission to any Ur- or Earth-Mother, one outgoes mental sets when, piece by piece, one must

> press
> in under a deeper dark until
> the curtained sex
> the arch, the streaming buttress
> have become
> the self's unnameable and shaping home.

"Shaping"—as with another descent by Tomlinson into a dark interior (*Movements,* 1972), where "the going down / Is to a city of shapes, not a pit of shades," the affinity, one now sees, is not only with Bunting's shaped, interlocking sense of a habitable land, but with the form-seeking art of David Jones. In his work of prose and poetry, *The Anathemata* (1952), where a line of consciousness is traced from prehistoric millenia to the centuries after Christ, his rescue of concreteness and focused ground from wasteland neglect exactly complements Tomlinson's view of the mind as "a hunter of forms, binding itself, in a world that must decay, to present substance" (*Oppositions*, 1969). For Jones also, speaking of the poet's role in the preface to *The Anathemata*, "the 'forms' . . . that he's after, will be found to be part of vast, densely wooded, inherited and entailed domains."[9] Although that historical density leads to the excess of allusiveness that Tomlinson notes, it is also Tomlinson who provides the judicious standard with which to evaluate the distinctive powers of an Anglo-Welsh Londoner entering upon the "inherited . . . domains" of an enlarged, particularized Britain.

II

In a letter of 1952, Jones sets *The Anathemata* far apart from self-absorbed writing—"psychological" poetry and modern "personal" experience. To him, it is "a lucid, impersonal statement with regard to those things which have made us *all*—of this island":[10] the especially British experience of the sea, the Celtic past, and the pre-Reformation church. A communal inheritance is therefore voyaged toward, like a perpetual homecoming, in the several books of *The Anathemata*, where landfall in Britain is to be achieved via myth, folklore, history, etymology, crafts, and sciences. But these are literary voyages of the consciousness that are sustained by a sacramental Catholicism. Thus sailors to Britain across the ages may be tossed by storms, as in the books called *Middle-Sea and Lear-Sea* and *The Lady of the Pool*, but while Christ upholds, the bark of human mind will not be lost. So, what is seen in Ruskin and Tomlinson as a secular yet religious fidelity to intelligence, as it ventures through nature's intricacy, is, in Jones's art, more explicitly a Christian faith that gives constant intelligibility and ratification to the world of time.

In *The Sense of the Past*, Tomlinson observes a damage to concreteness by Jones's use "of typologies, of historic, mythic or literary anticipations"[11] of Christ's coming. While that remains true, it is also evident that Jones celebrates Christ's corporeality as a giving value and illumination to physical nature. In the book called *Keel, Ram, Stauros*, the Cross is prefigured in the timbers of a Greek ship sailing to Britain—

>   the central *arbor*
> the quivering elm on which our salvation sways.
> *Baum*, baulk
>   ridging the straked, dark
> inverted vaults of her.

Despite the prefiguring, however, Jones displays a muscular and etymological delight in the grain of wood and words. There is a carpenterlike exactness in joining solid fact to eternity at "the intersected place" in a way that avoids Eliot-like spirituality, with its intersection of the timeless with time and its would-be transcendence of nature. Indeed, throughout *The Anathemata,* one feels the influence of the different Eliot who mattered also to Tomlinson: that is, the man for whom, in "the mind of Europe," time and history have a cumulative worth, superannuating neither "Shakespeare, or Homer, or the rock drawing of the Magdalenian draughtsmen." Jones's God does not forsake anything either across time as he "brights" the fragments unearthed after "the Magdalenian splendours," as with "the juxtaposed forms, brighting the vaults of Lascaux." In *Rite and Foretime,* one is incited to follow the course of God's "brighting" across the vast span of time that includes the geological upheavals after Britain's Ice Age. Here, by contrast with Tomlinson's illumination of facts' rocky opacity, with relation reproven at every instance, Jones's instinct for the concrete, mobile, and present can only find expression through his portrayal of God's light rippling within a stationary past: a fixed spread from which no single item is lost in the divine numbering of particulars. Whatever the multitudes, "From before all time / the New Light beams for them":

> Piercing the eskered silt, discovering every stria, each score
> and macula, lighting all the fragile laminae of the shales.
> However Calypso has shuffled the marked pack, veiling with
> early the late.
> Through all unconformities and the sills without sequence,
> glorying all the under-dapple.
> Lighting the Cretaceous and the Trias, for Tyrannosaurus
> must somehow lie down with herbivores, or, the poet lied,
> which is not allowed.
> However violent the contortion or whatever the inversion
> of the folding.
> Oblique through the fire-wrought cold rock dyked from
> convulsions under.
> Through the slow sedimentations laid by his patient creature
> of water.
> Which ever the direction of the strike, whether the hade is
> to the up-throw or the fault normal.
> Through all metamorphs or whatever the pseudomorphoses.

It is as if a Ruskinian grasp of rock-structures has been joined to a Hopkins-like pleasure in nature's tiniest idiosyncrasy ("glorying all the under-dapple") and all has been given voice through Whitman's kind of extendable verse-line. Yet there is a central firmness, a pinioning of all the geological facts and prosaic oddness to a logical clarity as Jones reiterates a way through obstacle—"through the fire-wrought cold rock ... Through the slow sedimentations ... Through all metamorphs." It is the unmystical reasonableness with which the author also encourages the reader not to waver as the verse negotiates breaks in geological history. The "sills" of lava that, against chronological sequence, have been thrust up between rocks; the "unconformities" that arise when flat rock forms protrusions of a different age from adjacent terrain: none of this (nor any confusion wrought by history's mixing-up the order of strata, like a Calypso enchantress) can stop human—and divine—perception of the truth as it moves along the pathway of clear "continuings." Indeed, nothing is too difficult or meticulous for an undeceived God who lights up the "eskers" (ridges of clay, sand, or gravel deposits), the "strike" (the horizontal trend of a fault), the "hade" (the angle between the fault plane and the vertical), or the "pseudomorphoses" (when one mineral takes the appearance of another).

Yet even if Jones leaps to no timeless transcendence, he is—as becomes visible in the light of Tomlinson's and Lawrence's perception of the contraries that necessarily play against each other in the time-bound world—overready to span abysses and imagine reconciliations across time in the spirit of Christian love. Thus, like an immense prefiguring of Isaiah's prophecy that the calf shall lie down with the lion, the wolf with the lamb, "Tyrannosaurus must somehow lie down with herbivores": that is, dinosaurs of the Triassic Period (225 to 193 million years ago) become extinct and lay down their bones in the same Cretaceous Period (136 to 65 million years ago) as carnivorous animals. It is an instance of the way that Jones, without a more exact regard for the space and difficulty that must be traversed before relation becomes possible, later offers promiscuous fantasy in *The Lady of the Pool*—the mythologizing of the cockney narrator into Earth Mother, Roman deity, and Britannia, so that her sailor lover can be imagined voyaging home through her body into the multilayered historical density of London.

Jones's strength lies elsewhere, in his feeling for the unexaggeratedly specific, as when he writes that God's self-limiting for mankind in the Passion of Christ was "on this hill / at a time's turn / not on any hill / but on this hill." That is to celebrate, as in *Sherthursdaye and Venus Day*, the God who, by taking flesh, has defined the bounds and containment into which spiritual presence can enter. One remembers the tutelars of place in Tomlinson's poetry: his words, like the unegotistic self, emptied of insistence to receive a fullness. So also with Jones, there is emptying yet replenishment when a guardian "Genius" enters a Roman household—and, simultaneously, Christ's new Church ("new-gens"):

> As a *paterfamilias* among his own on his own festal-night
> empties out to the Genius of the place
>   he in this place
> empties himself
>   to the Lar of this place
> of this household
>   in session, here
> under the roof-beam at the bright hearth of this Lar,
> Here to the Genius of this *familia* of new-gens founders
> Inaugurally met.

All is specifically "here" ("this place ... this household ... this *familia*") with a sense of *thisness* that Tomlinson also articulates. But the latter poet, in A Given Grace (1966), does not rely on Christian particularity when two cups and the clarified self ("you, who are challenged / and replenished by / those empty vessels") embody refreshment of a different religious kind:

> Two cups,
> a given grace,
> afloat and white
> on the mahogany pool
> of table. They unclench
> the mind, filling it
> with themselves.

Nature's grace rather than a Christian God's: the distinction is even clearer when the household utensils in Tomlinson's *Annunciations* (1989) are suddenly lit by a revelatory sunray.

As with the starlight in *Briggflatts* ("Then is Now"), the millenially distant touches the domestically near when this "angel of appearances" tells how

>   "each cup
> dish, hook and nail
> now gathers and guards the sheen
> drop by drop
> still spilling over
> out of the grail of origin".

7: To Marry with a Land

Where "grail" brings one back to cup—to a gatherable source rather than a holy legend—one is a long way from Jones's tendency to mythic excess: what Tomlinson calls an "imaginative over-crowding . . . relentless typological parallels."[12] He refers not just to *The Anathemata* but also to the earlier book, *In Parenthesis* (1937), where the "densely wooded . . . domains" and "tangled brake" of the Celtic-Roman-Saxon inheritance make their appearance as thickening myth. The timespan may be shorter—the period from December 1915, when a group of Welsh Fusiliers finish training in England, up to their doomed attack on Mametz Wood during the Somme offensive of July 1916, but allusion extends chronology by setting the soldiers in a high order of warriors that stretches back through England's past battles to prehistory. "My fathers were with the Black Prince of Wales . . . I was the spear in Balin's hand." Thus runs a fragment of the long boast spoken by the soldier Dai Greatcoat, amplified by extensive annotation by which Jones invokes the Welsh bard Taliesin and the Germanic *Widsith*. Therefore, against the twentieth century's "loppings off of meanings" and thinning of connotation—as Jones sees it in his preface to *The Anathemata*—he sets the dense conflation of the Great War with all wars and Western Front soldiers with heroes from *Morte d'Arthur* or *The Mabinogion*. Distances and discontinuities are readily overleaped when Jones celebrates Lance-Corporal Aneirin Lewis's insistence (like a Shakespearean Fluellen) on the "Disciplines of the Wars" without seeming to be aware that a moral issue is involved as regards the military follies committed in the name of such "disciplines."

Yet an historically allusive poet like Jones, who takes epigraphs from Aneurin's seventh-century poem, *Y Goddodin,* about a fated Welsh assault on Ida's northern kingdom at Catraeth, is not to be confused with a naïve visionary like his character Aneirin Lewis, "for whom Troy still burned, and sleeping kings return." Jones, like Gurney, has also an unfantastic, durable sense of the past alive in the present—of a bold, civilized vigor, refusing to die and independent of myth or archetype, as it negotiates its way with stylistic care through wasteland fact. Hence, for example, the narrative is verbally alert to the immediacy of the moment when the new soldiers move forward to the frontline under the whispered guidance of Lieutenant Jones. Loving care must here be unsentimentally on its guard as the officer, priestlike, teaches his "ministrants" the steps of a vital catechism that they whisper as they go:

> Step down—
> step down and keep a bit left—keep your rifles down—mind
> the wire

> mind the wire—
> be careful of the wire.
>   The long professed sergeant of engineers; '04, Time Expired, out since the Marne; tempered to night watchings, whole armoured against this sorry place; considerate of sluices, revetting frames and corrugated iron; of sapping to his second line, of mines and countermines, who dreamed of pontoons in open places, of taking over from the cavalry; stood at the trench head, and kindly, in a quiet voice, guided their catechumen feet:
>   Seem pretty bitched—but they'll soon shape—get 'em in quickly corporal, it's not too healthy here.

The novice soldiers may be "catechumens," but Jones earns that framework of suggestion by the moral toughness that he accumulates in the sentence beginning, "The long professed sergeant . . . ," for, between the subject and the long-delayed main verb, there gathers the hardiness of the NCO's sensibility—an enactment of the way by which, "tempered," "armoured," and "considerate," the delicacy of a man measures up to the iron mechanics of his profession. Hotspur-like, his mind may be full "of sapping . . . of mines and countermines . . . of taking over from the cavalry"; yet Jones, by semi-evoking a Shakespearean soldier's dream "Of palisadoes, frontiers, parapets, / Of basilisks, of cannon, culverin,"[13] places the sergeant firmly within the civilized needs of the present. Slangily kind, he watches over the tired men without any of the mythic heightening that Jones offers later when Private Ball, on sentry duty, is "brother-keeper, and ward-watcher" to his fellows, the "long-barrow sleepers"—a remembrance of the Celtic armed sleepers, about whom Jones's notes give lengthy exposition and connect to Blake's theme in his picture, *The Ancient Britons*.

The narrative is more watchfully awake, however, when Corporal Lewis distributes rations to his section of men. He grandly "makes divisions, he ordains" and has the manner of Moses in the wilderness, who chided the Israelites with the cry, "Hear now, ye rebels; must we fetch you water out of this rock?"[14] Now, though, Lewis's manner—like his rebuke to soldiers who want cigarettes and complain that they have been given pipe tobacco ("You whoresons / must we fetch you immaculate *Abdullas* out of this earth")—has a demotic vigor played against it:

> Come off it Moses—dole out the issue.
> Dispense salvation,
> strictly apportion it,

> let us taste and see,
> let us be renewed,
> for christ's sake let us be warm.
> O have a care—don't spill the precious
> O don't jog his hand—ministering;
> do take care.
> O please—give the poor bugger elbow room.

It was surely of such a passage that Jones was thinking when he told a correspondent that he had tried to make cockney speech in the work *"not realistic"* yet with a *"real enduring shape that won't be embarrassing"* (his italics).[15] Indeed it is an "enduring shape," a firm, kind constancy inside the bounds of contingency, that stylistically becomes apparent as the soldiers' demands and their swearing energetically admit the tone of prayer: "don't spill the precious." Despite the Christian grace suggested by "*the* precious," language avoids any pious preciousness. That would be to push and insist—to go beyond the imaginably sayable instead of gradually winning, line by line, from the cries of the soldierly jostlers a civilized concern for person and place that is vigorously antimaudlin: "O please—give the poor bugger elbow room."

With style governed by circumstance, the urgency of the moment lets in prayer even more strikingly towards the end of *In Parenthesis*. There Dai Greatcoat, shot in the bowel during the attack on the wood, is being carried under fire with extreme difficulty by two stretcher-bearers. No Greatcoat-type boasts are possible when terrain must be hugged in frightened-grateful intensity: "down on hands on hands down and flattened belly and face pressed and curroodle mother earth." So, in words of cursing caution from one bearer to another, a man does not merely "cradle" but "curroodle" earth with relishing *r*'s—the vehemence that, at a particular moment, shapes human prayer and grounds it in local fact, rather than delivering its speaker completely to the embrace of an Earth-Mother: "Pray her hide you in her deeps . . . . Maiden of the digged places / let our cry come unto thee." Prayer is neither submersion nor transcendence, but it is that reaching toward relation within grounded limit that one sees in Jones's last book, *The Sleeping Lord* (1974). There the danger is not bullets, but the "bland megalopolitan light" of the western world after a second war; this time it is a Poundian vocabulary that Jones draws upon, notably from *Canto XLV*. For if "with usura is no clear demarcation / and no man can find site for his dwelling," that idea—minus Pound's obsession with usury—helps set the "sweet remembered demarcations" of *The Sleeping Lord* against the world's would-be centralizers.

Thus, in the section, *The Tutelar of the Place,* a delight in boundary and dwelling is the basis for prayer to a guardian spirit: "She that loves place, time, demarcation, hearth, kin, enclosure, site, differentiated cult." She is also "one mother of us all," but no generalized mythic matriarch when one considers her distinct, separate attributes:

> mother of particular perfections
> queen of otherness
> mistress of asymmetry
> patroness of things counter, parti, pied, several
> protectress of things known and handled
> help of things familiar and small

Hopkins's "pied beauty" has its place in this shapely identity, and Tomlinson's urban tutelary ("our lady of the nameless metals . . . guardian / Of all that our daily contact stales and fades") also has a kinship. Yet Tomlinson is also a reminder that Jones's particularities are not, except for remarkable moments, presented on the move— piece interlocking with piece, word with word, language with land. For that kind of active marrying one must go to the "ceaseless pairings" of Tomlinson's *Winter Encounters* (1960) where, "Meshed / Into neighbourhood by such shifting ties, / The house reposes." One must also go to the linkages and dwelling offered by another "house," the Quaker meetinghouse in Cumbria that provides the title of Bunting's *Briggflatts*. Through this "house" of encounter, where constancy is built on vanishings, a lineage is rediscovered, another voyage home undertaken. Native ground and language are to be meshed by a further, extraordinary precision.

III

The first lines of *Briggflatts* hold together nature's fact and human word so closely that the bold imperatives—

> Brag, sweet tenor bull,
> descant on Rawthey's madrigal

—are also tenderly exact. For "Brag" affectionately risks braggartry, like Aneirin Lewis's great boast, only to startle the reader back to perception of its accuracy. The springtime bellow of the bull that the poet remembers from his schooldays in Sedbergh fifty years before, does indeed, when heard, have its "sweet tenor" note. Moreover, this is not a solo vaunt, but a variation on a communal theme—a "descant" on and acoustic revelation of the River Rawthey's many voices in its water and stones. So, by the poet's and humanity's variation (our verbal dancing-away from nature's wordless actuality), one comes back to, and distinguishes, the separate elements of one music: "each pebble its part / for the fells' late spring."

This has a moral dimension in the poem. As the "spring" theme of part 1 leads to the "summer" of the poet's adulthood in part 2, there is a veering from the whole. By expediency and deadened response, the human being fails to grip with a land. Therefore lines in part 2 such as

> Starfish, poinsettia on a half-tide crag,
> a galliard by Byrd

offer the surprise—and the music—of consciousness regaining a small hold "on" place. After earlier slackening (where Bunting portrays the mesh of word with land as "ravelled and worn past splice, / yarns falling to staple," like the defeated Viking Eric Bloodaxe with his vaunts), nakedness of vision is the basis for a new weave and clothing. So "Starfish," uncovered on shore (and on the bare, clean monosyllables of the text's "half-tide crag") spreads open the mind to thought of an inland plant in the multisyllabic "poinsettia." The slight shock of another association ("a galliard by Byrd") takes one closer to the odd yet proper appositeness by which the human, in all its named identity, could dance with nature.

Yet the oddness, the incongruity, signals the gap that still exists in the poem before a language of human naming can again concur with nature's "animal" fact. Tomlinson, in *Adam* (1969), speaks of the process by which "Flower-maned beasts, beasts of the cloud, / Beasts of the unseen, green beasts"—all the singularities of the created world—look to our necessary utterance: "We bring / To a kind of birth all we can name / And, named, it echoes in us our being." For Bunting in part 2, after an Adamic Fall from such speech, the human-animal congruence can only be articulated with a jolt—as when, in a moment recalled from his Middle East experience in the Second World War

> swift desert ass startled by the
> camels' dogged saunter
> figures sudden flight of the descant
> on a madrigal by Monteverdi.

Like the descant of the Briggflatts bull, a variation from the whole is revelation of it: a jumping away, with swiftness against saunter, that returns the "startled" mind from desert to European civilization, from animal variety to the multivocal named profusion of "a madrigal by Monteverdi." It is also a musical figuring that is not Eliotic (hierarchical and transcendent in "The dance along the artery / The circulation of the lymph . . . figured in the drift of stars") but is Tomlinson-like in counterpoint—as with *Nine Variations in a Chinese Winter Setting* (1955), where pine scent is played against "snow-clearness" and where one hears the "creak of trodden snow / Against a flute." For Bunting in part 2, this has to be a music reached toward out of contraries and dissonance, as when he sees how

> rat, grey, rummaging
> behind the compost heap has daring
> to thread, lithe and alert, Schoenberg's maze.

Juxtapositions have their own daring. The anonymous, articleless rat entering a human speech of names and recognitions, takes one beyond incongruity toward a matched exactness, as "*thread*" becomes sinuously "li*the*," then acoustically "al*er*t" enough to penetrate the "Schoen*ber*gian maze."

The thread of a verbal weave begins to be fashioned, and, on such an occasion, Pound's poetic example is not far away. "Lithe turning of water, / sinews of Poseidon . . . Glass-glint of wave in the tide-rips against sunlight." To these lines from *Canto II*, one can justly add these from *Canto XVII*: "silver beaks rising and crossing / prow set against prow, / stone, ply over ply." Here is the suggestion of a sinewy interplay in speech that points Tomlinson toward Williams and Bunting toward a text nearer home—the "plaited lines" of seventh-century Gospels written out in posthumous tribute to Cuthbert, saint of the monastery at Lindisfarne island off the Northumbrian coast. It is, after all, particularly appropriate that a poem with the name of a Quaker meetinghouse (though one never mentioned in the work itself) should remember, with religious rather than Christian contemplation, the interlacing art of a text where names and words seem at moments to disappear inside a dense foliage of decoration.[16] Bunting significantly has noted the weave of the "cross-carpet pages"[17] that introduce each Gospel and the intricacies in the major "initial" pages of each Gospel itself, where, for example, at the beginning of St. Mark, the three columnar letters of "Initium" ("Initium evangelii Iesu Christi"), like the first three of St. John's ("In principio erat verbum"), are difficult to distinguish among a tracery of knots, frets, spirals, and pelta. The Word can hardly be seen inside a world of naturelike abundance and complexity.

7: To Marry with a Land

So Bunting is precise when he refers in *Briggflatts* to an "initial, / lot in Lindisfarne plaited lines." But he has also been precise at the beginning of the poem when he evoked the close texture of an experience from childhood. Then a boy and girl journey under sacks on the mason's lorry from Sedbergh to Hawes. This is not only the weave of body against body—"Stocking to stocking, jersey to jersey"—but of life and death as, pressed close against the load of carved headstones, "they kiss under the rain / bruised by their marble bed." There is also an interlocking speech of animal, human and inanimate, as they

> hear the horse stale,
> the mason whistle,
> harness mutter to shaft,
> felloe to axle squeak,
> rut thud the rim,
> crushed grit.

Word on word, thing on thing, each piece clinches to make a wheel move on the road. It is that sense of existing in a full, tangible entirety that Bunting suggests later when the journey is over. With the girl's parents in bed, the children dry their clothes before the fire: "He has untied the tape / of her striped flannel drawers / before the range." A naked, rain-washed literalness is bared in "tape," "striped flannel," and "range"; and by that cleansed uncovering, in style and content, the senses—through ear, speech, toe, fingertip, and genitals—can be said to come "home" to new clothing:

> Naked
> On the pricked mat
> his fingers comb
> thatch of his manhood's home.
>
> Gentle generous voices weave
> over bare night
> words to confirm and delight
> till bird dawn.
> Rainwater from the butt
> she fetches and flannel
> to wash him inch by inch,
> kissing the pebbles.
> Shining slowworm part of the marvel.

The human discovers its place in the "thatch" and "weave"—the inch-by-inch particularity of nature where, as with Rawthey's "madrigal" ("each pebble its part / for the fells' late spring"), the boy's "pebbles" and hair are, in their waking puberty, only parts of a larger music. So too "*Gentle generous voices*" gradually, uninsistently, reach towards the celebratory cries of birdsong.

That "Shining slowworm" is not just phallic, but is image of a humble yet undaunted regard for body and substance. It is the "Shining" of an animal and human concreteness, engaged with and loved. In part 2, love has been cheapened to mere convenience and become "discarded," like a wool unusable for spinning because it has not yet been carded, combed, and washed. But one sees a way to a "Shining" disentanglement and a combing when

> Riding silk, adrift on noon,
> a spider gleams like a berry
> less black than cannibal slug
> but no less pat under elders
> where shadows themselves are a web.

Borne on mere thread, subject to time's whim ("adrift on noon"), the spider as voyager is nevertheless "*Riding* silk"—adventurously and luxuriously unabashed by frailty. It is that bright thread of delicate toughness—followed through nature's network of slugs, elders, shadows—that intimates for Bunting a human-animal way back to a clarified, loving speech. Thus he presents the courageous vulnerability of Pasiphae, daughter of the Cretan king, Minos, who gave herself to the god-bull and begot the minotaur. Part 3 also shows it there, with further mingling of myth and history, in the Persian version of Alexander the Great journeying up a mountain to meet the Archangel. Having fallen down, he recovers his senses by a spring where, "snaking his flank" (but no snake of the Fall), the slowworm reappears—to speak of his twining through crops, as if he were one of the interlacing figures from the Lindisfarne Gospels: "Ripe wheat is my lodging. I polish / my side on pillars of its transept." Here, without dependence on myth, Bunting shows recovery for a frictional yet smoothing engagement with the world in its rain-washed clarity. That was seen in the personal memories of part 1, but part 4, evoking a larger Northumbrian past within the present, shows such engagement to be even more tightly made.

This is a land that the sensibility inhabits with a newly interknitted garment—as Bunting intimates when, like Jones in his use of *Y Gododin*, he draws on Aneurin. The Welsh bard is heard numbering the dead at the battle of Catraeth. But Jones's Aneurin-derived epigraphs in celebration of soldiers past and present marching to their doom, have none of the crisscross tensions that make up the tough, unrecking gladness of Bunting *against* such reckoning-up; he says, "I hear Aneurin number the dead and rejoice." His is an unregretful openness to fate and time, a nakedness also to the fact of flesh's vulnerability and physical zest as it bulks within, bodies forth, a clothing of realization:

> I see Aneurin's pectoral muscle swell under his shirt,
> pacing between the game Ida left to rat and raven,
> young men, tall yesterday, with cabled thighs.

The "cabled" quality of such garment has extra strands when history adds to bardic heroism that of Britain's Christian saints. Aneurin and Taliesin make their stay against death's dark, but Aidan, founder of the monastery on Lindisfarne and his ascetically enduring successor Cuthbert "put on daylight." This is the bold vitality of a love without self-regard that follows in the lineage of St. Columba at Iona and St. Columbanus, the uncompromising missionary:

> Columba, Columbanus, as the soil shifts its vest,
> Aidan and Cuthbert put on daylight,
> wires of sharp western metal entangled in its soft
> web, many shuttles as midges darting;
> not for bodily welfare nor pauper theorems
> but splendour to splendour, excepting nothing that is.

Sharp metal "entangled" in a soft web: this has the dawning toughness and delicacy of a love for all creation by which, in further daylight, the poet sees the sun rise "on an acknowledged land." He does so in further clarifying of the "entangled" elements in his own and country's sensibility. Part 4 continues by his image of a love persistent against the dark unknown because it is brave enough not to insist on permanence. It is like a slow-burning fire banked against the autumn night "till day"—with a sense of impermanence and of a constancy beyond that:

> Applewood, hard to rive,
> its knots smoulder all day.
> Cobweb hair on the morning,
> a puff would blow it away.

The "autumn" of this poetic "autobiography" is leading to the "winter" of age in part 5. But now Bunting's more confident readiness to poise on the page the images of "Applewood" and "Cobweb hair"— to set them in space, as when he says in part 5, "Sing, / strewing the notes on the air"—has the quality of substance and ephemera, generous daring and vulnerable delicacy, which finds a kinship in nature: "Mist sets lace of frost / on rock for the tide to mangle." There shall be no regret for what the flux destroys; but, equally, there shall be a quick eye, a nimble tongue, to celebrate the vanishing, reappearing design in which nature is clothed:

> Even a bangle of birds
> to bind sleeve to wrist
> as west wind waves to east
> a just perceptible greeting—
> sinews ripple the weave,
> threads flex, slew, hues meeting,
> parting in whey-blue haze.

Only Tomlinson has more extensively offered such a masterful idiom of instabilities and balancings. With Bunting, the ever-changing fabric of birds, wind, and color is rendered as plosively tight, when bodies seem to knit the air they circle ("bangle of birds / to bind"), yet shimmers with potential loosening—except that "west" greets "east" with "*ju*st perceptible" assonance, and "wrist" seems to fill, physically ripple within, the verbal sleeve of "*w*est *w*ind *w*aves." It is like the moment Tomlinson speaks of in *The Double Rainbow* (1981) where "words become / brides of the weather"—a marriage made possible in Bunting's syllabic seascape by the agility with which diphthong translates to a defter consonant ("*th*reads *fl*ex") and "slew" slides, only to be saved from mere evanescence by the perilous, trembling balance of "h*ue*s meeting, parting in whey-blue-haze."

Yet flux engages with land, and, in Bunting's Northumberland (where grit shapes the shore "as a mason / fondles and shapes his stone"), shepherds lead "demure dogs / from Tweed and Till and Teviotdale, / with hair combed back from the muzzle." All belong to a firmly located lineage of human and animal relation: "dogs from Redesdale and Coquetdale / taught by Wilson or Telfer." Northern place-names, like those of Cumbrian dog-trainers from the past, bulk large and unashamed. Yet now the relation between nameless animal fact and human naming is more subtly groomed and combed than when a galliard by Byrd suddenly became neighbor to a starfish on a crag.

Moreover, names and human speech are now entwined with wordless existence across a greater space as the poet looks to the stars above Northumberland's islands. The winter constellations that carry man's naming and shaping into the sky—Orion the Hunter, Procyon the Little Dog, Capella the Goat—seem to move within the same fabric as the smaller agitations of the animals below. So what decisively "strides" must go with "shuffle" and "shift": all part of that knit texture, that combing of speech and speechless, by which the universe is seen to journey:

> Orion strides over Farne.
> Seals shuffle and bark,
> terns shift on their ledges,
> watching Capella steer for the zenith,
> and Procyon starts his climb.

It is the abrasive and smoothed grip of word and thing that Tomlinson evokes in the poem *Orion over Farne* (1989). There, with a memory of Bunting, "constellation / On hunted constellation grinds and growls." But such stars at the end of *Briggflatts* are removed to greater distances and their nonhuman singularity. There is only a small light flickering back across bygone millenia—and, more personally, across the poet's own fifty years of remembered love. Nevertheless, that "tremulous thread spun in the hurricane" is a frailty and strength hazarded against the dark:

> Furthest, fairest things, stars, free of our humbug,
> each his own, the longer known the more alone,
> wrapt in emphatic fire roaring out to a black flue.
> Each spark trills on a tone beyond chronological compass,
> yet in a sextant's bubble present and firm
> places a surveyor's stone or steadies a tiller.
> Then is Now. The star you steer by is gone,
> its tremulous thread spun in the hurricane
> spider floss on my cheek; light from the zenith
> spun when the slowworm lay in her lap
> fifty years ago.

Like Shakespeare's "star to every wandering bark," this image of love is both unpossessively distant yet navigably near. Fragile yet steadying, the "bubble" holds, the vision flickers in the balance. After the journeys of the poem, from Sedbergh to Hawes, to the Arctic with Bloodaxe, to the Mediterranean and the Middle East with the adult poet, and then out to sea from the Northumbrian coast, the self takes its bearings—threads its way clearly into the shifting permanence of the weave. To be part of that texture, with its disquiet and calming, sureness and uncertainty, is to make ready, finally, in the coda of

Briggflatts, for further voyaging: "Blind, we follow . . . to fields we do not know."

IV

One need not invoke here any Larkinesque idea of "unfenced existence." Bunting's achievement is best measured by remembering Tomlinson's way of seeing the self in its movement out from egotism and stale assumptions: "Released / From knowing to acknowledgement." It is like the "acknowledged land" on which the sun rises in *Briggflatts*. But, as seen in this and previous chapters, such realization of a geographical and moral terrain—a disciplining concreteness, a tradition beyond the self through which the self can speak with new individuality—has also been the discovery of other English poets. Ivor Gurney, Edward Thomas, and D. H. Lawrence followed Hopkins in escaping from, or transforming, a romanticism of sublimities and melancholies, so that their energy could again contact the world of the particularized, factually definite, and objectively other: all that is the province of passionate reason and exact encounter in the kind of romanticism that, at their best, was offered by Coleridge, Blake, and Wordsworth.

The clarity of this lineage (and our being able to see Ruskin's key place, together with Whitman and Pound) owes its special sharpness to Tomlinson, as poet and critic. For all his affinities with Bunting—and for all he has learned from Williams—about localism, acceptance of the chance-given, or lineal flexibility, it is Tomlinson—and no other—who has provided so wide-ranging an awareness of inheritances and potentialities.

Just as many of his poems are thresholds by which the reader enters a pluralistic world, so his work overall is a unique point of access to the varied ways in which others have struggled towards, achieved, or lapsed from articulation of phenomenal existence. There *is* a moral standard here, particularly in the way that his poetry guards place and substance from brutalization or transcendence. Earth, time, and body are not to be soared beyond—by revolutionary politics, neoromantic symbolism, mystic Anglicanism, or surrealistic Hinduism. But it is a mark of Tomlinson's undogmatic moral sense that other writers' practice, seen in the light of his own, should invite from one no narrow judgement, but rather a width of discriminations. Now, for example, the Eliot of temporal struggle in *The Waste Land* seems more than ever distinct from the poet of *Four Quartets*. In the same way, one is now even more unlikely to mistake the Christian ethic of late

Eliot for Jones's incarnatory Catholicism, with its affirmation of time, space and fact.

Tomlinson's art points to connections as well as differentiations. One sees, for example, the aesthetic and scientific lineage that leads from Coleridge to Ruskin, Hopkins, Williams, Moore, Lawrence, and Jones. Yet connections and relations, as Tomlinson so often shows, become most clearly visible when one also respects the separateness of things. The human is not to be merged, sleepingly, with the sensuous world, because only through a wakeful awareness of the sharply singular can human reason and instinct dance with the nonhuman in all its changes and constancy. To stay aware is the finest—though secular—religious tutelage: moving with the grain of things, not mindlessly, but alertly admitting, in new fullness, the "Flower-maned beasts, beasts of the cloud, / Beasts of the unseen." Just as the poem, for him, is "the field of action" in Williams's sense—bearing witness to the particularized imprint by which each occasion marks it—it is also, in Moore's sense, the syllabic recipient of the strange, concrete otherness and bestiary that shapes it (a reminder of the way that Jones's shaped layout brings him closer to the wit of Moore than to the Anglo-Welshness of Edward Thomas). Tomlinson's poetry therefore extraordinarily illuminates not only the "beasts" of fauna and flora that enter the poetry of Moore, Lawrence, and Bunting, but also the self struggling out from submergence by animal babel and bird's cry in *The Waste Land,* toward human voice and community.

Ultimately, Tomlinson's direction is towards the communal. He, above all, exemplifies the movement from insularity, parochialism, exile, or alienation, toward a center: a nativeness that crystallizes itself by an internationalism (especially American objectivity) and a language of the present that, without exaggeration or strain, has learned how to reinherit the past. One sees his parallelism with and apt admiration for those like Octavio Paz and Hugh MacDiarmid who have also sought to bring their countries out of a cultural isolation into a mainland. But, as always with Tomlinson, it is the practical means that occupy him: the moment-by-moment way, without grand leaps, by which the consciousness finds a path through resistance and enters into a greater, branching whole—locality again connected to the universal, but with the nonfanciful invigoration by which people recreate cities and become newly aware guardians of neglected place. In *At the Edge* (1981), Tomlinson's keen pastoral reaches beyond the woodland scene where it begins:

> Edges are centres: once you have found
> Their lines of force, the least of gossamers

> Leads and frees you, nets you a universe
> Whose iridescent weave shines true
> Because you see it, but whose centre is not you:

In "the least of gossamers," one may be rightly reminded of Bunting's "tremulous thread." But Tomlinson's own distinctive touch and mastery could not be clearer. As the nonegotistic "you" chimes with "*u*niverse" (rhymingly "shines tr*ue*" in sharp-eyed attunement), "*y*ou"—and we—look into a radiating center. Through his work, also, we see a plurality of artists gathered together and lit in all their distinctness. It is he who nets us a universe of realization.

Notes

Chapter 1. A Lucid Darkness

1. Charles Tomlinson, "The Poet as Painter" (introductory essay), *Eden: Graphics and Poetry* (Bristol: Redcliffe Press, 1985), 10.
2. Charles Tomlinson and Richard Swigg, "Tomlinson at Sixty" (an interview), in Kathleen O'Gorman, ed., *Charles Tomlinson: Man and Artist* (Columbia: University of Missouri Press, 1988), 223. This is a reprint of "Charles Tomlinson at Sixty: In Conversation with Richard Swigg," *Poetry Nation Review* 14, no. 3 (November 1987): 58–61.
3. Alan Ross and Charles Tomlinson, "Words and Water: The Poetry of Charles Tomlinson," *London Magazine* 20 (January 1981): 26.
4. Ezra Pound, *Literary Essays of Ezra Pound* (London: Faber and Faber, 1954), 154.
5. Charles Tomlinson, *Some Americans: A Personal Record* (Berkeley and London: University of California Press, 1981), 105.
6. Quoted (from an 1856 diary entry) in Patricia Ball, *The Science of Aspects* (London: Athlone Press, 1971), 63.
7. Tomlinson, "The Poet as Painter," 14.
8. Ball, *The Science of Aspects*, 58.
9. John Ruskin, *Modern Painters*, in *The Works of John Ruskin*, ed. E. T. Cook and Alexander Wedderburn (London and New York: Grant Allen, 1904), 3:233.
10. Ibid., 3:205, 219.
11. Ibid., 343.
12. Charles Tomlinson, "Pages from an Italian Journal," *Poetry* 89, no. 3 (December 1956): 186.
13. Ruskin, *Modern Painters*, 3:204.
14. Ibid., 1:563.
15. Ibid., 3:235, 240, 244, and 234.
16. John Ruskin, *Praeterita*, in his *Works* (London and New York: George Allen, 1908), 226.
17. Ruskin, *Modern Painters*, 3:359.
18. Ibid., 3:342.
19. Ibid., 3:222: "Black or clear, monstrous or violet-coloured, cold salt water it is always, and nothing but that."
20. Ibid., 4:373.
21. Ibid., 4:479–80.
22. Ibid., 1:561.
23. Ibid., 1:566–67.
24. Charles Tomlinson, *Oppositions, The Way of a World, Collected Poems* (Oxford and New York: Oxford University Press, 1985), 189.
25. Constable's lecture at Hampstead, 16 June 1833, as recounted in C. R. Leslie,

Memoirs of the Life of John Constable (1843; reprinted London and New York: Dent/Everyman, 1911), 285.

26. Ruskin, *Modern Painters*, 1:553.
27. Ibid., 554.
28. Ibid., 1:490.
29. Ibid., 1:590.
30. Ruskin, *Praeterita*, 314.
31. Ruskin, *Modern Painters*, II:209.
32. See Gerard Manley Hopkins, *Gerard Manley Hopkins: Selected Letters*, ed. Catherine Philips (Oxford: Clarendon Press, 1990), 18; Hopkins's letter to A. W. M. Baillie, 10 July 1863: "I am sketching (in pencil chiefly) a good deal. I venture to hope you will approve of some of the sketches in a Ruskinese point of view." See also Tomlinson's remarks in an interview with Sean Street, recorded for Two Counties Radio, Southampton, England, December 1980: "I got very interested [when he was younger] in Ruskin's book *Modern Painters*, particularly those early sections . . . Truth of Leaves, Truth of Light, Truth of Water. . . . Hopkins at one point in his career says, 'I am keeping a journal from a Ruskinese point of view.' And suddenly I started to keep a journal from a Ruskinese point of view."
33. Gerard Manley Hopkins, *The Journals and Papers of Gerard Manley Hopkins*, ed. Humphrey House and Graham Storey (London and New York: Oxford University Press, 1959), September 1871 entry, 215.
34. Ibid., 230.
35. Ibid., 223.
36. Ibid., 208.
37. Ibid., 233.
38. Ibid.
39. Donald Davie, *The Purity of Diction in English Verse* (London: Chatto and Windus, 1952), 175.
40. Tomlinson, "Pages from an Italian Journal," 186.
41. These unpublished lines remain in the possession of the poet. Note the Ruskinian phrasing of "I instance / Only bowl and water-jug, white porcelain" by comparing it with: "I will instance only the San Pietro Martire, which, if not the most perfect, is at least the most popular of Titian's landscapes," Ruskin, *Modern Painters*, 1:171.

Chapter 2. "Thus Men Make a Mountain"

1. Charles Tomlinson, *Observation of Facts*, in his *The Necklace, Collected Poems* (Oxford and New York: Oxford University Press, 1985), 11:

> The house encloses: or fails to signify
> As being bodied over against one,
> As something one has to do with.

It directly echoes: "The tree is no impression, no play of my imagination, no value depending on my mood; but it is bodied over against me and has to do with me, as I with it—only in a different way"; Martin Buber, *Ich und Du* (1923). Tomlinson used the translation *I and Thou*, trans. Ronald Gregor Smith (Edinburgh: T. & T. Clark, 1937; revised version, 1966), 8.

2. Interview, January 1961, in Peter Orr, ed., *The Poet Speaks* (London: Routledge and Kegan Paul, 1964), 251.

3. Tomlinson, "The Poet as Painter," 12.

4. Orr, ed., *The Poet Speaks*, 251.

5. John M. Slatin, *The Savage's Romance: The Poetry of Marianne Moore* (University Park and London: Pennsylvania State University Press, 1986), 181–84.

6. Charles Tomlinson, "Abundance, Not Too Much: The Poetry of Marianne Moore," *Sewanee Review* 65 (Autumn 1957): 684.

7. Tomlinson, *Some Americans*, 33–34.

8. Translated as "instead of style / an austere disposition of / bolts"; from *Brooklyn Bridge*, in Vladimir Mayakowsky, *The Bedbug and Selected Poetry*, trans. Max Hayward and George Reavey (London: Weidenfeld and Nicholson, 1960), 170.

9. As told to me by Charles Tomlinson, May 1981, Newcastle-under-Lyme.

10. Tomlinson, *Some Americans*, 3.

11. Ruskin, *Modern Painters*, 1:554.

12. Tomlinson, "Abundance, Not Too Much," 678.

13. Charles Tomlinson, "Fate and the Image of Music: An Examination of Rosenberg's Plays," *Poetry Nation* 3 (1974): 64.

14. Ibid., 66.

15. Tomlinson, "Abundance, Not Too Much," 679.

16. Charles Tomlinson, "Introduction: Marianne Moore, Her Poetry and Critics," in his *Marianne Moore: A Collection of Critical Essays* (Englewood Cliffs, N.J., and London: Prentice-Hall, 1969), 8.

17. Isaac Rosenberg, *The Collected Works of Isaac Rosenberg*, ed. Ian Parsons (London: Chatto and Windus, 1979; reprinted 1984), 139.

18. Tomlinson, "Fate and the Image of Music," 61.

19. Tomlinson, ed., *Marianne Moore: A Collection of Critical Essays*, 3.

20. Moore's diary entry concerning John Dewey, 1920; quoted in Lisa M. Steinman, "Modern America, Modernism, and Marianne Moore," *Twentieth Century Literature* 30, no. 2–3 (Summer/Fall 1984): 210.

21. Tomlinson, *Some Americans*, 76–77.

22. Ibid., 77.

23. See Moore's "Poetry," 1921 version, in her *Collected Poems* (London: Faber and Faber, 1951).

24. Clifton Johnson, *What To See in America* (New York: Macmillan, 1919), 534.

25. M. C. Carey, "The Octopus in the Channel Islands," London *Graphic*, 25 August 1923, 282.

26. Francis Ward, "Poison Gas in Nature: The Lesser Octopus": *Illustrated London News*, 11 August 1923, 270.

27. John Ruskin, *Frondes Agrestes: Readings in "Modern Painters," Chosen at Her Pleasure by the Author's Friend, The Younger Lady of the Thwaite, Coniston* (Orpington and London: George Allen, 1896), 118.

28. This does not seem to be a direct quotation, but possibly a version of "Every tree had a water system of its own spreading far and wide like miniature Amazons and Mississippis"; John Muir, *The Mountains of California* (1894; reprinted Harmondsworth: Penguin, 1985), 184.

29. Walter Dwight Wilcox, *The Rockies of Canada* (New York and London: G. Putnam's Sons, 1909), 17.

30. Johnson, *What To See in America*, 514.

31. Ibid., 445–46.

32. Wilcox, *The Rockies of Canada*, 28.

33. Ibid., 130: "They are small horses with very great endurance and ability.... Some of them have 'glass eyes,' or a colourless condition of the retina, supposed to

be the result of too much in-breeding. . . . In winter, most of the horses are driven from the mountains and pastured among the foothills, where they paw away the snow and find abundant nourishment in the 'bunch grass.'"

34. Ruskin, *Frondes Agrestes*, 118–19.
35. Ibid., 119.
36. Ibid., 124.
37. See William Carlos Williams on Marianne Moore: "A poem such as 'Marriage' is an anthology of transit. It is a pleasure that can be held firm only by moving rapidly from one thing to the next"; William Carlos Williams, *Selected Essays of William Carlos Williams* (1954; reprinted New York: New Directions, 1969), 123.
38. Ruskin, *Frondes Agrestes*, 44.
39. Ibid., 110–11.
40. Ibid., 132.
41. Ibid., 128.
42. This, like all of the following quotations from Ruskin concerning Geneva, comes from his *Praeterita*, 321–25.
43. Ibid., 324.
44. Quoted in Vivienne Koch, "The Peaceable Kingdom of Marianne Moore," *Poetry Quarterly* 12, no. 1 (Spring 1950): 47. In this issue (which also contains an uncollected poem by Tomlinson called simply "Poem"), Koch goes on to say: "It is precisely Marianne Moore's 'sociality which could not be pent within the bounds of the actual.' It is her social shuttling from the actual to the imagined, or from what is imaginable in the actual, to its actuality, that is at once the key and the meaning to her charmed movement between the human and the animal kingdom."

Chapter 3. In the Tutelary Spirit

1. Letter to Witold von Hulewicz, November 1925, quoted by J. B. Leishman in his "Introduction" to Rainer Maria Rilke, *Sonnets to Orpheus*, trans. J. B. Leishman (London: Hogarth Press, 1936), 20–21.
2. This is as Tomlinson has told me (May 1981, Newcastle-under-Lyme). Therefore a footnote to the poem's title in M. L. Rosenthal, gen. ed. (Rosemary Sullivan, ed. of the "Late Moderns" section), *Poetry in English: An Anthology* (New York and Oxford: Oxford University Press, 1987), 1080, is incorrect in locating the hall as "Alfoxden, a house near the town of Nether Stowey, rented by William Wordsworth while he worked on the *Lyrical Ballads*."
3. Tomlinson, *Some Americans*, 24.
4. Charles Tomlinson, "Introduction," in William Carlos Williams, *William Carlos Williams: Selected Poems* (1976; reprinted Harmondsworth: Penguin, 1983), 14.
5. D. H. Lawrence, *Phoenix: The Posthumous Papers of D. H. Lawrence*, ed. Edward D. McDonald (1936; reprinted London: William Heinemann, 1961), 335.
6. Bram Dijkstra, *The Hieroglyphics of a New Speech: Cubism, Stieglitz, and the Early Poetry of William Carlos Williams* (Princeton: Princeton University Press, 1969), 99–100.
7. The photograph was taken by Ken Lambert and was used on the front cover of the first edition of Charles Tomlinson, *The Way In and Other Poems* (London and New York: Oxford University Press, 1974).
8. Tomlinson, "Introduction," in Williams, *Selected Poems*, 16: "If, as with Emerson, Williams seems to 'ask the fact for the form,' the form, once it comes, is free of the fact, is a *dance above the fact*."

9. William Wordsworth, *The Prelude*, book 1 (1850 version), in his *The Prelude: A Parallel Text*, ed. J. C. Maxwell (1971; reprinted Harmondsworth: Penguin Education, 1975), 53.
10. Tomlinson, "Introduction," in Williams, *Selected Poems*, 13.
11. Charles Tomlinson, "Letter to Dr. Williams," *Spectrum* (Fall 1957): 58–59.
12. Ralph Waldo Emerson, "Poetry and Imagination," in his *The Works of Ralph Waldo Emerson*, ed. George Sampson (London: G. Bell and Sons, 1913), 3:210.
13. Charles Tomlinson, *The Poem as Initiation* (Hamilton, N.Y.: Colgate University Press, 1967).
14. Ralph Waldo Emerson, "The American Scholar," in his *The Collected Works of Ralph Waldo Emerson* (Cambridge: Belknap Press of Harvard University, 1971), 1:67.
15. Jed Rasula and Mike Erwin, "An Interview with Charles Tomlinson," *Contemporary Literature*, 16 (Autumn 1975): 406.
16. William Carlos Williams, *The Autobiography of William Carlos Williams* (1951; reprinted New York: New Directions, 1967), 333.
17. Tomlinson, "Introduction," in Williams, *Selected Poems*, 19.
18. Mr. Tomlinson worked as an estate agent's clerk in Stoke-on-Trent and for many years contributed angling notes to the local newspaper, the *Evening Sentinel*.
19. Charles Tomlinson, "Words and Water," *London Magazine*, 10 January 1981, 26.
20. P. J. Kavanagh, "Introduction," in Ivor Gurney, *Collected Poems of Ivor Gurney*, ed. P. J. Kavanagh (1982; reprinted Oxford and New York: Oxford University Press, 1985), 16.

Chapter 4. Between Paradise and History

1. All dates for Gurney's poems in this chapter are derived from the Kavanagh edition of his *Collected Poems*, with its six sections: 1. From *Severn and Somme* (1917). From *War's Embers* (1919); 2. 1917–1919; 3. From *Rewards of Wonder* (1919–1920); 4. 1919–1922; 5. September 1922–1925; 6. 1926 and after.
2. Lawrence, *Phoenix*, 304.
3. Charles Tomlinson, *The Sense of the Past: Three Twentieth Century Poets* (Liverpool: Liverpool University Press, 1983), 5.
4. Charles Tomlinson, "Ivor Gurney's 'Best Poems,'" *The Times Literary Supplement*, 3 January 1986, 12.
5. Ivor Gurney, *Ivor Gurney: War Letters*, ed. R. K. R. Thornton (1983; reprinted London: Hogarth Press, 1984), 40.
6. Ibid., 25.
7. Ibid., 73.
8. Ibid., 56.
9. Ibid.
10. Ibid., 170.
11. Ibid., 180.
12. Charles Tomlinson, *Poetry and Metamorphosis* (Cambridge, London, and New York: Cambridge University Press, 1983), 42.
13. Tomlinson, "Ivor Gurney's 'Best Poems.'"
14. Although not published in Gurney, *Collected Poems*, this poem can be found in Tomlinson, "Ivor Gurney's 'Best Poems.'"
15. Tomlinson, *Some Americans*, 11.
16. Gurney, *War Letters*, 234.

17. Charles Tomlinson, review of Eleanor Farjeon, *Edward Thomas: The Last Four Years*, and of Helen Thomas, *As It Was* and *World without End*, *Poetry* 95, no. 1 (October 1959): 52–53.
18. Edward Thomas, *In Pursuit of Spring* (London: Thomas Nelson and Sons, 1914), 86.
19. Ibid., 87–88.
20. See especially John C. Kemp, *Robert Frost: The Poet as Regionalist* (Princeton: Princeton University Press, 1979).
21. Edward Thomas, review of *North of Boston*, *English Review* (August 1914); reprinted in his *A Language Not to Be Betrayed: Selected Prose of Edward Thomas*, ed. Edna Longley (Manchester: Carcanet Press, 1981), 129.
22. Thomas, *In Pursuit of Spring*, 207: "Though born and bred a Clapham Junction man, I have become indifferently so."
23. Tomlinson, *Poetry and Metamorphosis*, 24.
24. Thomas, *A Language Not to Be Betrayed*, 131.
25. See Tomlinson, "Ivor Gurney's 'Best Poems'": "Except for Lawrence, it is hard to think of any other English poet who has known what to do with Whitman."

Chapter 5. Contraries and Relations

1. Charles Tomlinson, "Art and Chaos," *Nine* 2 (Winter 1949–50): 52. A footnote says: "*Nightbook* is written in the form of a long prose-poem, illustrated by the author. The intended effect is much the same as that of a Blake prophetic book, words and pictures being interdependent. The work takes for its theme the role of the moon as a cosmological religious symbol, arriving at an overtly pagan synthesis. The extract given is from the introductory section, *Art and Chaos*, a diagnosis of the arts of moon-sickness."
2. Charles Tomlinson, review of William Blake's *Vala*, ed. H. M. Margoliouth, *Poetry* 90, no. 5 (August 1957): 321–25.
3. Lawrence, "The Reality of Peace," in his *Phoenix*, 692.
4. D. H. Lawrence to Edward Marsh, 18 November 1913, in his *D. H. Lawrence, The Letters of D. H. Lawrence II*, ed. George J. Zytaruk and James T. Boulton (London and New York: Cambridge University Press, 1981), 103.
5. D. H. Lawrence, *Women in Love*, ed. David Farmer, Lindeth Vasey, and John Worthen (Cambridge, London, New York, New Rochelle, Melbourne, and Sidney: Cambridge University Press, 1987), 356–57.
6. Lawrence, *Phoenix*, 139.
7. D. H. Lawrence, *Twilight in Italy* (1916; reprinted Harmondsworth: Penguin, 1960), 54.
8. D. H. Lawrence, *The Ladybird*, in his *Three Novellas* (1924; reprinted Harmondsworth: Penguin, 1974), 35.
9. Lawrence, *Phoenix*, 567.
10. Ibid., 568.
11. Ibid., 567.
12. Lawrence, *Letters II*, 183–84,
13. D. H. Lawrence to Henry Savage, Autumn 1913, in D. H. Lawrence, *The Collected Letters of D. H. Lawrence*, ed. Harry T. Moore (London and Melbourne: Heinemann, 1962), 1:241.
14. Ibid.
15. Lawrence, *Letters II*, 182–83.

16. Lawrence, *Women in Love*, 421.
17. Ibid., 434.
18. D. H. Lawrence, *Studies in Classic American Literature* (1924; reprinted London: Heinemann, 1964), 118.
19. Ibid., 138.
20. Ibid.
21. Ibid., 10°.
22. D.H. Lawrence, *The Captain's Doll*, in his *Three Novellas*, 239–40.
23. Keith Sagar, *D. H. Lawrence: A Calendar of His Works* (Manchester: Manchester University Press, 1979), 101–2.
24. As in D. H. Lawrence, *The Complete Poems of D. H. Lawrence*, ed. Vivian de Sola Pinto and Warren Roberts (London: Heinemann, 1964), 1:372, where *Humming-Bird* is given a location ("Española") and, therefore, by implication, a date when Lawrence was in New Mexico. But, as Sagar points out (*D. H. Lawrence: A Calendar of His Works*, 102), the poem was published in May 1921, well before Lawrence went to America.
25. D. H. Lawrence, *The Symbolic Meaning: The Uncollected Versions of "Studies in Classic American Literature"*, ed. Armin Arnold (Fontwell, Arundel: Centaur Press, 1962), 262.
26. Lawrence, *Studies in Classic American Literature*, 162.
27. Lawrence, *The Symbolic Meaning*, 64.
28. Ibid., 64.
29. Ibid.
30. D. H. Lawrence, *Mornings in Mexico* and *Etruscan Places* (1927 and 1932, respectively; reprinted Harmondsworth: Penguin, 1960), 166.
31. Ibid., 167.
32. Pound, *Literary Essays*, 154.
33. Lawrence, *Studies in Classic American Literature*, 6.
34. Tomlinson, *The Poem as Initiation*, 5.
35. Lawrence, *Mornings in Mexico* and *Etruscan Places*, 65–69.
36. Ibid., 78.
37. John Cage, *Silence: Lectures and Writings* (London: Calder and Boyers, 1973), 73.
38. Ibid., 143. See also Tomlinson and Swigg, "Tomlinson at Sixty," 23–31: "I'd discovered Webern and Schoenberg just when I started fragmenting my lines, spacing them out with breath-pauses and hesitations, caught up very consciously into the fabric of the whole, like Webern's use of silences. I also enjoyed John Cage's lecture *On Nothing* . . . which is a sort of talkathon arranged around silences ('I have nothing to say / and I am saying it / and that is / poetry . . .'). He breaks up his sentences, lets in the pauses, actually makes you see that silence as well as the words is a created thing—'What we re-quire / is / silence / ; / but what silence re-quires / is / that I go on talking / . / . . . .' It's all very witty and more than witty. I suppose this kind of thing could become tediously self-conscious, as some Cage is, though he seems to be attacking the idea of self—certainly the egotistical sublime."
39. D. H. Lawrence, *The Plumed Serpent* (1926; reprinted London: Heinemann, 1970), 75–76; Kate Leslie is reading the words of Don Ramón.

Chapter 6. Ends and Beginnings

1. T. S. Eliot, *Charles Tomlinson Reads "The Waste Land" by T. S. Eliot*, sound cassette (Keele University, 1989).

2. Octavio Paz, "Poetry and History," in his *Octavio Paz: Selected Poems*, ed. Charles Tomlinson (Harmondsworth: Penguin, 1979), 15.

3. "Octavio Paz in England" (introductory talk), in Octavio Paz and Charles Tomlinson, *Octavio Paz Talks to Charles Tomlinson*, sound cassette (Keele University, 1989).

4. Charles Tomlinson's introductory note to *Assassin* and *Swimming Chenango Lake*, in *Let the People Choose*, ed. James Gibson (London: Harrap, 1973), 174: "In 'Assassin' I visualize the denial of relationship, the attempt to go against the grain of humanity and achieve a kind of mystical transcendence by cold will. . . . I had in mind also Che Guevera's phrase, 'We must transform ourselves into cold and efficient killing machines.' Since he is so widely and uncritically admired, the moral is self-evident." See also Rasula and Erwin, "An Interview with Charles Tomlinson," 409: ". . . history is certainly an arc that resists completion, though men are always trying to fix it through revolution or mystical transcendence. I see the assassination of Trotsky in *The Way of a World* ['Assassin'] as an attempt to transcend time, almost as a caricature of mysticism, an attempt to have the future *now* on one's own terms and the result of trying to complete *that* circle is inhumanity—as when Che Guevara for whatever "good" reasons decided 'We must transform ourselves into cold and efficient killing machines.'"

5. Isaac Deutscher, *The Prophet Outcast: Trotsky: 1929–1940* (London, New York, and Toronto: Oxford University Press, 1963), 499.

6. Letter from Charles Tomlinson to Richard Swigg, 19 March 1987.

7. Tomlinson drew on Wilson for another poem, *Above Manhattan* (1984). As he says in his commentary on the poem recorded on Charles Tomlinson, *Charles Tomlinson Reads His Poems*, sound cassette (Keele University, 1985): "It was from Edmund Wilson's book *In Defense of the Iroquois* I first learned that the people who work at building the skyscrapers of Manhattan are often Iroquois Indians."

8. Tomlinson and Swigg, "Tomlinson at Sixty," 228.

9. Lawrence, *Phoenix*, 335.

10. Lawrence, *Studies in Classic American Literature*, 51.

11. Ibid.

12. See Robert L. Carringer, *The Making of Citizen Kane* (London: John Murray, 1985), 18ff., about the early drafts of the *Citizen Kane* script.

13. Joseph Conrad, *Heart of Darkness* in his *Youth: A Narrative and Two Other Stories* (London and Edinburgh: Thomas Nelson and Sons, 1955), 163 and 165.

14. See Tomlinson's comments in "Reading *The Waste Land*", a talk recorded on Eliot, *Charles Tomlinson Reads "The Waste Land"*, sound cassette: "This is a poem that, like the rapid cutting in some films, only releases its larger meaning as you reexperience it."

15. Charles Tomlinson and Michael Schmidt, "Charles Tomlinson in Conversation," *Poetry Nation Review* 5, no. 1 (October 1977): 36.

16. Ibid.

17. Thomas Carlyle, *The French Revolution* (1837; reprinted London: Dent, 1899), 3:209. Carlyle speaks of "a fair young creature, sheeted in red smock of murderess; so beautiful, serene, so full of life."

18. André Chénier, *A Charlotte Corday*, in his *Poésies* (Paris: Nelson Éditeurs, 1949), 358–61.

19. Jules Michelet, *Histoire de la Révolution Française* (Paris: Chamerot, 1853), 343.

20. Ibid., 344.

21. Ibid.

22. Ibid.
23. Ibid., 350–51:

"Que haïssiez-vous en lui?—Ses crimes."
"Croyez-vous donc avoir tué tous les Marats?—Celui-là mort, les autres auront peur, peut-être."
"Apparemment, vous vous étiez d'avance bien exercée . . .—O le monstre! s'écria-t-elle. Il me prend pour un assassin!"

24. 1850 version, in Wordsworth, *The Prelude: A Parallel Text*, 411 and 399.
25. Hilaire Belloc, *Danton: A Study* (1899: reprinted London: Nisbet and Co., 1928), 237.
26. Ibid., 46–47.
27. Tomlinson's word: on Paz and Tomlinson, *Octavio Paz Talks to Charles Tomlinson*, sound cassette.
28. Niccolò Machiavelli to Francesco Vittorio, 10 December 1513, in his *Opere Complete di Niccolò Machiavelli* (Firenze: Passigli, Borghi, e Compagni, 1831), 872.
29. Maurice Merleau-Ponty, *Signs*, trans. Richard C. McCleary (Evanston, Il.: Northwestern University Press, 1964), 221; translated from his *Signes* (1960).
30. Maurice Merleau-Ponty, *The Primacy of Perception*, ed., James M. Edie (Evanston, Ill.: Northwestern University Press, 1964), 25; translated by Edie and others from studies published 1947–61. Note Tomlinson's remarks in Rasula and Erwin, "An Interview with Charles Tomlinson," 416: "I'd always wanted to find some way of explaining how we build our structures on the sensed and the given. Then one day, in a friend's flat in New York, I turned up Merleau-Ponty's *The Primacy of Perception* and the little essay in it that seemed to say all I'd wanted to say. It says it for poetry and much more, and it makes one see how poetry is of a piece with other human activities. I return, time and again, to the central point of that essay where Merleau-Ponty says,

By these words, the "primacy of perception," we mean that the experience of perception is our presence at the moment when things, truths, values are constituted for us; that perception is a nascent logos; that it teaches us, outside all dogmatism, the true condition of objectivity itself; that it summons us to the tasks of knowledge and action. It is not a question of reducing human knowledge [and here I put in poetry] to sensation, but of assisting at the birth of this knowledge, to make it as sensible as the sensible, to recover the consciousness of rationality.

That, for me, with the whole essay behind it, is one of our great defenses of poetry."
31. Merleau-Ponty, *Signs*, 218.
32. Machiavelli, *Opere*, 872.
33. Merleau-Ponty, *Signs*, 221.
34. Ibid., 222.
35. William Carlos Williams, *In the American Grain* (1925; reprinted New York: New Directions, 1956), 69.

Chapter 7. To Marry with a Land

1. Tomlinson, *The Sense of the Past*, 19.
2. Charles Tomlinson, "Poetry Today," in Boris Ford, ed., *The Modern Age*, vol. 7 of *The Pelican Guide to English Literature* (1961; reprinted Harmondsworth: Penguin, 1963), 458.

3. Charles Tomlinson, "The Middlebrow Muse" (review of *New Lines*), *Essays in Criticism* 7 (April 1957): 215. Brian John, *The World as Event: The Poetry of Charles Tomlinson* (Montreal and Kingston, London and Buffalo: McGill-Queen's University Press, 1989), 106, traces "suburban mental ratio" to William Blake's *There Is No Natural Religion*: "If it were not for the Poetic or Prophetic character the Philosophic & Experimental would soon be at the ratio of all things, & stand still unable to do other than repeat the same dull round over again."

4. Quoted by Tomlinson in "Poetry Today," 458. The full quotation runs: "Nobody wants any more poems about philosophers or paintings or novelists or art galleries or mythology or foreign cities or other poems. At least I hope nobody wants them."

5. See Fiordiligi in *Così fan tutte*. The reply, it seems, is not just to Amis but to Larkin, of whom Tomlinson comments in "Poetry Today," 458, that he now publicly indulges "a dislike of Mozart and 'a mild xenophobia.'"

6. Tomlinson, "The Middlebrow Muse," 214.

7. Adrian Stokes, *The Stones of Rimini* in his *The Critical Writings of Adrian Stokes*, ed. Lawrence Gowing (London: Thames and Hudson, 1978), 1:192.

8. Tomlinson gives a location for the poem on his *Charles Tomlinson Reads His Poems*, sound cassette (Keele University, 1985).

9. David Jones, "Preface," to his *The Anathemata* (1952; reprinted London and Boston: Faber and Faber, 1979), 20.

10. David Jones to Jim Ede, 17 December 1952, printed in his *Dai Greatcoat: A Self-Portrait of David Jones in His Letters*, ed. René Hague (London and Boston: Faber and Faber, 1980), 155.

11. Tomlinson, *The Sense of the Past*, 14.

12. Ibid.

13. William Shakespeare, *King Henry IV, Part 1*, 2.3.

14. *Numbers* 20:10.

15. David Jones to René Hague, 2 December 1935, printed in his *Dai Greatcoat*, 80.

16. For her commentary on the whole corpus, I am especially indebted to Janet Backhouse, *The Lindisfarne Gospels* (1981; reprinted Oxford: Phaidon Press, 1989). For his discussion of *Briggflatts'* woven texture, I am also indebted to Peter Makin, "*Briggflatts* and *Beowulf*," *Scripsi* 4, no. 3 (1986): 225–41.

17. See the extract from Bunting's 1976 interview with Duncan Bush and Paul Merchant, quoted in Carrol F. Terrell, ed., *Basil Bunting: Man and Poet* (Orono, Maine: National Poetry Foundation/University of Maine, 1980), 244.

Bibliography

Books

Auden, W. H. *Collected Poems*. Edited by Edward Mendelson. London: Faber and Faber, 1976.

Backhouse, Janet. *The Lindisfarne Gospels*. Oxford: Phaidon Press, 1981; reprinted 1989.

Ball, Patricia. *The Science of Aspects*. London: Athlone Press, 1971.

Bedient, Calvin. "On Charles Tomlinson." In *British Poetry since 1960*, edited by Michael Schmidt and Grevel Lindop. South Hinksey, Oxford: Carcanet Press, 1972.

———. *Eight Contemporary Poets*. Oxford: Oxford University Press, 1974.

Belloc, Hilaire. *Danton: A Study*. 1899; reprinted London: Nisbet and Co., 1928.

Blake, William. *The Poems of William Blake*. Edited by W. H. Stevenson. Text by David V. Erdman. London: Longman, 1980.

Buber, Martin. *I and Thou*, trans. 1937 Ronald Gregor Smith; reprinted in revised version Edinburgh: T. & T. Clark, 1966.

Bunting, Basil. *Collected Poems*. Oxford and New York: Oxford University Press, 1978; reprinted 1987.

Carlyle, Thomas. *The French Revolution*. 1837; reprinted London: Dent: 1899.

Carringer, Robert L. *The Making of Citizen Kane*. London: John Murray, 1985.

Chénier, André. "A Charlotte Corday", in *Poésies*. Paris: Nelson Éditeurs, 1949.

Conrad, Joseph. *Youth: A Narrative and Two Other Stories*. London and Edinburgh: Thomas Nelson and Sons, 1955.

Cookson, William. "Charles Tomlinson." In *Contemporary Poets of the English Language*, edited by Rosalie Murphy. London and Chicago: St. James Press, 1970.

Davie, Donald. *The Purity of Diction in English Verse*. London: Chatto and Windus, 1952.

———. *Thomas Hardy and British Poetry*. London: Routledge and Kegan Paul, 1973.

———. *Under Briggflatts: A History of Poetry in Great Britain 1960–1988*. Manchester: Carcanet Press, 1989.

Deutscher, Isaac. *The Prophet Outcast: Trotsky: 1929–1940*. London, New York and Toronto: Oxford University Press, 1963.

Dijkstra, Bram. *The Hieroglyphics of a New Speech: Cubism, Stieglitz, and the Early Poetry of William Carlos Williams*. Princeton: Princeton University Press, 1969.

Donoghue, Denis. *The Ordinary Universe: Soundings in Modern Literature*. London: Faber and Faber, 1968.

Edwards, Michael. "Charles Tomlinson." In *Twentieth Century Poetry: Third Level Course, Unit 31: Donald Davie, Charles Tomlinson, [and] Geoffrey Hill*. Milton Keynes: The Open University Press, 1976.

——. *Poetry and Possibility*. London: Macmillan, 1988.

Eliot, T. S., *The Complete Poems and Plays*. London: Faber and Faber, 1969.

Emerson, Ralph Waldo. "The American Scholar", in *The Collected Works of Ralph Waldo Emerson I*. Cambridge: Belknap Press of Harvard University.

——. *Poems*. London: Routledge, 1898.

——. "Poetry and the Imagination", in *The Works of Ralph Waldo Emerson III*, ed. George Sampson. London: G. Bell and Sons, 1913.

Ford, Boris (ed.). *The Modern Age*, vol. 7 of *The Pelican Guide to English Literature*. Harmondsworth: Penguin, 1961; reprinted 1963.

Frost, Robert. *The Poetry of Robert Frost*. Edited by Edward Connery Lathem. London: Jonathan Cape, 1976.

Gurney, Ivor. *Collected Poems of Ivor Gurney*. Edited by P. J. Kavanagh. Oxford, New York: Oxford University Press, 1985.

——. *War Letters*, ed. R. K. R. Thornton. London: Hogarth Press, 1983; reprinted 1984.

Hopkins, Gerard Manley. *Gerard Manley Hopkins: Selected Letters*, ed. Catherine Phillips. Oxford: Clarendon Press, 1990.

——. *The Journals and Papers of Gerard Manley Hopkins*, ed. Humphrey House and Graham Storey. London and New York: Oxford University Press, 1959.

——. *The Poems of Gerard Manley Hopkins*. Edited by W. H. Gardner and N. H. Mackenzie. London and New York: Oxford University Press, 1967.

John, Brian. *The World as Event: The Poetry of Charles Tomlinson*. Montreal and Kingston, London and Buffalo: McGill-Queen's University Press, 1989.

Johnson, Clifton. *What To See in America*. New York: Macmillan, 1919.

Jones, David. *The Anathemata: Fragments of an Attempted Writing*. London, Boston: Faber and Faber, 1979.

——. *In Parenthesis*. London and Boston: Faber and Faber, 1989.

——. *The Sleeping Lord and Other Fragments*. London: Faber and Faber, 1975.

Kemp, John C. *Robert Frost: The Poet as Regionalist*. Princeton: Princeton University Press, 1979.

Kenner, Hugh, *A Sinking Island: The Modern English Writers*. London: Barrie and Jenkins, 1988.

King, P. R. *Nine Contemporary Poets: A Critical Introduction*. London: Macmillan, 1979.

Kirkham, Michael. "Charles Tomlinson." In *British Poetry since 1970*, edited by Michael Schmidt and Peter Jones. Manchester: Carcanet Press, 1980.

——. "Philip Larkin and Charles Tomlinson: Realism and Art." In *The Present*, vol. 8 of *The New Pelican Guide to English Literature*, edited by Boris Ford. Harmondsworth: Penguin, 1983.

Koch, Vivienne. "The Peaceable Kingdom of Marianne Moore", in *Poetry Quarterly* 12, no. 1 (Spring 1950).

Larkin, Philip. *The Whitsun Weddings*. London: Faber and Faber, 1964.

Lawrence, D. H. *The Captain's Doll*, in *Three Novellas*. 1924; reprinted Harmondsworth: Penguin, 1974.

——. *The Collected Letters of D. H. Lawrence I*, ed. Harry T. Moore. London and Melbourne: Heinemann, 1962.

———. *The Complete Poems of D. H. Lawrence*. 2 volumes. Edited by Vivian de Sola Pinto and Warren Roberts. London: Heinemann, 1972.

———. *The Ladybird*, in *Three Novellas*. 1924; reprinted Harmondsworth: Penguin, 1974.

———. *The Letters of D. H. Lawrence II*, ed. George J. Zytaruk and James T. Boulton. Cambridge, London, New York, New Rochelle, Melbourne and Sidney: Cambridge University Press, 1981.

———. *Mornings in Mexico* and *Etruscan Places*. 1927 and 1932 respectively; reprinted Harmondsworth: Penguin, 1960.

———. *Phoenix: The Posthumous Papers of D. H. Lawrence*, ed. Edward D. McDonald. 1936; reprinted London: Heinemann, 1961.

———. *Studies in Classic American Literature*. 1924; reprinted London: Heinemann, 1964.

———. *The Symbolic Meaning: The Uncollected Versions of "Studies in Classic American Literature"*, ed. Armin Arnold. Fontwell, Arundel: Centaur Press, 1962.

———. *Twilight in Italy*. 1916; reprinted Harmondsworth: Penguin, 1960.

———. *Women in Love*. 1921; edited in new reprint by David Farmer, Lindeth Vasey, and John Worthen: Cambridge, London, New York, New Rochelle, Melbourne and Sidney: Cambridge University Press, 1987.

Leslie, C. R. *Memoirs of the Life of John Constable*. 1843; reprinted London and New York: Dent/Everyman, 1911.

Machiavelli, Niccolò. *Opere Complete di Niccolò Machiavelli*. Firenze: Passigli, Borghi e Compagni, 1831.

Marvell, Andrew. *The Poems of Andrew Marvell*. Edited by Hugh MacDonald. London: Routledge and Kegan Paul, 1952.

Mayakowsky, Vladimir. *The Bedbug and Selected Poetry*. trans. Max Hayward and George Reavey. London: Weidenfeld and Nicholson, 1960.

Merleau-Ponty, Maurice. *The Primacy of Perception*, ed. James M. Edie. Evanston, Ill.: Northwestern University Press, 1964.

———. *Signs*, trans. Richard C. McCleary. Evanston, Il.: Northwestern University Press, 1964.

Michelet, Jules. *Histoire de la Revolution Française*. Paris: Chamerot, 1853.

Moore, Marianne. *Collected Poems*. London: Faber and Faber, 1951.

Muir, John. *The Mountains of California*. 1894; reprinted Harmondsworth: Penguin, 1985.

O'Gorman, Kathleen, ed. *Charles Tomlinson: Man and Artist*. Columbia: University of Missouri Press, 1988.

Oppen, George. *Collected Poems*. London: Fulcrum Press, 1972.

Orr, Peter (ed.). *The Poet Speaks*. London: Routledge and Kegan Paul, 1964.

Paz, Octavio. *Early Poems 1935–1955*. Translated by Muriel Rukeyser and others. Bloomington and London: Indiana University Press, 1963.

———. *The Collected Poems 1957–1987*. Edited by Eliot Weinberger. Manchester: Carcanet Press, 1988.

Pope, Alexander. *Poetical Works*. Edited by Herbert Davies. London, New York, and Toronto: Oxford University Press, 1966.

Pound, Ezra. *The Cantos of Ezra Pound*. London: Faber and Faber, 1975.

———. *Collected Shorter Poems*. London: Faber and Faber, 1958.

———. *Literary Essays of Ezra Pound*. London: Faber and Faber, 1954.

Press, John. *A Map of Modern English Verse*. London: Oxford University Press, 1969.

———. *Rule and Energy: Trends in British Poetry since the Second World War*. London: Oxford University Press, 1963.

Rilke, Rainer Maria. *Sonnets to Orpheus*, trans. J. B. Leishman. London: Hogarth Press, 1936.

Rosenberg, Isaac. *The Collected Works of Isaac Rosenberg*. Edited by Ian Parsons. London: Chatto and Windus, 1969.

Rosenthal, M. L. *The New Poets: American and British Poetry since World War II*. New York: Oxford University Press, 1967.

———, ed. *Poetry in English: An Anthology*. New York and Oxford: Oxford University Press, 1987.

Ruskin, John. *Frondes Agrestes: Readings in "Modern Painters", Chosen at Her Pleasure by the Author's Friend, The Younger Lady of the Thwaite, Coniston*. Orpington and London: George Allen, 1896.

———. *Modern Painters*, in *The Works of John Ruskin*, ed. E. T. Cook and Alexander Wedderburn. London and New York: Grant Allen, 1904.

———. *Praeterita*, in *The Works of John Ruskin*, ed. E. T. Cook and Alexander Wedderburn. London and New York: Grant Allen, 1908.

Sagar, Keith. *D. H. Lawrence: A Calendar of His Works*. Manchester: Manchester University Press, 1979.

Slatin, John M. *The Savage's Romance: The Poetry of Marianne Moore*. University Park and London: Pennsylvania State University Press, 1986.

Stevens, Wallace. *The Collected Poems of Wallace Stevens*. London: Faber and Faber, 1966.

Thomas, Dylan. *Collected Poems 1934–1952*. London: Dent, 1955.

Swigg, Richard and Tomlinson, Charles. "Charles Tomlinson at Sixty", in *Charles Tomlinson: Man and Artist*. Columbia: University of Missouri Press, 1988.

Terrill, Carroll F. (ed.). *Basil Bunting: Man and Poet*. Orono, Maine: National Poetry Foundation/University of Maine, 1980.

Thomas, Edward. *The Collected Poems of Edward Thomas*. Edited by R. George Thomas. Oxford and New York: Oxford University Press, 1985.

———. *In Pursuit of Spring*. London: Thomas Nelson and Sons, 1914.

———. *A Language Not to Be Betrayed: Selected Prose of Edward Thomas*, ed. Edna Longley. Manchester: Carcanet Press, 1981.

———. Review of *North of Boston*, in *English Review*, August 1914. Reprinted in *A Language Not to Be Betrayed: Selected Prose of Edward Thomas*, ed. Edna Longley. Manchester: Carcanet Press, 1981.

Tomlinson, Charles. *Annunciations*. Oxford and New York: Oxford University Press, 1989.

———. *Collected Poems*. Oxford and New York: Oxford University Press, 1985.

———. *Eden: Graphics and Poetry*. Bristol: Redcliffe Press, 1985.

———, ed. *Marianne Moore: A Collection of Critical Essays*. Englewood Cliffs, N.J., and London: Prentice-Hall, 1969.

———. *Notes from New York and Other Poems*. Oxford and New York: Oxford University Press, 1984.

———. *Relations and Contraries.* Aldington, Kent: Hand and Flower Press, 1951.
———. *The Return.* Oxford and New York: Oxford University Press, 1987.
———. *Translations.* Oxford and New York: Oxford University Press, 1983.
———, ed. *William Carlos Williams: Selected Poems.* 1976; reprinted Harmondsworth: Penguin, 1983.
Watkins, Evan. *The Critical Act: Criticism and Community.* New Haven: Yale University Press, 1978.
Weatherhead, A. Kingsley. *The British Dissonance: Essays on Ten Contemporary Poets.* Columbia: University of Missouri Press, 1983.
Whitman, Walt. *Leaves of Grass.* Edited by Harold W. Blodgett and Sculley Bradley. London: University of London Press, 1965.
Whittier, John Greenleaf. *The Poetical Works of Whittier.* Boston: Houghton Mifflin, 1975.
Wilcox, Walter Dwight. *The Rockies of Canada.* New York and London: G. F. Putnam's Sons, 1909
Williams, William Carlos. *The Autobiography of William Carlos Williams.* 1954; reprinted New York: New Directions, 1967.
———. *The Collected Poems of William Carlos Williams 1909–1939.* Edited by A. Walton Litz and Christopher MacGowan. New York: New Directions, 1986.
———. *The Collected Poems of William Carlos Williams 1939–1962.* Edited by Christopher MacGowan. New York: New Directions, 1988.
———. *In the American Grain.* 1925; reprinted New York: New Directions, 1956.
———. *Selected Essays of William Carlos Williams.* 1954; reprinted New York: New Directions, 1969.
Wordsworth, William. *The Poetical Works of Wordsworth.* Edited by T. Hutchinson and E. de Selincourt. Oxford and New York: Oxford University Press, 1961.

Reviews and Articles

Betjeman, John, et al. "Fifteen Ways of Looking at a Tomlinson." *Poetry Nation Review* 5, no. 1 (October 1977): 40–50. (The other contributors are George Oppen, Peter Levi, John Press, Vittorio Sereni, Michael Kirkham, Donald Wesling, Ronald Hayman, Geoffrey Strickland, Frederick Busch, Michael Dibb, Alasdair Clayre, Ruth Grogan, Marjorie Perloff and John Berger; this was part of the magazine's tribute, "Charles Tomlinson at 50: A Celebration.")
Clayre, Alasdair. "The Poetry of Charles Tomlinson." *London Magazine* 3, no. 2 (May 1963): 47–57.
Davie, Donald. Review of *Seeing is Believing. Essays in Criticism* 9, no. 2 (April 1959): 189–95; reprinted in *The Poet in the Imaginary Museum,* by Donald Davie. Manchester: Carcanet Press, 1977.
Edwards, Michael. "The Poetry of Charles Tomlinson.: *Agenda* 9, no. 2–3 (Spring–Summer 1971): 126–41.
———. "Charles Tomlinson: Notes on Tradition and Impersonality." *Critical Quarterly* 3, no. 2 (Summer 1973): 133–44.
Gitzen, Julian. "Charles Tomlinson and the Plenitude of Fact." *Critical Quarterly* 13, no. 4 (Winter 1971): 355–62.

Grogan, Ruth A. "Charles Tomlinson: The Poet as Painter." *Critical Quarterly* 19, no. 4 (Winter 1977): 71–77.

———. "Charles Tomlinson: The Way of His World." *Contemporary Literature* 19, no. 4 (1978): 472–96.

Kenner, Hugh. Review of *The Necklace*. *Poetry* 88, no. 5 (August 1956): 324–28.

———. Review of *Seeing is Believing*. *Poetry* 93, no. 5 (February 1959): 335–40.

Paz, Octavio. "The Graphics of Charles Tomlinson" (introductory essay), In *Black and White: The Graphics of Charles Tomlinson*. Cheadle, Cheshire: Carcanet Press, 1976. Reprinted in *On Poets and Others*, by Octavio Paz (Manchester: Carcanet Press, 1987) under the title "The Graphics of Charles Tomlinson: Black and White."

———. "El asesino y la eternidad." *Vuelta* 62 (January 1982): 52.

Ross, Alan, and Charles Tomlinson. "Words and Water: The Poetry of Charles Tomlinson," in *London Magazine* 20, January 1981.

Stacey, Robert. "Gael Turnbull and Charles Tomlinson: Two British Poets in Canada." *Northward Journal* 50–51 (1990): 50–59.

———. "Towards Encounter: Charles Tomlinson and Canadian Painting." *Northward Journal* 50–51 (1990): 91–110.

Steinman, Lisa M. "Modern America, Modernism, and Marianne Moore," in *Twentieth Century Literature* 30, no. 2–3 (Summer/Fall 1984).

Swigg, Richard. "Charles Tomlinson: The Cutting Edge." *The Gadfly* 6, no. 2–3 (May–August 1983): 47–58.

———. Review of *Collected Poems* and *Eden*. *Prospice* 18 (August 1986): 130–37.

———. "Charles Tomlinson's Keele Recordings." In *Charles Tomlinson on Cassette* (a booklet accompanying the recordings of the *Complete Poems*). Keele: Keele University, 1987.

———. Review of *The Return*. *Scripsi* 5, no. 3 (April 1989): 83–85.

Tomlinson, Charles. "Art and Chaos," in *Nine* 2, Winter 1949–50.

———. Introductory note to *Assassin* and *Swimming Chenango Lake*, in *Let The People Choose*, ed. James Gibson. London: Harrap, 1973.

———. "Letter to Dr. Williams," in *Spectrum*, Fall 1957.

Ward, Francis. "Poison Gas in Nature: The Lesser Octopus," in *The Illustrated London News*, 11 August 1923.

Williams, William Carlos. Review of *Seeing is Believing*. *Spectrum* 2, no. 3 (1958): 189.

Young, Alan. "Rooted Horizon: Charles Tomlinson and American Modernism." *Critical Quarterly* 24, no. 4 (Winter 1982): 67–73.

Bibliographical Appendix

Charles Tomlinson: Selected Works, in Chronological Order of Publication

Poetry

Relations and Contraries. Aldington, Kent: Hand and Flower Press, 1951.

The Necklace. Swinford, Eynsham, Oxford: The Fantasy Press, 1955. Reprinted, with introduction by Donald Davie, London and New York: Oxford University Press, 1966.

Seeing is Believing. New York: McDowell, Obolensky, 1958. Reprinted London: Oxford University Press, 1960. (The Oxford edition omitted *Beauty and the Beast* and enlarged the collection with *Winter Encounters, How Still the Hawk, Gli Scafari, The Gorge, Rose-Hips, At Delft, At Holwell Farm, Stone Walls: at Chew Magna, Sconset, Fire in a Dark Landscape, Aqueduct, Encounter,* and *Epitaph.*

Versions from Fyodor Tyutchev, 1803–1873 (with Henry Gifford). London and New York: Oxford University Press, 1960.

A Peopled Landscape. London and New York: Oxford University Press, 1963.

Castilian Ilexes: Versions from Antonio Machado, 1875–1939 (with Henry Gifford). London, New York, and Toronto: Oxford University Press, 1963. Reprinted Harmondsworth: Penguin, 1974.

Poems by Austin Clarke, Charles Tomlinson, Tony Connor. London and New York: Oxford University Press, 1964.

American Scenes and Other Poems. London and New York: Oxford University Press, 1966.

The Matachines: New Mexico. Cerrillos, N.M.: San Marcos Press, 1968.

The Way of a World. London, New York, and Toronto: Oxford University Press, 1969.

Penguin Modern Poets 14: Alan Brownjohn, Michael Hamburger, Charles Tomlinson. Harmondsworth: Penguin, 1969.

America West Southwest. Cerrillos, N.M.: San Marcos Press, 1970.

Ten Versions from "Trilce" by César Vallejo (with Henry Gifford). Cerrillos, N.M.: San Marcos Press, 1970.

Renga: A Chain of Poems (coauthor with Octavio Paz, Jacques Roubaud, and Edoardo Sanguineti). Paris: Éditions Gallimard, 1971; Mexico: Joaquín Mortiz, 1972; New York: George Braziller, 1972; Harmondsworth: Penguin, 1979.

Written on Water. London: Oxford University Press, 1972.

The Way In and Other Poems. London, New York, and Toronto: Oxford University Press, 1974.

The Shaft. Oxford, London, and New York: Oxford University Press, 1978.

Selected Poems, 1951–1974. Oxford, London, and New York: Oxford University Press, 1978.

Airborn/Hijos del Aire (coauthor with Octavio Paz). Mexico: Martin Pescador, 1979; London: Anvil Press Poetry, 1981.

The Flood. Oxford, New York, Toronto, and Melbourne: Oxford University Press, 1981.

Translations. Oxford and New York: Oxford University Press, 1983.

Notes from New York and Other Poems. Oxford and New York: Oxford University Press, 1984.

Collected Poems. Oxford and New York: Oxford University Press, 1985. This edition omitted *Relations and Contraries*, apart from *Poem*. Beginning with *The Necklace*, it concluded with *The Flood*. *Notes from New York* was included in the 1987 edition.

The Return. Oxford and New York: Oxford University Press, 1987.

Annunciations. Oxford and New York: Oxford University Press, 1989.

Graphics

Words and Images. London: Covent Garden Press, 1972.

In Black and White: The Graphics of Charles Tomlinson. Cheadle, Cheshire: Carcanet Press, 1976.

Eden: Graphics and Poetry. Bristol: Redcliffe Press, 1985.

Recordings of Poetry and Conversations
(all published on cassette by Keele University, Staffordshire, England)

Charles Tomlinson Reads His Poems. 1985. Recorded 17 September 1985.

Charles Tomlinson Reads His Stoke Poems. 1985. Recorded 18 September 1985.

Charles Tomlinson Reads His Poems on Music. 1987. Recorded 11 November 1987.

Charles Tomlinson: The Complete Poems 1955–1984. 1987. Ten cassettes recorded on the following dates: *The Necklace*, 17 September 1985; *Seeing is Believing*, 6 January 1986; *A Peopled Landscape*, 7 January 1986; *American Scenes and Other Poems*, 2 April 1986; *The Way of A World*, 3 April 1986; *Written on Water*, 29 July 1986; *The Way In and Other Poems*, 30 July 1986; *The Shaft*, 17 December 1986; *The Flood*, 18 December 1986; and *Notes from New York and Other Poems*, 21 July 1987.

The Return. 1989. Recorded 15 September 1987.

Annunciations. 1989. Recorded 12 April 1989.

Charles Tomlinson: The Complete Poems 1955–1989. 1989. An expanded edition of the 1987 *Complete Poems*, with the inclusion of *The Return* and *Annunciations*.

The Modern Age: Hugh Kenner and Charles Tomlinson in conversation. 1988. Recorded 24 June 1988.

Octavio Paz Talks to Charles Tomlinson. 1989. Recorded May 1989. Tomlinson's introductory talk on the cassette, "Octavio Paz in England," was recorded July 1989.

Charles Tomlinson Reads "The Waste Land" by T. S. Eliot. 1989. Recorded 11 April 1989, together with the two talks by Tomlinson, "Eliot, Pound and *The Waste*

Land: The Narrative of a Relationship" and "Reading *The Waste Land*," which accompany his reading of the poem.

Notes on His Own Poetry

[*A Peopled Landscape*]. *The Poetry Book Society Bulletin* (Summer 1963).

Introductory Note on *Swimming Chenango Lake* and *Assassin*. In *Let the People Choose*. Edited by James Gibson. London: Harrap, 1973.

[*The Way In and Other Poems*]. *The Poetry Book Society Bulletin* (Autumn 1974).

[*The Shaft*]. *The Poetry Book Society Bulletin* (Spring 1978).

[*The Return*]. *The Poetry Book Society Bulletin* (Winter 1978).

Interviews and Conversations

Interview with Peter Orr, 4 January 1961. In *The Poet Speaks*, edited by Peter Orr. London: Routledge and Kegan Paul, 1964.

"Robert Creeley in conversation with Charles Tomlinson." *The Review*, 10 (January 1964): 24–35.

Interview with Ian Hamilton in the series "Four Conversations." *London Magazine*, 4, no. 6 (November 1964): 82–85.

"An Interview with Charles Tomlinson," by Jed Rasula and Mike Erwin. *Contemporary Literature*, 16, no. 4 (Autumn 1975): 405–16.

"Charles Tomlinson in Conversation" with Michael Schmidt. *Poetry Nation Review*, 5, no. 1 (October 1977): 35–40.

"Words and Water: Charles Tomlinson and His Poetry," with Alan Ross. *London Magazine*, 20, no. 10 (January 1981): 22–39. Reprinted in *Charles Tomlinson: Man and Artist*, edited by Kathleen O' Gorman. Columbia: University of Missouri Press, 1988.

"Charles Tomlinson at Sixty: In conversation with Richard Swigg." *Poetry Nation Review*, 14, no. 3 (November 1987): 58–61. Reprinted in *Charles Tomlinson: Man and Artist*, edited by Kathleen O'Gorman. Columbia: University of Missouri Press, 1968.

"A Human Balance: An Interview with Charles Tomlinson," by Bruce Meyer. *The Hudson Review*, 43, no. 3 (Autumn 1990): 437–48.

Memoir

Some Americans: A Personal Record. Berkeley and London: University of California Press, 1981.

Lectures

The Poem as Initiation: An Address delivered at Phi Beta Kappa Convocation, Colgate University, 30 October 1967. Hamilton, N.Y.: Colgate University Press, 1968.

Isaac Rosenberg of Bristol (the Southey Lecture, delivered at Christ Church, Bristol, 1981). Bristol: Bristol Branch of the Historical Association, 1982.

The Sense of the Past: Three Twentieth-Century British Poets (the Kenneth Allott

Lecture, delivered at the University of Liverpool, 21 October 1982). Liverpool: Liverpool University Press, 1983.

Poetry and Metamorphosis (the Clark Lectures, delivered at the University of Cambridge, January–February 1982). Cambridge, London, and New York: Cambridge University Press, 1983.

Articles

"Coleridge: *Christabel*." In *Interpretations: Essays on Twelve English Poems*, edited by John Wain. London: Routledge and Kegan Paul, 1955.

"Pages from an Italian Journal." *Poetry*, 89, no. 3 (December 1956): 183–87.

"Abundance, Not too Much: The Poetry of Marianne Moore" *Sewanee Review*, 65, no. 4 (Autumn 1957): 677–87.

"America: Imagination and the Spirit of Place." *National Review*, 11, no. 6 (12 August 1961): 86–87.

"Poetry Today." In *The Modern Age*, Vol. 7 of *The Pelican Guide to English Literature*, edited by Boris Ford. Harmondsworth: Penguin, 1961.

"Poets and Mushrooms: A Retrospect of British Poetry in 1961." *Poetry*, 100, no. 2 (May 1962): 104–121.

"Yeats and the Practising Poet." In *An Honoured Guest: New Essays on W. B. Yeats*, edited by Denis Donoghue and J. R. Mulryne. London: Edward Arnold, 1965.

"An Introductory Note on the Poetry of George Oppen." *Grosseteste Review*, 6, no. 1–4 (1973): 233–39.

"Not in Sequence of a Metronome." *Agenda*, 10–11, no. 4 (Winter 1972): 53–54.

"Fate and the Image of Music: An Examination of Rosenberg's Plays." *Poetry Nation*, 3 (1974): 57–69.

"Some Aspects of Poetry Since the War." In *The Present*, vol. 8 of *The New Pelican Guide to English Literature*, edited by Boris Ford. Harmondsworth: Penguin, 1983.

"Of Charles Reznikoff." In *Charles Reznikoff: Man and Poet*, edited by Milton Hindus. Orono, Maine: National Poetry Foundation, 1984.

"Ivor Gurney's 'Best Poems.'" *The Times Literary Supplement*, 3 January 1986, 12.

"Some Presences on the Scene: A Vista of Post-War Poetry." In *On Modern Poetry: Essays Presented to Donald Davie*, edited by Vereen Bell and Laurence Lerner. Vanderbilt: Vanderbilt University Press, 1988.

"Wallace Stevens and the Poetry of Scepticism." In *American Literature*, vol. 9 of *The New Pelican Guide to English Literature*, edited by Boris Ford. Harmondsworth: Penguin, 1988.

Reviews

"Mr. Pound on Literature" (review of *Literary Essays of Ezra Pound*, edited by T. S. Eliot). *Spectator*, 192 (19 February 1954): 212.

"The Middlebrow Muse" (review of *New Lines: An Anthology*, edited by Robert Conquest). *Essays in Criticism*, 7 no. 2 (April 1957): 208–16.

"Poet without an Audience" (review of *The Letters of William Blake*, edited by Geoffrey Keynes; *William Blake's "Vala"*, edited by H. M. Margoliouth; *William Blake: The Finger on the Furnace* by Laura DeWitt James). *Poetry*, 90, no. 5 (August 1957): 321–25.

"Edward Thomas" (Review of *The Last Four Years* by Eleanor Farjeon, and *As It Was* and *World Without End* by Helen Thomas). *Poetry,* 95, no. 1 (October 1959): 52–54.

"The Tone of Pound's Critics" (review of *Poet in Exile* by Noel Stock; *Ezra Pound and Sextus Propertius* by J. P. Sullivan; *The Confucian Odes of Ezra Pound* by L. S. Dembo; *Ezra Pound: The Poet as Sculptor* by Donald Davie). *Agenda* 4, no. 29 (October–November 1965): 46–49.

"Experience into Music: The Poetry of Basil Bunting" (Review of *Loquitur, The Spoils* and *Briggflatts* by Basil Bunting). *Agenda*, 4, no. 5–6 (Autumn 1966): 11–17.

"Dr. Williams' Practice" (review of *The W. C. Williams Reader*, edited by M. L. Rosenthal; *Penguin Modern Poets 9: Denise Levertov, Kenneth Rexroth, William Carlos Williams*; *William Carlos Williams: A Collection of Critical Essays*, edited by J. Hillis Miller). *Encounter*, 29 (November 1967): 66–70. An excerpt from the review was reprinted in *William Carlos Williams: The Critical Heritage*, edited by Charles Doyle. London and Boston: Routledge and Kegan Paul, 1980.

"Of Native Things" (review of *The Autobiography of William Carlos Williams*). *The Listener*, 81, no. 20 (February 1969): 242.

"Marianne Moore: Her Poetry and Her Critics" (review of *The Complete Poems of Marianne Moore*). *Agenda*, 6, no. 3–4 (Autumn–Winter 1968): 137–42. (It should be noted that although this review shares a title and several paragraphs with Tomlinson's introductory essay in *Marianne Moore: A Collection of Critical Essays*—see below under "Anthologies Edited"—it is essentially not the same).

"A Rich Sitter: The Poetry of Lorine Niedecker" (review of *North Central* by Lorine Niedecker). *Agenda*, 7, no. 2 (Spring 1969): 65–67.

"Poetry and Possibility: The Work of Robert Duncan" (review of *The First Decade, Derivations, The Opening of the Field, Roots and Branches* by Robert Duncan). *Agenda*, 8, no. 3–4 (Autumn–Winter 1970): 159–70.

"The Poet as Translator" (review of *The Violet in the Crucible: Shelley and Translation*, by Timothy Webb). *The Times Literary Supplement*, 22 April 1977, 474.

"Looking Out for Wholeness" (review of *The Complete Poems 1927–1979* by Elizabeth Bishop). *The Times Literary Supplement*, 3 June 1983, 575.

"Discovering Cézanne" (review of *Cézanne by Himself*, edited by Richard Kendall). *Modern Painters*, 2, no. 1 (Spring 1989): 109–13.

"Poetry and Friendship" (review of *Becoming a Poet: Elizabeth Bishop with Marianne Moore and Robert Lowell* by David Kalstone). *Parnassus*, 16, no. 2 (1991): 102–7.

Anthologies Edited

Marianne Moore: A Collection of Critical Essays. Englewood Cliffs, N.J., and London: Prentice-Hall, 1969.

William Carlos Williams: A Critical Anthology. Harmondsworth: Penguin, 1972.

William Carlos Williams: Selected Poems. Harmondsworth: Penguin, 1976; reprinted 1983.

Octavio Paz: Selected Poems. Harmondsworth: Penguin, 1979.

The Oxford Book of Verse in English Translation. Oxford and New York: Oxford University Press, 1980.

Poems of George Oppen. Newcastle-upon-Tyne: Cloud, 1990.

Index

Abercrombie, Lascelles, 120
Adam, 136, 143–44, 229
Aeneas, 30
After Apple-Picking (Frost), 132
Agassiz, Louis, 64
Alberta, 67
Alexander, 212, 232
Allegria, L' (Ungaretti), 162
Alps, the, 28, 66–67
Alton Locke (Kingsley), 26
Ambulances (Larkin), 216
America, 38, 50, 63, 65, 67–68, 74, 76–77, 79, 86–87, 95, 148–49, 166, 172, 174, 180–81, 184–85, 194–96, 213, 219
"American Scholar, The" (Emerson), 100
Amulet, The (Rosenberg), 60
Anathemata, The (Jones), 12, 220–25
Ancient Britons, The (Blake), 226
Anecdote of the Jar (Stevens), 39
Aneurin, 225, 232–33
Apocalyptic poets, 214
Apollinaire, Guillaume, 161
Arcis-sur-Aube, 203, 205–7
Arctic, the, 235
Ariadne, 61
Arizona, 68, 74
Arras, 128
Arundel Tomb, An (Larkin), 216–17
Atlantic Ocean, 57–58, 62
Auden, W. H., 218–20; *In Praise of Limestone*, 219; *Missing*, 218; *Musée de Beaux Arts*, 218; *New Year Letter*, 219–20
Audubon, John James, 64
Autobiography of William Carlos Williams, The (Williams), 104
Autumn (Williams), 199
Aztecs, 178–79, 184, 192

Baby Tortoise (Lawrence), 169
Bach, Johann Sebastian, 123

Bacon, Francis, 64
Ball, Patricia, 25
Bare Line of the Hill, The (Gurney), 141–42
Barn, The (Edward Thomas), 129
Bastard Peace, A (Williams), 99
Baudelaire, Charles, 20
Beethoven, Ludwig van, 191
Belloc, Hilaire, 120, 123, 125, 205; *Courtesy*, 123; *Danton: A Study*, 205; *The South Country*, 120
Bertolani, Paolo, 108–12, 188
Bettesworth Book, The (Sturt), 130
Biography (Masefield), 120
Black Earth (Melancthon) (Moore), 59–61, 63
Blake, William, 13–14, 144, 146–54, 186; *The Ancient Britons*, 226; *The Divine Image*, 148; *The Lamb*, 147–48; *The Marriage of Heaven and Hell*, 147; *Milton*, 150; *Mock On, Mock On, Voltaire, Rousseau!*, 149; *Proverbs of Hell*, 147, 151; *Songs of Innocence and Experience*, 147, 151; *Vala, or The Four Zoas*, 147
Boccioni, Umberto, 58
Boone, Daniel, 213
Borgia, Cesare, 210
Bourne, George. *See* Sturt, George
Boy's Will, A (Frost), 131–32
Briggflatts (Bunting), 15, 125, 217, 228–36
Britain, 120, 128, 221–22
Britannia, 223
British Isles, 15, 19
Broadway Pageant, A (Whitman), 181
Brooklyn, 52–53
Brooklyn Bridge, 52, 59
Buber, Martin, 38
Bunting, Basil, 15, 125, 214, 217, 228–36
Buñuel, Luis, 192
Burnt Norton (Eliot), 230

Byrd, William, 125–26, 229
Byron, George Gordon, Lord, 25–26

Cage, John, 180, 245 n.38
Calvin, John, 72
Cambridge, 13, 20, 146, 192
Canada, 19, 67, 156
Cántaro roto, El (The Broken Waterjar) (Paz), 187–88
Canto I (Pound), 144
Canto II (Pound), 22–23, 57, 128, 230
Canto XXI (Pound), 24
Canto XLV (Pound), 227
Canto LXXIV (Pound), 22, 174
Capella, 234–35
"Captain's Doll, The" (Lawrence), 163
Carlsbad Caves, 220
Carlyle, Thomas, 197
Catholicism, 15, 110, 182, 221, 237
Catraeth, 225, 232
"Cavalcanti" (Pound), 22, 174
Celts, 221, 225–26
Cézanne, Paul, 13, 25, 30, 46, 61, 70, 73–75, 79, 107, 146, 159, 173, 218
Champlain, Samuel de, 213
Chapman, George, 126
Château de Muzot, 79
Chénier, André, 197–99, 201
Christ, 32, 220–21, 223–24
Chronophotography, 58
Cinna (Corneille), 200
Citizen Kane (Welles), 192–95
Claude Lorrain, 25
Cockcrow (Edward Thomas), 129
Code, The (Frost), 132
Coleridge, Samuel Taylor, 81, 237
Colorado, 75
Comedian as the Letter C, The (Stevens), 39, 128
Conquest, Robert, 34
Conrad, Joseph, 194
Constable, John, 13, 29–31, 36, 56–57, 156
Cooper's Hill, 118
Cooperstown, 174
Corday, Charlotte, 112, 197–203, 208
Corneille, Pierre, 200
Così fan tutte (Mozart), 248 n.5
Cotswolds, the, 119–20, 125, 127
Courtesy (Belloc), 123
Crane, Hart, 128

Cranham Hill, 118
Crèvecoeur, Hector St. John, 64, 167
Crickley Hill, 118
Crimson Cyclamen, The (Williams), 90
Crossing Brooklyn Ferry (Whitman), 122
Cuban missile crisis, 53
Cubists, 13
Cuento de dos jardines (A Tale of Two Gardens) (Paz), 187
Cumbria, 228, 234
Cypresses (Lawrence), 172–74

Dana, Richard Henry, 163
Danton, Georges-Jacques, 15, 112, 185, 201, 203–8
Danton: A Study (Belloc), 205
David, Jacques-Louis, 202
Davie, Donald, 34
Dearness of Common Things, The (Gurney), 141
Death of the Hired Man, The (Frost), 132–33
Demuth, Charles, 90
Desert Music, The (Williams), 13, 79
Deserted Village, The (Goldsmith), 111
De Soto, Hernan, 213
Deutscher, Isaac, 191
Digging (Edward Thomas), 136
Dijkstra, Bram, 90
Divine Image, The (Blake), 148
Dockery and Son (Larkin), 215
Dream Pang, A (Frost), 131
Dryden, John, 27
Duino Elegies (Rilke), 36, 79
Dulac, Germaine, 192
Dürer, Albrecht, 51–52
Durham, County, 219
Dymock, 118
Dynasts, The (Hardy), 128

Eagle in New Mexico (Lawrence), 178
Earth Mother, 220, 223, 227
Earthy Anecdote (Stevens), 40
Eden, 21–22, 119, 143–44, 206, 219–20
Elephants (Moore), 59
Elgar, Edward, 118
Eliot, T. S., 13–15, 60, 136, 185–86, 195, 207, 213, 222, 230, 236–37; *Burnt Norton*, 230; *Four Quartets*, 15, 185, 207, 236; *Little Gidding*, 185, 207; *The Love Song of J. Alfred Prufrock*, 136;

Portrait of a Lady, 136; "Tradition and the Individual Talent," 60, 185, 222; *The Waste Land*, 15, 136, 185–86, 213, 236–37
Emerson, Ralph Waldo, 100–101
Empson, William, 13
Endymion (Keats), 26–27
England, 57, 81, 86, 114, 116, 126, 128–31, 155, 214, 216, 218
England (Moore), 57
Epistle to Burlington (Pope), 27, 85
Etruria, 23
Etruria Vale, 19, 20, 23, 113
Etruscan Places (Lawrence), 152, 174
Etruscans, 173, 174
Evening Land, The (Lawrence), 172
Ezra Pound: Selected Poems (Pound), 22

Fables (La Fontaine), 73
"Facts and Considerations on the Strata of Mont Blanc" (Ruskin), 25
Fall, the, 220, 229
Farnham, 130
Felling a Tree (Gurney), 126–28, 140
Fern Hill (Dylan Thomas), 36
Fiascherino, 47–49, 55, 112, 160
Fiesole, 61–63, 74, 97, 156, 172
Fifty Faggots (Edward Thomas), 140–41
First Time In (Gurney), 124–25
Fish (Lawrence), 170–72
Fish, The (Moore), 53–55, 63, 67, 128
Fitzwilliam Museum, 146
Flanders, 125
Florence, 208, 210
Florentines, 210–11
Fontainebleu, 31
Four Quartets (Eliot), 15, 185, 207, 236
Framilode, 118
Frampton, 118
France, 19, 118–19, 121, 141, 208
French Revolution, The (Carlyle), 197
Frondes Agrestes (Ruskin), 66, 69–71, 77, 83
Frost, Robert, 14, 39, 117, 129–36, 138–40; *After Apple-Picking*, 132; *A Boy's Will*, 131–32; *The Code*, 132; *The Death of the Hired Man*, 132–33; *A Dream Pang*, 131; *The Ghost House*, 131; *Home Burial*, 133–34; *A Hundred Collars*, 132; *Mending Wall*, 133, 136; *Mowing*, 132; *My November Guest*, 131; *North of Boston*, 39, 129, 131–32, 138, 140; *A Servant to Servants*, 135; *A Tuft of Flowers*, 131; *The Vantage Point*, 131; *The Wood-Pile*, 138–40
Fuller, R. Buckminster, 180

Galla Placidia, 24
Geneva, 71–74
Georgianism, 117, 120, 125, 129
Georgian Poetry (Marsh), 120
"Georgian Poetry, 1911–12" (Lawrence), 120
Georgic tradition, 27
Germany, 166
Ghost House, The (Frost), 131
Gibson, Wilfrid, 120
Gli Scafari, 160–61
Girovagi (Wanderer) (Ungaretti), 162
Gloucester, 118, 127
Gloucestershire, 47, 51, 117–18, 126
Gloucestershire regiment, 120
Gododdin, Y (Aneurin), 225
Gogh, Vincent Van, 160
Graphic, London, 66
Greek landscape, 27
Greeks, 28
Guevara, Che, 188
Gulf of Spezia, 160
Gurney, Ivor, 14, 117–31, 141–45, 170, 236; *The Bare Line of the Hill*, 141–42; *The Dearness of Common Things*, 141; *Felling a Tree*, 126–28, 140; *First Time In*, 124–25; *Hedger*, 125–26; *Henry David Thoreau*, 126; *The Lock-Keeper*, 125; *Looking There*, 126; *Near Vermand*, 119–20; *Of the Sea*, 128; *Portraits*, 126; *Roads—Those Roads*, 141; *The Sea Borders*, 121; *Signallers*, 122–23, 170; *The Silent One*, 123–24; *Tewkesbury*, 141; *Up There*, 141; *The Valley Farm*, 142; *Walt Whitman*, 126; *Washington Irving*, 126

Hacia el Comienzo (Toward the Beginning) (Paz), 187
Hampshire, 134
Hand of Man, The (Stieglitz), 90
Hardy, Thomas, 128
Harmonium (Stevens), 139
Harvey, Will, 118, 121
Hawes, 231, 235

Hawthorne, Nathaniel, 14
Haymaking (Edward Thomas), 129–30
Heart of Darkness (Conrad), 194
Hedger (Gurney), 125–26
Heine, Heinrich, 20
Heloïse, 189
Henry David Thoreau (Gurney), 126
Here (Larkin), 217, 236
Hill, Geoffrey, 214
Himno entre ruinas (*Hymn among the Ruins*) (Paz), 186
His Shield (Moore), 59
Holloway, John, 120
Holmes, Oliver Wendell, 26
Home Burial (Frost), 133–34
Homer, 27, 36
Hopi, 74, 75, 179, 215
Hopi Antelope Dance, 179
Hopkins, Gerard Manley, 13–14, 31–36, 122, 222, 228, 236–37; *Journals and Papers of Gerard Manley Hopkins*, 31–34; *Pied Beauty*, 32, 228; *That Nature is a Heraclitean Fire*, 33–34; *To What Serves Mortal Beauty*, 32; *The Wreck of the Deutschland*, 33
Howells, Herbert, 118
Hudson, W. H., 64
Hugh Selwyn Mauberley (Pound), 157
Hugo, Victor, 20
Huizipochtli, 176
Humming-Bird (Lawrence), 167–69
Hundred Collars, A (Frost), 132
Hungarians, 20
Hymn among the Ruins (*Himno entre ruinas*) (Williams), 186

I and Thou (Buber), 240 n.1
Ida, King, 225
Idea of Order at Key West, The (Stevens), 46
Idéntico, Lo (*One and the Same*) (Paz), 187
Idler, The (Johnson), 27
Illustrated London News, 64
In Country Sleep (Dylan Thomas), 36
In Defense of the Iroquois (Wilson), 246 n.7
In Parenthesis (Jones), 122, 225–27
In Pursuit of Spring (Edward Thomas), 130–31, 134

"In the American Grain" (Lawrence), 86, 193
In the American Grain (Williams), 86, 193, 213
"Introduction to These Paintings" (Lawrence), 159–60
Iona, 233
Irving, Washington, 126
Israelites, 150, 226
Italy, 19, 23, 36, 79, 163, 166, 210

Jackson, Andrew, 126
Jefferies, Richard, 129
Jefferson, Thomas, 126
Johnson, Clifton, 65, 68
Johnson, Samuel, 27
Jones, David, 15, 122, 214, 220–28, 237; *The Anathemata*, 15, 220–25; *In Parenthesis*, 122, 225–27; *The Sleeping Lord*, 227–28
Jonson, Ben, 126
Journals and Papers of Gerard Manley Hopkins, The (Hopkins), 31–34
Journey to Love (Williams), 13, 79
Junction of the Greta and the Tees, The (Turner), 130

Kavanagh, P. J., 117
Keats, John, 26, 34, 39, 131
Kemp, Lysander, 188
King, Clarence, 64
King Henry IV, Part I (Shakespeare), 226
Kingsley, Charles, 26
Kosmos (Whitman), 123

"Ladybird, The" (Lawrence), 153, 156
La Fontaine, Jean de, 73
Lake Agnes, 67
Lake District, 220
Lake Guatavita, 68
Lake Louise, 67–68
Lamartine, Alphonse, 20
Lamb, The (Blake), 147–48
Lares, Roman, 37, 79
Larkin, Philip, 13, 34, 214–18, 236; *Ambulances*, 216; *An Arundel Tomb*, 216–17; *Dockery and Son*, 215; *Here*, 217, 236; *The Whitsun Weddings*, 216
La Serra, 23, 108–12, 116
La Spezia, 111, 160
Lawrence, D. H., 14, 25, 65, 86, 105,

120, 145, 151–60, 162–63, 166–79, 181–82, 184, 193, 223, 236–37; *Baby Tortoises,* 169; "The Captain's Doll," 163; *Cypresses,* 172–74; *Eagle in New Mexico,* 178; *Etruscan Places,* 152, 174; *The Evening Land,* 172; *Fish,* 170–72; "Georgian Poetry, 1911–12," 120; *Humming-Bird,* 167–69; "In the American Grain," 86, 193; "Introduction to These Paintings," 159–60; *The Ladybird,* 153, 156; *Mornings in Mexico,* 176–77, 179; *The Mosquito,* 167; *New Heaven and Earth,* 167; "Nottingham and the Mining Countryside," 153; "The Novel," 154; *The Plumed Serpent,* 181, 184; *The Rainbow,* 152, 160, 162, 177; *The Shades of Spring,* 152; *Snake,* 169; *Studies in Classic American Literature,* 65, 163, 167–68, 175, 194; *Turkey-Cock,* 172; *Twilight in Italy,* 154
Leatherstocking Tales, The (Cooper), 194
Leaves of Grass (Whitman), 64
Lee, Robert E., 126
Lerici, 160, 218
Letters from an American Farmer (Crèvecoeur), 167
Liguria, 47, 160–61
Lincoln, Abraham, 189
Lindisfarne Gospels, 230, 232
Lindisfarne Island, 230, 233, 235
Little Englandism, 34, 214
Little Gidding (Eliot), 185, 207
Lob (Edward Thomas), 129, 136
Lock-Keeper, The (Gurney), 125
London, 13, 20, 23, 73, 126, 129, 134, 186, 216
Long Ships Lighthouse, The (Turner), 29
Looking There (Gurney), 126
Louis XVI, 205–6
Love Song of J. Alfred Prufrock, The (Eliot), 136
Lubbock, Percy, 160
Lux, Adam, 198

Mabinogion, The, 225
Macbeth (Shakespeare), 191, 196
MacDiarmid, Hugh, 218, 237
Machiavelli, Niccolò, 15, 112, 207–13
Maisemore, 118, 127
Malatesta, Sigismondo, 209

Malverns, the, 119
Mametz Wood, 225
Marey, Étienne-Jules, 58
Marinetti, Filippo, 162–63
Marmion (Scott), 28
Marriage of Heaven and Hell (Blake), 147
Marsh, Edward, 120
Marvell, Andrew, 85
Marx, Karl, 191
Marxists, 191–92
Mary, 189
Masefield, John, 120
Maud (Tennyson), 26
May 23 (Edward Thomas), 137
Mayakowsky, Vladimir, 52, 59
Mediterranean Sea, 23, 27, 174, 219, 235
Melville, Herman, 14, 163
Memoirs of a Surrey Labourer (Sturt), 130–31
Mending Wall (Frost), 133, 136
Mercian Hymns (Hill), 214
Mercury, 27
Merleau-Ponty, Maurice, 211–12
Mesa Verde, 75
Mexicans, 20
Mexico, 19, 79, 94, 181–84, 186–88, 192, 196
Mexico City, 191
Michelangelo, 147, 152
Michelet, Jules, 200–201
Middle East, 229, 235
Midlands, 19, 118
Middleton Murry, John, 129
Mill-Water, The (Edward Thomas), 135–36
Milton (Blake), 150
Mind Is an Enchanting Thing, The (Moore), 50, 58
"Mind of Europe," 14
Minos, 232
Minotaur, the, 61, 232
Minsterworth, 118
Missing (Auden), 218
Moby Dick (Melville), 65, 162
Mock On, Mock On, Voltaire, Rousseau! (Blake), 149
Moctezuma, 174, 189
Modern Painters (Ruskin), 24, 26–31, 59, 69
Mont Blanc, 25
Monteverdi, 229–30

Mont Ste. Victore, 30, 73
Moore, Marianne, 13–14, 25, 37–39, 49–61, 63–69, 71, 75, 99, 128, 237; *Black Earth* (Melancthon), 59–61, 63; *Elephants*, 59; *England*, 57; *The Fish*, 53–55, 63, 67, 128; *His Shield*, 59; *The Mind Is an Enchanting Thing*, 50, 58; *An Octopus*, 63–69, 168; *The Plumet Basilisk*, 68; *The Steeple-Jack*, 50–53, 63, 128; *When I Buy Pictures*, 50
Morning (Williams), 99
Mornings in Mexico (Lawrence), 176–77, 179
Morte D'Arthur (Malory), 225
Moses, 61, 178, 212, 226
Moses (Rosenberg), 61, 178
Mosquito, The (Lawrence), 167
Mountain, The (O'Keeffe), 64
Mount Rainier, 63
Mount Shasta, 64
"Movement," the, 13, 34
Mowing (Frost), 132
Mozart, Wolfgang Amadeus, 125, 214, 248 n.5
Muir, John, 67
Musée de Beaux Arts (Auden), 218
Muybridge, Eadweard, 58
My November Guest (Frost), 131
Myth, 13, 22–23, 76, 87, 194, 222, 225, 232
"Myth of America," 194
"Myth of England," 120

National Parks Portfolio, 65
National Parks Service, 64
Navajo, 176, 179–81
Navajo Dance of the Sprouting Corn, 176
Near Vermand (Gurney), 119–20
Nether Stowey, 81
Never Until the Mankind Making (Dylan Thomas), 35
New Hampshire, 129, 131, 133
New Heaven and Earth (Lawrence), 167
New House, The (Edward Thomas), 129
New Jersey, 23, 78, 85–86, 99, 113
New Lines (Conquest), 34, 214
Newman, Cardinal, 64
New Mexico, 64, 167, 177–78, 181
New Year Letter (Auden), 219–20
New York, 73, 85, 90, 186

Norman builders, 141
Normandy, 197, 201
North of Boston (Frost), 39, 129, 131–32, 138, 140
Northumberland, 234
Northumbria, 15, 230, 235
"Nottingham and the Mining Countryside" (Lawrence), 153
"Novel, The" (Lawrence), 154

Oaxaca, 93, 181
Octavio Paz: Selected Poems (Paz), 186
Octavio Paz Talks to Charles Tomlinson (Paz and Tomlinson), 187
Octopus, An (Moore), 63–69, 168
Odysseus, 209
Odyssey, The (Homer), 27
Of Being Numerous (Oppen), 87, 204
Of the Sea (Gurney), 128
O'Keeffe, Georgia, 64
Oklahoma, 20
Old Man (Edward Thomas), 137–38
On A Raised Beach (MacDiarmid), 218
On Nothing (Cage), 245 n.38
On Something (Cage), 180
Oppen, George, 87, 204
Orchestra, The (Williams), 105–6
Oregon, 68
Orion, 234–35
Out of the Cradle Endlessly Rocking (Whitman), 111, 167
Ovid, 20
Owen, Wilfred, 119

Paris, 73, 197, 203, 206
Pasiphae, 232
Passaic River, 76
Pastoral (Williams), 96–97
Paterson (Williams), 76, 86, 100, 194
Pathetic Fallacy, 26, 29, 31, 44
Paumanok, 111
Pawnee ceremony, 176
Paz, Octavio, 14, 185–89, 192, 237; *El cántaro roto* (The Broken Waterjar), 187–88; *Cuento de dos jardines* (A Tale of Two Gardens), 187; *Hacia el Comienzo* (Toward the Beginning), 187; *Himno entre ruinas* (Hymn among the Ruins), 186; *Lo idéntico* (One and the Same), 187; *Octavio Paz: Selected Poems*, 186; *Octavio Paz Talks to*

Charles Tomlinson, 187; "Poetry and History," 185–86; *The Prisoner,* 192; *Sunstone (Piedra de Sol),* 189
Persephone, 189
Petrarch, 212
Pied Beauty (Hopkins), 32, 228
Pink Locust, The (Williams), 104–5
Pisa, 209
Plumed Serpent, The (Lawrence), 181, 184
Plumet Basilisk, The (Moore), 68
Poe, Edgar Allan, 14, 162
"Poetry and History" (Paz), 185–86
Poets of the 1950s (Enright), 214
Poor, The (Williams), 90, 96
Pope, Alexander, 85
Portrait of a Lady (Eliot), 136
Portraits (Gurney), 126
Poseidon, 23
Pound, Ezra, 15, 22–24, 37, 57, 60, 128, 157, 174, 209, 219, 230, 236; *Canto I,* 144; *Canto II,* 22–23, 57, 128, 230; *Canto XXI,* 24; *Canto XLV,* 227; *Canto LXXIV,* 22, 174; "Cavalcanti," 22, 174; *Ezra Pound: Selected Poems,* 22; *Hugh Selwyn Mauberley,* 157
Poussin, Nicolas, 25
Praeterita (Ruskin), 71–73
Prelude, The (Wordsworth), 27, 92, 100–101, 204–5
Primacy of Perception, The (Merleau-Ponty), 211, 247n.30
Prince, The (Machiavelli), 208
Prisoner, The (Paz), 192
Procyon, 234–35
Proletarian Portrait (Williams), 99
Prometheus, 34, 59, 148, 191–92
Prophet Outcast, The (Deutscher), 191
Protestant consciousness, 59
Protestantism, 59
Proverbs of Hell (Blake), 147, 151

Racine, Jean, 20
Rainbow, The (Lawrence), 152, 160, 162, 177
Rambler, The (Johnson), 27
Rasles, Père Sebastian, 213
Ravenna, 24
Rawthey River, 229, 231–32
Ray, Man, 192
Red Sea, 150

Red Wheelbarrow, The (Williams), 100–101
Resolution and Independence (Wordsworth), 27, 112–13
Rheims, 205–6
Rilke, Rainer Maria, 36, 79–80; *Duino Elegies,* 79; *Sonnets to Orpheus,* 79
Rimbaud, Arthur, 35
Roads (Edward Thomas), 141
Roads—Those Roads (Gurney), 141
Robespierre, Maximilien, 189, 201, 204
Rockies of Canada (Wilcox), 67–69
Rodin, Auguste, 152
Roman Campagna, 69
Roman Catholicism. *See* Catholicism
Romans, 141–42, 173–74, 210, 223, 225
Rome, 209–10
Rosa, Salvator, 25
Rosenberg, Isaac, 60–61, 178
Rossetti, Dante Gabriel, 131
Rousseau, Jean-Jacques, 72
Rural Elegance (Shenstone), 27
Ruskin, John, 13–14, 24–31, 34, 36–37, 39, 50, 52, 57, 59, 63–64, 66–67, 69–74, 76–77, 83, 100, 122, 221–22, 237; "Facts and Considerations on the Strata of Mont Blanc," 25; *Frondes Agrestes,* 66, 69–71, 77, 83; *Modern Painters,* 24, 26–31, 59, 69; *Praeterita,* 71–73
Rutherford, 85–86

Sade, Marquis de, 192
Sagar, Keith, 167
St. Aidan, 233
St. Columba, 233
St. Columbanus, 233
St. Cuthbert, 230
St. John, 230
St. Mark, 230
Saints' Everlasting Rest, The (Baxter), 64
Salève, the, 71–73
Sassoon, Siegfried, 119
Saussure, Horace Bénédict de, 72
Scarlatti, Domenico, 125
Schoenberg, Arnold, 106–8, 230
Science of Aspects, The (Ball), 25
Scott, Walter, 28
Scriabin, Aleksandr, 191
Sea Borders, The (Gurney), 121
Sea Drift (Whitman), 121, 170, 175

Seasons, The (Thomson), 27
Sea Symphony, A (Vaughan Williams), 120
Sedbergh, 228, 231
Sedge-Warblers (Edward Thomas), 136
Selected Poems (Pound). See *Ezra Pound: Selected Poems*
Selected Poems (Williams). See *William Carlos Williams: Selected Poems*
Servant to Servants, A (Frost), 135
Severn Estuary, 118
Severnside, 141
Shades of Spring, The (Lawrence), 152
Shakespeare, William, 122, 191, 196, 226, 235; *King Henry IV, Part I*, 226; *Macbeth*, 191, 196; *Sonnet CXVI*, 235
Shelley, Percy Bysshe, 26, 39, 80, 131, 191
Shelton Bar-Iron and Steelworks, 20, 113, 215
Shenstone, William, 27
Shetland, 218
Siena, 153
Signallers (Gurney), 122–23, 170
Signs (Merleau-Ponty), 211–12
Silent One, The (Gurney), 123–24
Six Significant Landscapes (Stevens), 40–41
Sleeping Lord, The (Jones), 227–28
Slumber Did My Spirit Seal, A (Wordsworth), 112
Snake (Lawrence), 169
Snow-Bound (Whittier), 101, 111
Snow Man, The (Stevens), 46–47, 65, 163
Snow Storm, The (Emerson), 101
Socrates, 189
Somerset, 81, 102
Somme offensive, 225
Somme River, 117
Song for Occupations, A (Whitman), 170
Song of the Open Road (Whitman), 122, 170
Songs of Innocence and Experience (Blake), 147, 151
Sonnet CXVI (Shakespeare), 235
Sonnets to Orpheus (Rilke), 79
South Country, The (Belloc), 120
South Country, The (Edward Thomas), 120
Spain, 186, 208

Sparkles from the Wheel (Whitman), 122
Spring and All (Williams), 96
Spring Strains (Williams), 106
Staffordshire, 19, 80, 116
Stalin, 182
Stalinist agent, 191
Steeple-Jack, The (Moore), 50–53, 63, 128
Stevens, Wallace, 13–15, 37–50, 57, 65, 77, 128, 163; *Anecdote of the Jar*, 39; *The Comedian as the Letter C*, 39, 128; *Earthy Anecdote*, 40; *Harmonium*, 39; *The Idea of Order at Key West*, 46; *Six Significant Landscapes*, 40–41; *The Snow Man*, 46–47, 65, 163; *Thirteen Ways of Looking at a Blackbird*, 41–43; *Valley Candle*, 40; *The Wind Shifts*, 44–45
Stieglitz, Alfred, 90
Stoke-on-Trent, 13, 19, 21–23, 65, 79, 90, 97, 113, 116, 118, 154, 215
Stokes, Adrian, 219
Stones of Rimini, The (Stokes), 219
Stowey, 81–85
Strawberry Hill, 84
Studies in Classic American Literature (Lawrence), 65, 163, 167–68, 175, 194
Sturt, George, 129–31; *The Bettesworth Book*, 130; *Memoirs of a Surrey Labourer*, 130–31; *The Wheelwright's Shop*, 129
Sunstone (*Piedra de Sol*) (Paz), 189
Surrealism, 13, 34, 186
Swinburne, Algernon Charles, 131
Switzerland, 25

Tales of Mystery and the Imagination (Poe), 162
Taliesin, 225
Tarquinia, 174
Tempers, The (Williams), 139
Tennessee, 39–40
Tennyson, Alfred, Lord, 26
Tewkesbury (Gurney), 141
That Nature is a Heraclitean Fire (Hopkins), 33–34
Theseus, 196, 212
Thirteen Ways of Looking at a Blackbird (Stevens), 41–43
This Compost (Whitman), 121
Thomas, Dylan, 13, 34–36, 70, 160, 214;

Fern Hill, 36; In Country Sleep, 36; Never Until the Mankind Making, 35; A Winter's Tale, 36

Thomas, Edward, 14, 117, 120, 129–31, 134–38, 140–41, 236–37; The Barn, 129; Cockcrow, 129; Digging, 136; Fifty Faggots, 140–41; Haymaking, 129–30; In Pursuit of Spring, 130–31, 134; Lob, 129, 136; The Manor Farm, 129; May 23, 137; The Mill-Water, 135–36; The New House, 129; Old Man, 137–38; Roads, 141; Sedge-Warblers, 136; The South Country, 120

Thoreau, Henry David, 64, 126

Three Choirs Festival, 118

Tlacolula, 183

To a Poor Old Woman (Williams), 99

To Daphne and Virginia (Williams), 105

To Elsie (Williams), 86–87

To the Finland Station (Wilson), 191

To What Serves Mortal Beauty (Hopkins), 32

Tomlinson, Alfred (Charles Tomlinson's father), 20, 113, 243 n.18

Tomlinson, Charles: at Cambridge, 20, 34, 146, 192; employed by Lubbock, 160; his father, 20, 113, 243 n.18; first visit to Italy, 23, 36, 160, 162; first visit to Mexico, 186; fishing, 20–21, 116; living in Gloucestershire, 118; schoolteacher in London, 23; visit to Moore, 52–53; visit to Williams, 85–86; youth in Stoke, 13, 19–22, 65

Tomlinson, Charles, works: Above Manhattan, 246 n.7; Adam, 136, 229; American Scenes, 75, 78; Annunciation, 224–25; Antecedents, 35, 70, 188, 207; Appearance, 209; Apples Painted, 155; Ariadne and the Minotaur, 61, 96; Arizona Desert, 74–75, 215; "Art and Chaos," 146–47, 152; The Art of Poetry, 41, 47; Assassin, 112, 185, 188–96, 213; At Holwell Farm, 83; The Atlantic, 57–58; At Stoke, 19; At the Edge, 237–38; At Trotsky's House, 181–82; Before the Dance, 179–81; Beginning of Another Home Holiday, 157; Bridges, 80–81; Canal, 97–99, 115; The Castle, 83; The Cavern, 220; Cézanne at Aix, 30, 46, 61, 70, 73, 75, 79, 107, 173, 218; Charles Tomlinson Reads His Poems, 248 n.8; Charles Tomlinson Reads "The Waste Land," 185, 246 n. 14; Charlotte Corday, 112, 185, 196–202, 208; Château de Muzot, 79; Cochiti, 177–78; The Commonest Objects, 36, 39, 100; The Compact: at Volterra, 23–24, 74; Constitution Day, 182; The Double Rainbow, 234; Eden, 153; Eden: Graphics and Poetry, 147; "Edward Thomas" (review), 129; Etruscan Shades, 152; Farewell to Van Gogh, 154, 160, 187; The Farmer's Wife, 64; Far Point, 156; Fiascherino, 47–49, 55, 112; Flute Music, 43; For Danton, 112, 185, 203–8; For Ivor Gurney, 118–19; For Miriam, 165–66, 177; Four Kantian Lyrics, 215; Foxes' Moon, 116; The Fox Gallery, 92–93; From the Motorway, 86; Frondes Agrestes: On Re-Reading Ruskin, 69–71; Geneva Restored, 71–74, 78, 112, 153; A Given Grace, 224; The Glacier, 163–64; Glass Grain, 55, 58, 156; Gli Scafari, 160–61; Hand at Callow Hill Farm, 80; High Summer, 178; How Still the Hawk, 158–59, 165, 177, 200; In Arden, 143–44; In Defence of Metaphysics, 80, 87; Interpretations, 20; "Introduction," William Carlos Williams: Selected Poems, 100; John Maydew or The Allotment, 20, 99, 113–16; The Lepidopterist, 192; Letter to Doctor Williams, 99; The Light and the Dark, 154; The Littleton Whale, 51–52, 92; Machiavelli in Exile, 112, 185, 207–13; Marat Dead, 202; The Marl Pits, 21–22; A Meditation on John Constable, 29, 30, 36, 57; The Metamorphosis, 143; More Foreign Cities, 153, 214–15; Movements, 78, 220; The Necklace, 13, 23, 30, 37–38, 47, 49–50, 148, 160; Nightbook, 146–47; Night-Piece: the Near and the Far, 55, 139–40; Nine Variations in a Chinese Winter Setting, 42–43, 230; Northern Spring, 49, 169; Notes from New York, 119; Observation of Facts, 38, 41, 47; "Octavio Paz in England," 187; Ode to Arnold Schoenberg, 106–8; Old Man's Beard, 137; One and the Same (Lo idéntico), 187; On the Hall at Stowey, 81–85; On

the Tlacolula Bus, 181; Oppositions, 29, 220–21; Orion Over Farne, 235; ... Or Traveller's Joy, 137; Over Brooklyn Bridge, 52–53, 59; Over Elizabeth Bridge, 20; Oxen: Ploughing at Fiesole, 61–63, 74, 97; "Pages from an Italian Journal," 26; Paring the Apple, 56–57, 159; Peace Between Us, William Blake, 153–54; A Peopled Landscape, 35, 78, 99, 112–13; Los Pobrecitos, 182–83; Poem ("It falls onto my page"), 169; Poem ("Wakening with the window"), 35, 157; The Poem as Initiation, 176; Poem for My Father, 116–17, 119; Poem of the Neighbours, 151, 184; Poetry and Metamorphosis, 123, 136, 144; "Poet Without an Audience" (review of Blake's Vala), 147; Portobello Carnival 1973, 20; Project 95, 192; Prometheus, 191; The Race, 135; Reflections, 56; Relations and Contraries, 146, 148, 151–57; The Return, 23, 47; Return to Hinton, 99, 102–4; Rose-Hips, 56; The Ruin, 37, 80; Sea Change, 45–47; Sea Poem, 112–13, 171–72; Seeing is Believing, 13, 30, 34, 37, 49, 55, 69–71, 75, 78–81, 83, 159–60, 173, 187–88, 214; 218; A Sense of Distance, 148–51, 156; The Sense of the Past, 214, 221; The Shaft, 220; The Slag Heap, 21–22; The Snow Fences, 164–65; Some Americans, 24, 64, 85–86; Something: A Direction, 207, 236; Steel: the night shift, 215; Stone Speech, 150, 218; Suggestions for the Improvement of a Sunset, 43–44; Swan, 155–56; Swimming Chenango Lake, 29–30, 96, 174–77; Tarquinia, 174; The Tax Inspector: at Tlacolula, 183–84; Terminal Tramps, 81; Through Binoculars, 154, 195; Tramontana in Lerici, 160, 218; Translations, 162; Travelling, 101; Up at La Serra, 23, 99, 107–12, 188; Ute Mountain, 75–77; Van Gogh, 160; Variation on Paz, 188; Wanderer (Girovagi), 162; The Way In, 81; The Way of a World, 106; Weeper in Jalisco, 182–83; The White Van, 33, 65; Winter Encounters, 228
Townsend, Aurelian, 126
"Tradition and the Individual Talent" (Eliot), 60, 185, 222
Trees (Williams), 106
Trotsky, Leon, 181–82, 188–93, 195–96
Tuft of Flowers, A (Frost), 131
Turkey-Cock (Lawrence), 172
Turner, J. M. W., 25–26, 28–30; The Junction of the Greta and the Tees, 30; The Long Ships Lighthouse, 29; The Upper Fall of the Tees, 29
Tuscany, 47
Twilight in Italy, 154
Two Years Before the Mast (Dana), 163
Tyrol, 51, 162–63

Ungaretti, Giuseppe, 162
Unique Forms of Continuity in Space (Boccioni), 59
United States of America, 51
Upon Appleton House (Marvell), 85
Upper Fall of the Tees, The (Turner), 29
Up There (Gurney), 141

Vala, or The Four Zoas (Blake), 147
Valley Candle (Stevens), 40
Valley Farm, The (Gurney), 142
Vantage Point, The (Frost), 131
Vaughan Williams, Ralph, 118, 120
View of a Lake (Williams), 87–88, 90
Virgil, 27
Volterra, 23
Voyages (Crane), 128

Waiting (Frost), 131
Walt Whitman (Gurney), 126
Wandsworth, 129
Washington, George, 126
Washington, state of, 63
Washington Irving (Gurney), 126
Waste Land, The (Eliot), 15, 136, 185–86, 213, 236–37
Webern, Anton, 187
Wedgwood, Josiah, 19–20
Welles, Orson, 192–95
Welsh Fusiliers, 225
Welsh soldiers, 124–25
What to See in America (Johnson), 65, 68
Wheelwright's Shop, The (Sturt), 129
When I Buy Pictures (Moore), 50

When Lilacs Last in the Dooryard Bloom'd (Whitman), 127
Whitman, Walt, 121–22, 127–28, 170–71; A Broadway Pageant, 181; Crossing Brooklyn Ferry, 122; Leaves of Grass, 64; Out of the Cradle Endlessly Rocking, 111, 167; Sea Drift, 121, 170, 175; A Song for Occupations, 170; Song of the Open Road, 122, 170; Sparkles from the Wheel, 122; This Compost, 121; When Lilacs Last in the Dooryard Bloom'd, 127
Whitsun Weddings, The (Larkin), 216
Whittier, John Greenleaf, 101, 139
Widsith, 225
Wilcox, W. D., 67–69
William Carlos Williams: Selected Poems, 100
Williams, William Carlos, 13–15, 23, 31, 38–39, 48, 50, 52, 75–79, 81, 85–91, 96–97, 99–101, 103–7, 112–13, 139, 147–48, 162, 166, 168, 171, 186, 193–94, 213, 219, 230, 236–37; The Autobiography of William Carlos Williams, 104; Autumn, 99; A Bastard Peace, 99; The Crimson Cyclamen, 90; The Desert Music, 13, 79; Hymn among the Ruins (Himno entre ruinas), 186; In the American Grain, 86, 193, 213; Journey to Love, 13, 79; Morning, 99; The Orchestra, 105–6; Pastoral, 96, 97; Paterson, 76, 86, 100, 194; The Pink Locust, 104–5; The Poor, 90, 96; Proletarian Portrait, 99; The Red Wheelbarrow, 100–101; Spring and All, 96; Spring Strains, 106; The Tempers, 39; To a Poor Old Woman, 99; To Daphne and Virginia, 105; To Elsie, 86–87; Trees, 106; View of a Lake, 87–88, 90; William Carlos Williams: Selected Poems, 100; Young Sycamore, 89–91
Wilson, Edmund: In Defense of the Iroquois, 246n.7; To the Finland Station, 191
Wiltshire, 129
Wind Shifts, The (Stevens), 44–45
Windsor Forest (Pope), 27
Winter, Fifth Avenue (Stieglitz), 90
Winter's Tale, A (Dylan Thomas), 36
Wood-Pile, The (Frost), 138–40
Wordsworth, William, 26–27, 92, 100–101, 112–13, 122, 130, 204–5; The Prelude, 27, 92, 100–101, 204–5; Resolution and Independence, 27, 112–13; A Slumber Did My Spirit Seal, 112
Wright, Elizur, 73

Xanadu, 193

Zeeland, 51
Zen, 180
Zuni, 179